# Learn Adobe Acrobat 4.0

# Learn Adobe Acrobat 4.0

## Cheryl Stinerock

Wordware Publishing, Inc.

ISBN 1-55622-772-8
10 9 8 7 6 5 4 3 2 1
0102

All inquiries for volume purchases of this book should be addressed to Wordware Publishing, Inc., at the above
address. Telephone inquiries may be made by calling:

(972) 423-0090

# Contents

Contents

Contents

# Chapter 1

# Adobe Acrobat 4.0 and PDF Files

## Introduction

Adobe® Acrobat® uses links, annotations, articles, thumbnails, bookmarks, electronic signatures, and more to convert a document that at one time was merely an output of the workflow into an actual part of the process. Once a document is converted to PDF (Portable Document Format), Acrobat provides you with tools that turn a static page into a document, which can change rapidly with the new demands in today's marketplace.

By using links and articles, you can eliminate the tedious process of leafing through pages and pages of text and instead provide readers with the ability to immediately access required information. Text, video, and sound annotations, links to web pages (URLs), an electronic signature process which retains each version of the document, enhanced security, and advanced form creation are only a few of the other features that have placed Adobe Acrobat and PDF files on the desktops of many businesses.

One of the most important qualities of the PDF file is the fact that it can be viewed, navigated, and printed on a wide variety of platforms. For that reason, Adobe offers versions of Acrobat for many different platforms, including Macintosh and Windows. Because of the high number of PDF users with Macs, much of the available documentation is apparently aimed primarily at them. At the present time, more and more users of Adobe Acrobat are found in a Windows-based environment and require answers to questions regarding typically used applications.

Although this book may reference, at times, the Macintosh platform, it will primarily cover those issues pertaining to Windows and applications available on that platform, such as Word, Excel, and PowerPoint. Some of those issues include:

■ PDF conversion techniques for Excel, Word, and PowerPoint documents

■ Available add-ins for Adobe Acrobat users on a Windows platform

■ Publishing documents created in a Windows environment on a web site

■ Creating and using forms in a Windows environment

# Installation of Adobe Acrobat

The installation process of Adobe Acrobat is fairly typical. Prior to installation, you should verify that your system has the minimum requirements for Acrobat, including:

■ i486 or Pentium-based processor

■ Windows 95, 98, or NT (including Service Pack 3 or later)

■ 16 MB of RAM on Windows 95 or 98

■ 24 MB of RAM on Windows NT (however, 32 MB RAM is suggested)

■ 80 MB of available space on the hard drive

■ CD drive

After you have determined that your system is appropriately equipped, you need to decide if you want Acrobat 4.0 to work with your other Microsoft applications, such as Word, Excel, and PowerPoint. If you want your applications to work with Adobe Acrobat and its macros and drivers, the sequence of application installation is very important: You must install Word, Excel, and PowerPoint prior to the installation of Acrobat 4.0 onto your system.

**Note:** *If you do not follow this sequence, you must reinstall Acrobat 4.0.*

After those issues are resolved, you can install Adobe Acrobat 4.0 onto your system by using the following steps:

1. First, close all applications.

2. Insert the Adobe Acrobat CD into the CD drive.

3. The setup process should begin automatically. If it does not, use My Computer or Explorer to navigate to the CD drive, then click on **ACROBAT4\Setup.exe**.

4. As you proceed, each screen in the Setup Shield will provide Next and Cancel buttons. To continue, press **Next**.

5. On one screen, you will be asked to select the type of installation you want:

   ■ Choose **Typical** if you want to install Acrobat, Acrobat Catalog, Acrobat Distiller, PDFWriter, PDFMaker, a few plug-ins, and online documentation.

   ■ Choose **Compact** if you only want to install Acrobat, Acrobat Distiller, PDFWriter, and PDFMaker.

   ■ To choose only those components you want on your system, choose **Custom**.

6. Finally, press **Finish** to complete the setup.

# Components of the Adobe Acrobat Suite

After the installation process has successfully completed, you'll find the following products in the Start menu, added onto the desktop, or added as print drivers.

## Adobe Acrobat

Acrobat is the main product contained in the Adobe Acrobat suite. Formerly known as "Acrobat Exchange," this software enables you to read, navigate, print, and edit a PDF file. Using Acrobat, you have the ability to add links, annotations, articles, bookmarks, etc., to your document. You also have the ability to transform a document into a form by using some of the tools available in Acrobat.

# Adobe Catalog

Using Adobe Catalog, you have the ability to create a searchable database of all the text contained in your documents. Important to note is the fact that all links, annotations, thumbnails, etc., should be added to the document prior to its addition to the catalog.

# Acrobat Distiller

If you want to convert a PostScript file into PDF format, you must use Acrobat® Distiller®. But you also have the option of using Distiller with many other types of files, including those created by MS Word, MS Excel, MS PowerPoint, Corel WordPerfect, Adobe FrameMaker, HTML files, text files, and certain image files (GIF, JPEG, TIFF, PCX, PNG, BMP).

In order for Distiller to properly function, your system must have a PostScript printer driver. The typical Adobe Acrobat installation includes an Adobe/PS driver.

When Distiller is used to create a PDF file, generally the graphics are of a higher quality than found on PDF files created by PDFWriter. For that reason, it is strongly suggested that you use PDF Distiller whenever your document includes graphics.

Distiller is available to you on your desktop as an application or as a print driver within MS Excel, MS Word, or MS PowerPoint. You can use it from the Print dialog box (found in the Microsoft applications), or you can drag and drop a file to the Distiller icon on the desktop. Automatically, Distiller will begin the conversion process.

# Acrobat PDFWriter

Acrobat's PDFWriter macro enables you to convert an existing file to PDF format in one quick step. When Adobe Acrobat is installed, the PDFWriter is automatically added as a printer driver to the applications available on your desktop. To use this macro:

Click on the **Acrobat PDFMaker** icon. This icon initiates the PDFWriter macro.

OR

Navigate to **File | Print** and choose a printer name of **Acrobat PDFWriter**.

When your documents contain primarily text, the PDFWriter macro is preferred. However, a document containing graphics, graphs, or charts should be converted to PDF format using Acrobat Distiller. Acrobat Distiller handles objects better than PDFWriter.

# Acrobat PDFMaker

Acrobat PDFMaker is basically a macro that enables you to convert a file from some Microsoft applications to PDF format using PDFWriter or Distiller. PDFMaker is installed only in the following applications: Word 97, Word 2000, PowerPoint 97, and PowerPoint 2000. After installation, this macro appears as an icon on the application's toolbar:

When you click on the PDFMaker icon, the PDFMaker dialog box will appear:

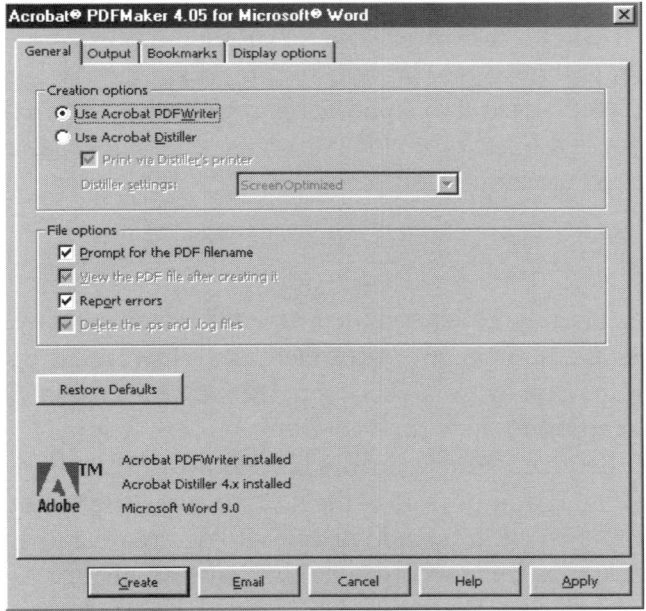

Here, you'll be provided with a number of formatting and conversion choices, including:

- Choice of conversion macro, either Distiller or PDFWriter

- Types of links which should be included (cross-reference and table of contents links, cross-documents links, footnote and endnote links, and Internet links)

- Automatic bookmark generation for headings
- Basic display options, including the appearance of the links (highlighted, color) and how the document should open (magnification level, page number)

### PDFWriter or Distiller?

If your document is primarily comprised of text, you will want to choose PDFWriter to convert your file to PDF format. In this case, the conversion will be done in a quick one-step process. The Word or Excel file will be converted from its original format to a PDF file.

However, if your document contains graphics, photographs, graphs, or charts, you will want to choose PDF Distiller to convert your file. In this case, the conversion will take place in a two-step process. First, PDFMaker and Distiller will convert your file into a PostScript file. From the Post-Script file, it will be converted into a PDF file. Important to note is the fact that Distiller will only use this two-step process when accessed through PDFMaker. When used as a standalone application, external to the Microsoft applications where PDFMaker is installed, Distiller still requires the input of a PostScript file.

## Acrobat Reader

If you have Adobe Acrobat installed on your system, then you have the ability to read/edit/navigate/print PDF files. However, if you distribute one of your documents to a user who does not have Acrobat, that user requires a method to view the PDF file—Acrobat Reader™.

Acrobat Reader is an application which provides users with the ability to view, navigate, and print PDF files. At no cost, Adobe provides a copy of Acrobat Reader to all interested people. If you create a PDF file that will be distributed to some users who do not have Acrobat or Acrobat Reader on their system, those users can acquire Acrobat Reader in two different ways:

1. Users can download a version of Adobe Reader 4.0 from the Adobe web site, www.Adobe.com, for any platform.

2. You (the creator of the PDF document) can distribute your platform's version of the Adobe Acrobat Reader 4.0 Installer along with your PDF documents. This installer can be found on the Adobe Acrobat CD in the directory Acroread\Installers\Acrd4enu.

Many users may find a visit to a web site to locate necessary software (even when the software is free) an interruption to their workflow. To enable them to view your PDF file as quickly as possible, it is suggested that you include a copy of Acrobat Reader with your distribution package.

If you decide to include the Acrobat Reader Installer along with your PDF documents and if your recipients are currently using a Windows platform, there are a few minimum system requirements. Prior to running the Acrobat Reader Installer, those users should be certain that their present systems include the following:

- i486 or a Pentium processor
- Windows 95, 98, or NT (**Note:** *If NT is used, Service Pack 3 or later is required.*)
- 8 MB RAM on Windows 95 or 98 (**Note:** *A minimum of 16 MB is suggested.*)
- 16 MB RAM on Windows NT (**Note:** *A minimum of 32 MB is suggested.*)
- 10 MB of available hard disk space

When PDF files are distributed along with the Acrobat Reader Installer, Adobe provides, at no cost, the "Includes Adobe Reader" logo. To obtain this logo, you must complete the Adobe Trademark License Agreement. (**Note:** *To sign this agreement, navigate to the "Using the Acrobat Logos" section on: www.adobe.com/products/acrobat/distribute.html.*) Additionally, Adobe requests that the following software and information be provided in the distribution package:

- The Acrobat Reader Installer (as provided by Adobe)
- The Acrobat Reader Electronic End User License Agreement (contained in the Acrobat Reader Installer program)
- Copyright and other proprietary notices included in Acrobat Reader
- The following attribution statement (which must appear on the package that includes Acrobat Reader):

"Acrobat® Reader Copyright © 1987–1999 Adobe Systems Incorporated. All rights reserved. Adobe, the Adobe logo, Acrobat, and the Acrobat logo are trademarks of Adobe Systems Incorporated."

# PDF Files and Adobe Acrobat

Adobe Acrobat works with PDF (Portable Document Format) files. In order to use Acrobat, you must convert your existing files to PDF format. If your files were in the PostScript format, then you would use the standalone version of Acrobat Distiller (found on your desktop after the typical Adobe Acrobat installation). If your files are created in a Windows application, you have the option of choosing PDFWriter or Distiller in the Print Setup dialog box. However, if your files are in a Word or PowerPoint (97 or 2000) format, you want to use the PDFMaker macro, which offers you the choice of conversion macros, PDFWriter, or Acrobat Distiller.

After the installation of Adobe Acrobat, you will notice that most of your Windows applications now include the options Acrobat PDFWriter and Acrobat Distiller under Printer Name. For the most part, any of your files created on a Windows-based system can be converted to PDF format without any difficulty.

## PDF Files — An Overview

A quick and easy definition for PDF files can be found in the basic meaning behind the acronym PDF. PDF stands for Portable Document Format. PDF files are documents formatted in such a way as to make them portable to and from a large assortment of computer systems.

If, for example, your work unit, Accounting (which uses a Windows-NT environment), is currently working on a project with the Design Group (which uses a Macintosh environment), there are most likely compatibility issues. If the project involves contracts/design layouts/etc., each area may be forced to provide hard copies of documents to ensure that the other group can read them. PDF documents, however, appear the same on either one of these systems. By using PDF documents, information, ideas, contracts, and design layouts can easily be e-mailed back and forth, viewed, and printed from each system.

The PDF file is independent of the hardware, operating system, and application software which initially created the file. This independence provides you, the user, with a great deal of flexibility concerning your work flow. By using PDF files, you no longer have to ask questions like, "Will the Legal Department be able to view this contract with their system?" Instead, the decision at hand is: Should the file be converted to PDF format using PDFWriter or Acrobat Distiller?

**Note:** *You may want to save the PDF files you create in the following sections for later use in this book.*

# Converting Word or PowerPoint Files to PDF Using PDFWriter

As mentioned, PDFWriter should be used when the document intended for conversion includes mostly text. To convert a Word 97, Word 2000, PowerPoint 97, or PowerPoint 2000 file to PDF format using PDFWriter:

1. Open the file you wish to convert.

2. Click the **PDFMaker** icon on the application's command bar.

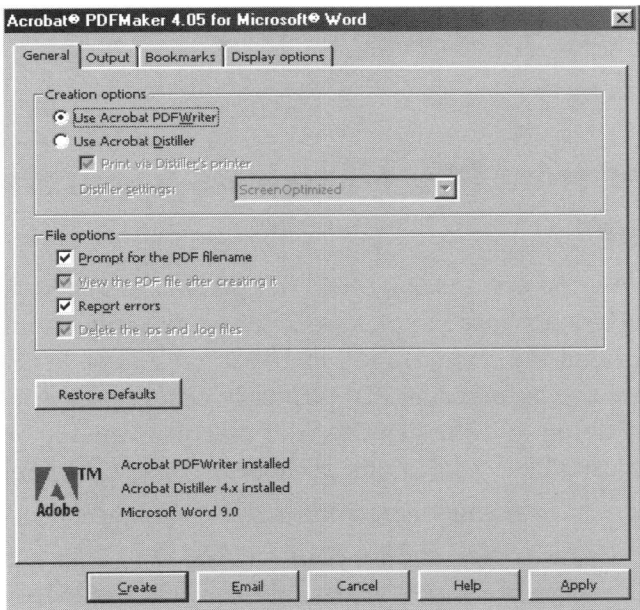

3. In the Acrobat PDFMaker dialog box, choose (on the General tab) the Creation option **Use Acrobat PDFWriter**. At this point, all options under the Output and Display options tabs are grayed out. Under the Bookmarks tab, the only option available is Destination Magnification. Evidently, PDFWriter is more limited in its conversion capabilities than Acrobat Distiller.

4. Under File options, choose **Prompt for the PDF filename** to be given the opportunity to choose the location of the resulting PDF file. If this option is not selected, this file will be added to the Windows temp directory.

5. Under File options, also choose **Report errors** to display an error window during the conversion process.

6. When all selections have been made, press the **Apply** button.

7. To begin the conversion process, press the **Create** button.

8. An Adobe PDFMaker dialog box appears, informing you that choosing PDFWriter makes certain features (bookmarks, links, etc.) unavailable. Here, you are given the opportunity to convert the file to PDF using Acrobat Distiller. Choose **Don't warn me again** to continue converting using PDFWriter.

9. The Save PDF File As dialog box appears. Choose the desired location of the resulting PDF file.

10. Click **Save**.

## Converting Files from Other Windows Applications to PDF Using PDFWriter

The Adobe Acrobat package will not install the PDFMaker macro in the other Windows-based applications. In some applications (such as Excel), you will find the menu option File | Create Adobe PDF, which enables you to create a PDF file using PDFWriter. In other applications, you will find the PDFWriter and the PDF Distiller macros available in the Print dialog box. To use PDFWriter in one of those other applications:

1. Open the file you wish to convert.

2. On the menu bar, choose **File | Print**. The Print dialog box appears on the screen. (If you are using Excel, choose **File | Create Adobe PDF**. After the Save PDF File As dialog box appears, skip to step 8.)

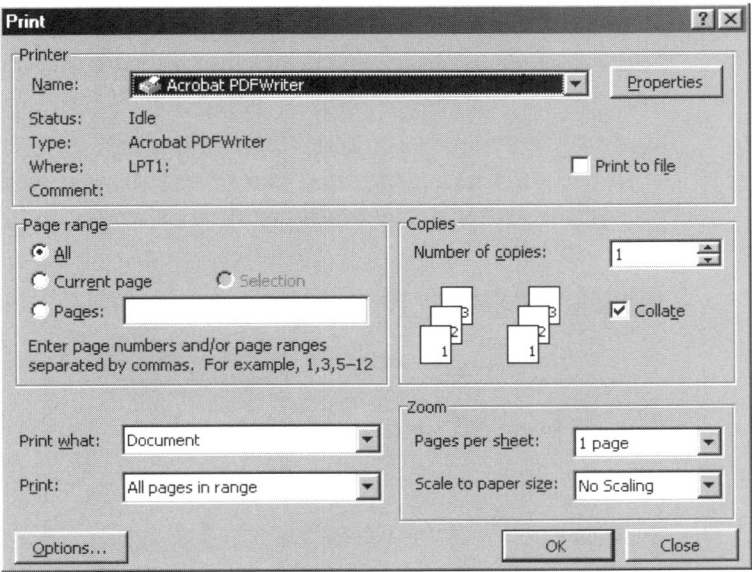

3. Click the drop-down arrow for the Printer Name box. The available printers will show in the selection box.

4. Select **Acrobat PDFWriter**.

5. Press the **Properties** button to access the Acrobat PDFWriter Properties dialog box. Here, you have the opportunity to choose options such as Page Setup, Compression Options, and Font Embedding.

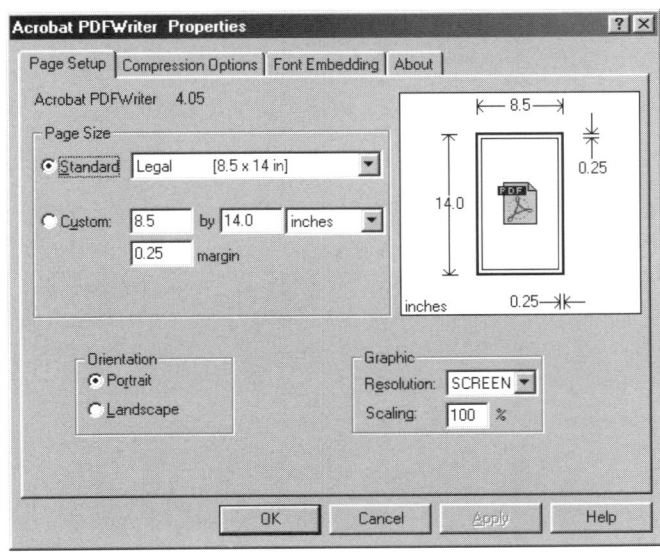

6. After you've made your selections, click **Apply** to apply your changes, and then **OK** to close this dialog box and return to the Print dialog box.

7. Make your selections in the Print dialog box, then click **OK** to proceed with the conversion process. The Save PDF File As dialog box appears, providing you with the ability to name the file and choose the placement of the file.

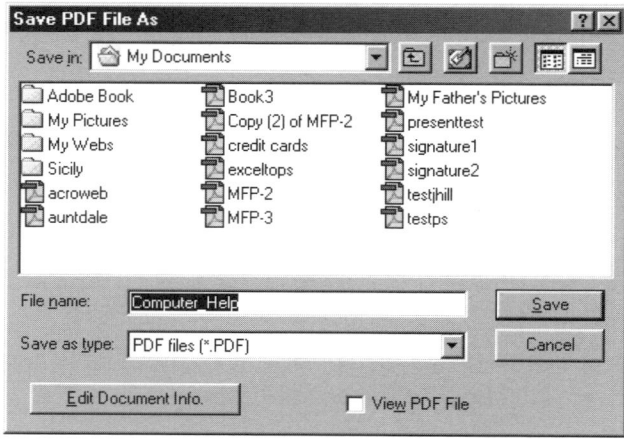

*Note:* *The conversion of this file creates a new PDF file and leaves the original file intact and in its original format.*

8. Click the **Edit Document Info** button to choose PDF document information such as the title, subject, author, and keywords.

9. Click **OK** to return to the Save PDF File As dialog box.

10. Click **Save** to create the PDF file with the requested name.

# Converting Word or PowerPoint Files to PDF Using Acrobat Distiller

When the document intended for conversion includes graphics, photographs, charts, etc., use Acrobat Distiller when converting it to PDF format. To convert a Word 97, Word 2000, PowerPoint 97, or PowerPoint 2000 file to PDF format using Acrobat Distiller:

1. Open the file you wish to convert.

2. Click the **PDFMaker** icon on the application's command bar. The Acrobat PDFMaker dialog box appears.

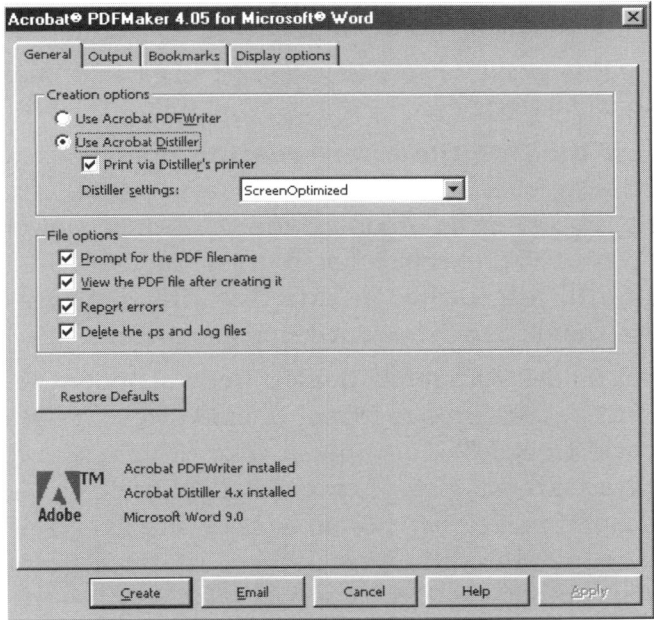

3. On the General tab, in the Creation options section, choose **Use Acrobat Distiller**.

*Note: To ensure that the file is converted via Acrobat Distiller, be sure to select the **Print via Distiller's printer** option directly underneath.*

4. Open up the Distiller settings selection box. Here, you are given three choices for three different quality types of output. Choose **Screen Optimized** for a small PDF file with lesser-quality resolution. This

setting is suggested if the output will be displayed on the Internet or if it will be eventually read on-screen.

Choose **Print Optimized** to create a larger file with better quality resolution. This setting is suggested for output that will be printed out using a desktop printer or will be copied to a CD.

Finally, choose **Press Optimized** to create the largest file with the best quality resolution. Use this setting if high-quality, professional output is required and intended for an imagesetter or a platesetter.

5. In the File options area, you are provided with the opportunity to choose the following settings: **Prompt for the PDF filename** displays a dialog box during the conversion process which allows you to choose the filename/destination folder of your PDF file.

*Note:* *If this option is not chosen, then this file will be added to the Windows temp directory.*

**View the PDF file after creating it** automatically launches Adobe Acrobat or Reader and displays your PDF file. **Report errors** brings up an error window during the conversion process to alert you of problems (the conversion process continues after each error is displayed). **Delete the .ps and .log files** removes these files immediately after the conversion completes.

6. Click on the Output tab to select General options (e.g., Should comments be converted to Notes? Should text boxes be converted to Article Threads?), Link options (e.g., What types of links should be converted/created: cross-document, Internet, etc.?), and Destination Magnification (Inherit Zoom — same size as original, Fit Page — resize to fit the entire page in the Acrobat window, Fit Width — resize to fit width in the Acrobat window, Fit Height — resize to fit height in the Acrobat window, or Fit Visible — resize so that text and graphics are visible in the Acrobat window).

7. Click on the Bookmarks tab to define what areas of the document will become bookmarks.

8. Click on the Display options tab to define the link appearance (e.g., Should the links be blue?) and the Document Open Options (e.g., Which page should be displayed when the document initially opens?).

9. When all selections have been made, press the **Apply** button.

10. To begin the conversion process, press the **Create** button.

11. The Acrobat PDFMaker for Word or PowerPoint dialog box appears, displaying the steps of the conversion process and your current position in this process. When a step completes, the word "done" or "skipped" appears to the right of the step.

12. When the conversion process nears completion, a Save PDF File As dialog box appears. Choose the filename and destination folder, then click **Save**. Your file is converted to a PDF file. If the View PDF File option was chosen, Acrobat or Acrobat Reader will launch and open your new PDF file.

# Converting Files from Other Windows Applications to PDF Using Acrobat Distiller

Although the PDFMaker macro is not available in the other Windows-based applications, other applications can use Acrobat Distiller to convert files to PDF format. To use Acrobat Distiller to convert a file to PDF format in one of these other applications:

1. Open the file you wish to convert.

2. Choose **File | Print** on the menu bar to access the Print dialog box.

3. In the Print dialog box, select **Acrobat Distiller** as your printer.

4. Click the **Properties** button to display a few setup choices prior to the conversion.

   In the Acrobat Distiller Properties dialog box, four tabs provide you with the option to set some preferences. The Paper tab enables you to change the paper size or the paper orientation. The Graphics tab provides options regarding resolution. The PostScript tab gives you the opportunity to choose between a few output formats: PostScript (optimize for speed), choose this option to reduce printing time; PostScript (optimize for portability), use this option if you require advanced printing options; Encapsulated PostScript (EPS), use this option if you plan to insert this document into another as a high-quality image or if this document will be printed from another location; and Archive format, choose this alternative if this document will be placed into long-term storage or wide distribution. Finally, the Watermarks tab gives you the opportunity to add a watermark to your final document, either your own or a watermark available on Adobe Acrobat.

5. After all selections are made, click **OK**.

   After the conversion is completed, Acrobat will launch, displaying the new PDF file.

6. To save the file, choose **File | Save As**.

7. In the Save As dialog box, choose the filename and the destination of the file.

8. Click **OK**.

# Converting Files from Windows Applications to PostScript Files

When Acrobat Distiller is used outside of your applications, a PostScript file is required. To create a PostScript file:

1. Open the file in an application other than Word or PowerPoint (such as Excel).

2. On the menu bar, choose **File | Print**.

3. In the Print dialog box, for the Printer name, choose **Acrobat Distiller**.

4. Click the **Properties** button.

5. In the resulting Acrobat Distiller Properties dialog box, choose the PostScript tab.

6. In the drop-down selection box for PostScript output format, choose **Encapsulated PostScript (EPS)**.

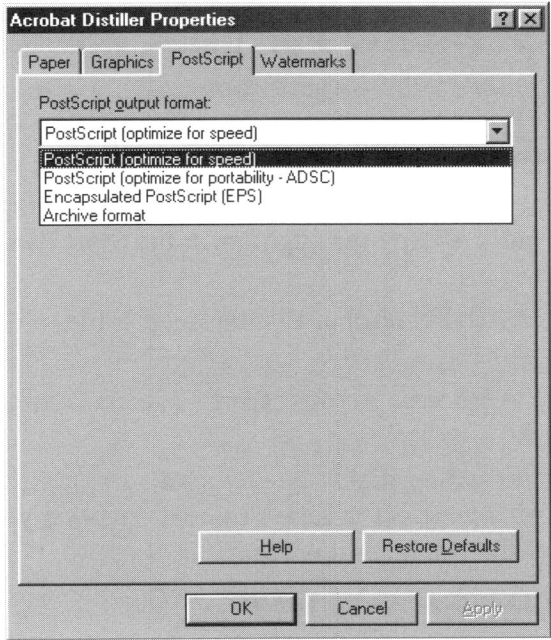

7. Choose **Apply**, then **OK** to close the Acrobat Distiller Properties dialog box.

8. In the Print dialog box, choose **Print to File**.

*Note: If you do not choose this option, the file will automatically be converted into a PDF file.*

9. Click **OK** to initiate the conversion process.

10. At this point, the Print To File dialog box appears on the screen. Choose the name of the file.

*Note: The extension of a PostScript file is .prn.*

11. Click **OK** to create the PostScript file.

# Converting PostScript Files to PDF Using Acrobat Distiller

If you have PostScript files on your computer, you can use a simple drag-and-drop process to quickly convert your files to PDF format. To convert a PostScript file to a PDF file:

1. Locate your PostScript file using My Computer (found on your desktop) or Windows Explorer (right-click the Start button and choose the Explore option).

2. Drag this file to the Acrobat Distiller icon situated on your desktop.

3. Drop this file onto the Acrobat Distiller icon. Acrobat Distiller is launched.

4. The Acrobat Distiller dialog box appears, providing you with a Progress bar and a progress description box, enabling you to watch the progress of the conversion process.

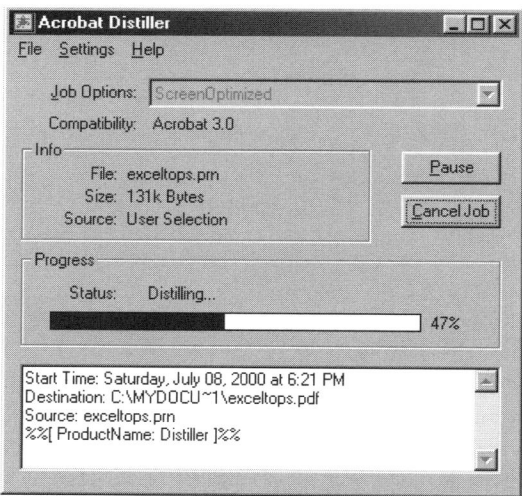

5. As the conversion process proceeds, the PostScript file is converted into a PDF file.

# Chapter 2

# Using the Adobe Acrobat Work Area

Before you begin incorporating Adobe Acrobat into your project, it's a good idea to become familiar with the Adobe Acrobat work area and the functionality it offers. By walking you through the work area, this chapter intends to familiarize you with the basic uses of Adobe Acrobat. While stepping through the exercises found on the following pages, provide yourself with more flexibility by creating a few sample documents.

## Adobe Acrobat User Interface — An Overview

After you have created your PDF file, you are ready to enhance it with links, annotations, etc., using Adobe Acrobat. When you initially launch Acrobat and open a PDF file, you will find the following workspace on your desktop:

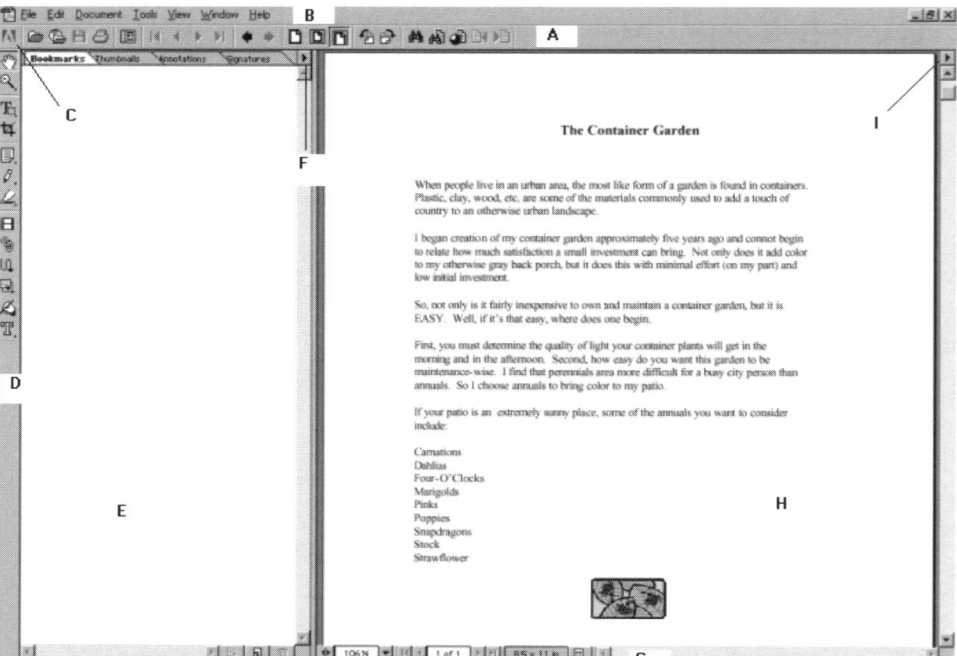

Provided in this workspace are:

A  Command bar

B  Menu bar

C  Adobe Online button

D  Toolbar

E  Navigation pane

F  Palette menu

G  Status bar

H  Document pane

I  Document Pane menu

Each of these nine areas provides you with increased functionality when navigating and working with PDF documents.

# Command Bar

The command bar contains icons, which enable you to quickly access commands available in Acrobat. When launched, Adobe Acrobat defaults to show the command bar above the document pane and below the menu bar.

When customizing your desktop, you may prefer to eliminate of the command bar or you may prefer to position it in another area of the desktop.

To hide the command bar:

On the menu bar, choose **Window | Hide Command Bar**.

OR

On the command bar, choose the **Show/Hide Navigation Pane** icon.

To show the command bar:

On the menu bar, choose **Window | Show Command Bar**.

OR

On the command bar, choose the **Show/Hide Navigation Pane** icon.

You also have the ability to move the command bar to a preferred area of the screen. To reposition the command bar:

1. Select the right or bottom edge, or the separator bar between  icon groups:

2. Using the left mouse button, click and drag the command bar to a new position.

3. Release the mouse button.

The command bar's icons provide you with quick and easy access to some of the most frequently used commands.

A few of these commands, including Open, Save, and Print, are commonly used in most computer applications. Other commands are typically found on Adobe applications, not Microsoft applications.

## Open

This command opens a chosen file.

## Open Web Page

This command enables you to select a web page or an entire web site (including the links), download it to your system, convert it to a PDF file, and then open it in Adobe Acrobat. After you choose this command, the Open Web Page dialog box appears.

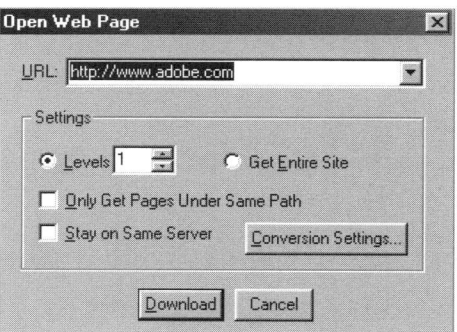

If you click on the Conversion Settings button, you will see a list of the file types this conversion process will recognize: PDF, FDF, GIF, HTML, JPEG, and plain text. Additionally, this function provides you with the ability to choose the general settings for the generated PDF file, the conversion settings for HTML and plain text files, and the page layout of the final downloaded file.

## Save

This command enables you to quickly save the file you currently have up on the screen. If you want to rename or redirect the file, you must choose the File | Save As option on the menu bar.

## Print

This is the typical Print command, found in most Windows-based applications. As in other applications, you have the option to choose from a few print drivers and to format the page as desired.

## Show/Hide Navigation Pane

Click this icon to toggle the navigation pane between visible and hidden.

## First Page

Use this command to navigate to the first page of the document currently on your screen.

## Previous Page

Use this command to navigate to the previous page of the document currently on your screen.

## Next Page

Click this icon to navigate to the next page of the document currently on your screen.

## Last Page

Use this command to navigate to the last page of the document currently on your screen.

## Go to Previous View

Click this icon to step backward through your viewing path. This feature enables you to step through a number of different documents mixed with a number of pages of each document. In total, Adobe remembers 64 separate steps (separate pages).

## Go to Next View

Click this icon to step forward through your viewing path. Again, up to 64 separate pages are retained in this feature.

## Actual Size

Click on this icon to show the actual size of the document currently visible on the screen. Although this icon usually returns the document to 100% magnification, if the creator formatted the document with a different page size, this icon will display the document in the formatted magnification.

## Fit in Window

Click on this icon to display the document fully in the work window.

## Fit Width

Choose this icon to expand the document to the width of the document pane. This type of screen formatting may cause the length of the document to extend beyond the viewing area of the pane.

## Rotate View 90 Degrees CCW

Choose this command to rotate the document 90 degrees in a counter-clockwise direction.

## Rotate View 90 Degrees CW

Choose this command to rotate the document 90 degrees in a clockwise direction.

## Find

Choose this command to locate a word or a text string within the current document.

## Search

Choose this command to search a full-text index of a collection of PDF documents. First, Acrobat Catalog must be used to create this full-text index, a comprehensive index of all the text found in a specified collection of documents. Only then can the Search command be used to query the contents of the index. After a search query is submitted, the results are displayed and rated in the Search Results window.

## Search Results

This command displays the Search Results window. Here, you can see which documents within the current collection contain matches. Additionally, the results are rated. For instance, those documents most likely to contain matches appear at the top of the list. Also, a circle is pictured next to each of the documents. The more filled-in the circle is, the more likely the search found matches in the document.

## Previous Highlight

This command is only enabled if you visit a web site that contains PDF files and offers a search engine that supports PDF Search Highlighting. PDF Search Highlighting shows you the results of a search by highlighting the results in the actual PDF document. Click this icon to navigate to the previous highlighted search result.

## Next Highlight ▶▤

This command is also only enabled if you visit a web site. Click this icon to navigate to the next highlighted search result.

# Menu Bar

The menu bar appears at the top of the screen when Adobe Acrobat is launched. If you prefer, you may choose to hide the menu bar in your work area.

To hide the menu bar:

Click **Window | Hide Menu Bar**.

To display the menu bar:

Press **F7**.

To access menu options:

This can be achieved by using the mouse, of course. However, if you find it more efficient to use keystrokes, you can access menu options by pressing Alt and the underlined letter of the menu option at the same time. For example, to access the File menu, press **Alt+F**.

The menu bar is divided into seven areas: File, Edit, Document, Tools, View, Window, and Help. Each of these areas contains commands and submenus, which assist you in manipulating the document. A black arrow to the right of the command indicates that the command includes submenus.

## File

This area contains basic file manipulation commands. Here, you have the ability to open, close, save, and print your document.

## Edit

The Edit menu provides a number of features which enable you to control the appearance of the document.

| File | |
|---|---|
| Open... | Ctrl+O |
| Open Web Page... | Ctrl+Shift+O |
| Close | Ctrl+W |
| Save | Ctrl+S |
| Save As... | Ctrl+Shift+S |
| Sign and Save... | |
| Revert | |
| Batch Process... | |
| Import | ▶ |
| Export | ▶ |
| Send Mail... | |
| Page Setup... | Ctrl+Shift+P |
| Print... | Ctrl+P |
| Document Info | ▶ |
| Preferences | ▶ |
| Adobe Online... | |
| 1 C:\My Documents\My Father's Pictures.pdf | |
| 2 C:\...\AcroHelp.pdf | |
| 3 C:\My Documents\acroweb.pdf | |
| 4 C:\...\Distparm.pdf | |
| Exit | Ctrl+Q |

| Edit | |
|---|---|
| Undo Move | Ctrl+Z |
| Cut | Ctrl+X |
| Copy | Ctrl+C |
| Paste | Ctrl+V |
| Delete | |
| Copy File To Clipboard | |
| Select All | Ctrl+A |
| Deselect All | Ctrl+Shift+A |
| Find... | Ctrl+F |
| Find Again | Ctrl+G |
| Search | ▶ |
| Properties... | Ctrl+I |

## Document

The commands in this area enable you to navigate the document, add or eliminate pages, or change the overall appearance of the pages.

| Document | |
|---|---|
| First Page | Ctrl+Shift+Pg Up |
| Previous Page | Ctrl+Pg Up |
| Next Page | Ctrl+Pg Dn |
| Last Page | Ctrl+Shift+Pg Dn |
| Go To Page... | Ctrl+N |
| Go Back Doc | Ctrl+Shift+<- |
| Go Back | Ctrl+<- |
| Go Forward | Ctrl+-> |
| Go Forward Doc | Ctrl+Shift+-> |
| Insert Pages... | Ctrl+Shift+I |
| Extract Pages... | |
| Replace Pages... | |
| Delete Pages... | Ctrl+Shift+D |
| Crop Pages... | Ctrl+T |
| Rotate Pages... | Ctrl+R |
| Number Pages... | |
| Set Page Action... | |

## Tools

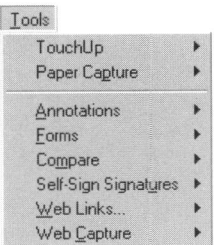

Here, the available commands provide you with the opportunity to further edit the appearance and content of your PDF document. Some features offered in this area include: self-sign signatures, annotations, and web links.

## View

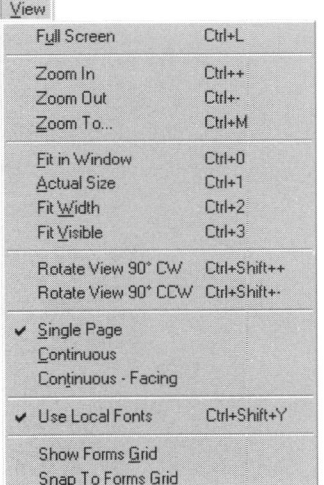

The commands in this menu control the view you have of the document. Here, you have the ability to control the size of the document showing on the screen, the actual position of the document on the screen, and how many pages show at one time.

## Window

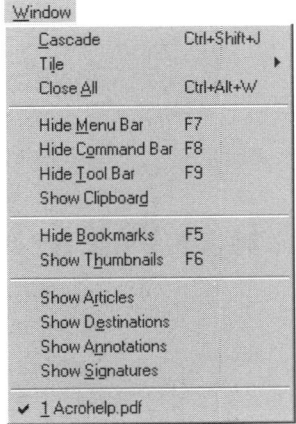

The Window menu enables you to control what type of information is displayed in the work area. For example, you can choose to show or hide the menu bar, toolbar, or command bar or you can choose to show or hide the tabs in the navigation pane (Bookmarks, Thumbnails, Annotations, Signatures).

## Help

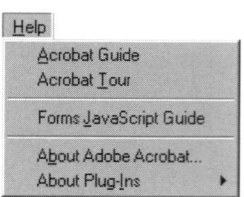

Here, Adobe provides you with a wealth of resources which assist you in your use of Adobe Acrobat. The documentation includes:

*Adobe Guide* — Detailed information regarding Adobe Acrobat.

*Acrobat Tour* — Quick walk-throughs of some of the basic areas of Adobe Acrobat, such as:

- Converting a document to PDF
- Navigating a PDF document
- Editing a PDF document
- Customizing PDF navigation
- Annotating a PDF document
- Creating a PDF form
- Distributing PDF files

*Forms JavaScript Guide* — Detailed explanation of how to use JavaScript with Acrobat Forms.

*About Plug-Ins* — A list of the Adobe Acrobat plug-ins, including:

- Acrobat Forms
- Acrobat Annotations
- Acrobat Movie
- Acrobat Scan
- Acrobat Weblink
- Acrobat Web Capture

# Adobe Online Button

The Adobe Online button appears to the left of the command bar in Adobe Acrobat. If you are connected to the Internet, clicking this icon automatically takes you to the Adobe web site. By using this icon, you can retrieve Acrobat fixes and updates, access Adobe online services, download additional documentation regarding this product, and acquire information regarding (and purchase, if interested) other Adobe products.

The first time you use this feature, you should run the included setup wizard:

1.  Click the **Adobe Online** button or select **File | Adobe Online** in the menu bar. The Adobe Online screen appears.

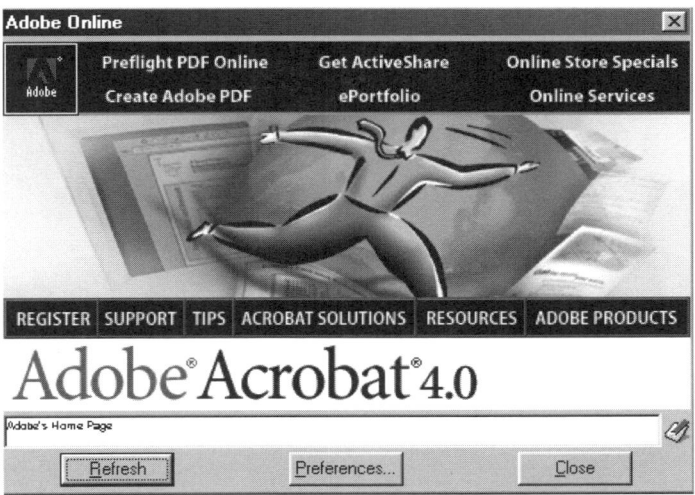

2.  Click **Preferences** to see the Adobe Online Preferences screen.

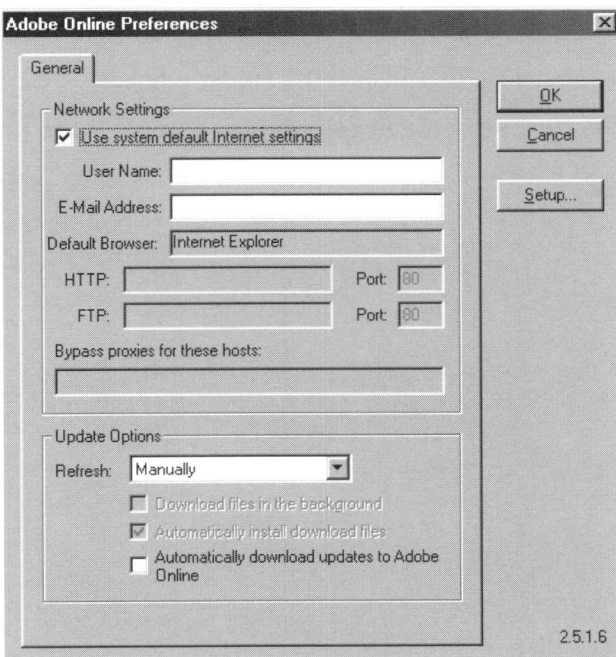

3. Input any specifics you want to include regarding your online connection, or choose **Use system default Internet settings**. Additionally, this dialog box provides you with the opportunity to change your Update Options.

4. Click **Setup** to run the setup process. The initial screen to guide you through the setup process appears.

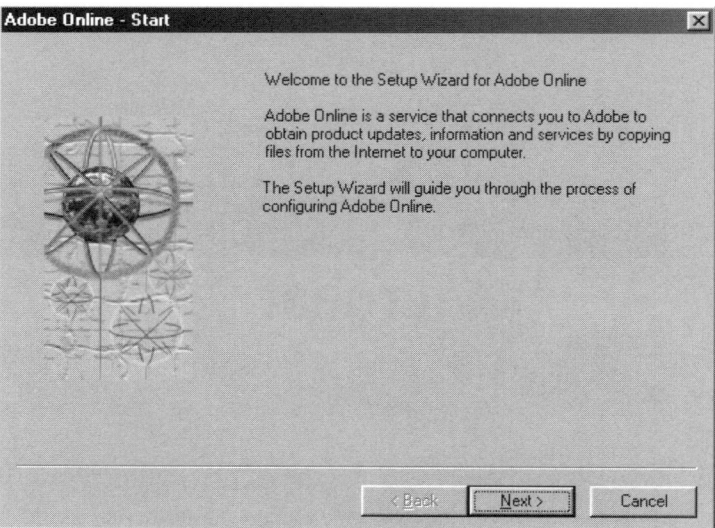

5. Continue the setup process by clicking **Next.**

6. On the final screen, click **Finish** to complete the process.

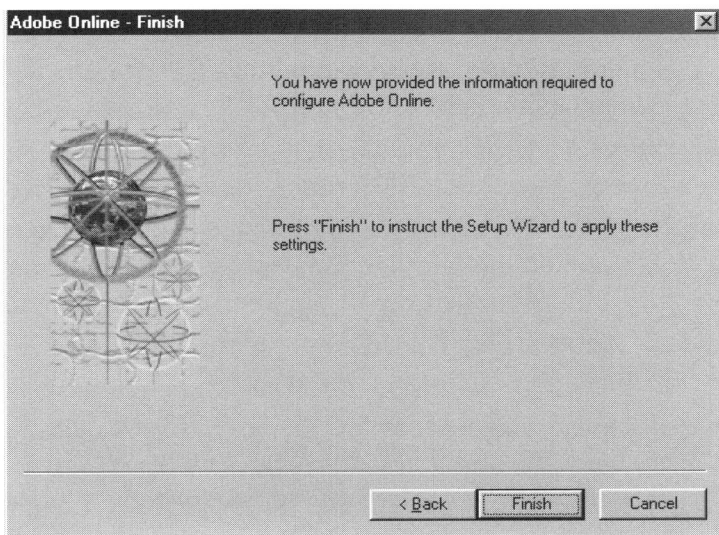

7. Click **OK** to close the Adobe Online Preferences screen.

8. Click **Close** to close the Adobe Online screen.

After your setup is completed, you can easily refresh online links in your documents. To refresh:

1. Click the **Adobe Online** button or select **File | Adobe Online** in the menu bar. The Adobe Online screen appears.

2. Click **Refresh** to automatically log on to specific areas of www.adobe.com.

Adobe Online provides you with a wealth of information. Some of the informative sections easily accessible from the Adobe Online button include:

- Register
- Support
- Tips
- Acrobat Solutions
- Resources
- Adobe Products

Additionally, Adobe Online provides you with the opportunity to try some of its online services and new products. Options quickly accessible from the Adobe Online button include:

- *Create Adobe PDF Online.* This service (for a fee) enables you to convert your files to PDF format online.

- *Preflight PDF Online.* Here, you have the opportunity to try this software online. Preflight analyzes your PDF documents and provides you with a detailed report pinpointing any problems.

- *Get Active Share.* This free online service enables you to add, edit, and manage photographs on the web.

- *ePortfolio.* Targeted toward the graphics/art field, this page provides you with the ability to search for a job or to search for an employee. The availability of a free online portfolio gives job seekers a global showcase for their work.

- *Online Store Specials.* This is the Adobe store.

- *Online Services.* Available here are free trials, online tools, and other services.

# Toolbar

The toolbar contains the tools required to edit and navigate the PDF document. To hide or show the toolbar, select **Window | Show/Hide Toolbar**. To use one of the tools:

Click the tool's icon.

OR

Type the letter associated with the tool.

***Note:*** *To find the letter associated with a tool, slowly move your cursor over the tool until the explanatory text appears. Along with the name of the tool, this text will include the tool tip letter.*

Some tools are hidden under other tools. A small arrow on the lower-right side of the tool indicates that there are hidden tools. To access those tools:

1. Left-click the tool's button.

2. When the list of hidden tools appears, position your cursor on the desired tool.

3. Release the mouse button to choose the tool.

To acquaint yourself with the wide range of functionality offered by these tools, choose a test PDF document of more than two pages (possibly one created during your reading of Chapter 1 — Adobe Acrobat 4.0 and PDF Files). Using a test document will give you the opportunity to try out a number of the options provided by these tools. In the following pages, each tool will be covered, from the Hand tool to the TouchUp tool, in the order they appear on the toolbar.

## Hand Tool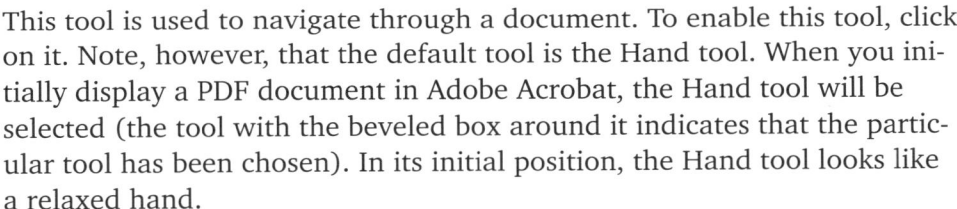

This tool is used to navigate through a document. To enable this tool, click on it. Note, however, that the default tool is the Hand tool. When you initially display a PDF document in Adobe Acrobat, the Hand tool will be selected (the tool with the beveled box around it indicates that the particular tool has been chosen). In its initial position, the Hand tool looks like a relaxed hand.

The appearance of the hand changes when its functionality changes. For example, when the Hand tool navigates over a link, it appears as a hand with a pointing finger. To move to the destination of the link, simply click on the link.

If the entire document is not visible on the screen, the appearance of the Hand tool will change to a hand in a clenched fist position as you drag the page on the screen. This cursor indicates that the current page can be moved to another position (up, down, left, right), enabling you to see the parts of the page that were previously out of the range of view.

To move the page to another position:

1. Grab the page by clicking and holding the left mouse button.

2. Pull the page into the desired position.

## Zoom-In Tool

When you initially select the Zoom-in tool, the cursor changes to a magnifying glass. As you use this tool, you can enlarge a non-specific area or a specific part of the document. Although in both cases the entire document is enlarged, choosing a specific area automatically displays that area on the screen, eliminating the need to scroll.

To generally enlarge the document:

1. Position the Zoom-in tool on the area you want to enlarge.
2. Click to enlarge this area.

To enlarge a specific area of the document:

1. Position the Zoom-in tool on the selected area.
2. Click and hold the left mouse button.
3. Drag the Zoom-in tool down and to the right, encasing the selected area in a dotted box.
4. Release the left mouse button.
5. You will see that the text on the screen is the area you encased in the box.

**Note:** *The entire document is enlarged, but the selected area is situated in the center of the screen.*

After the text has been enlarged a few times, the entire document will no longer be visible on the screen.

To see the rest of the document:

1. Choose the **Hand** tool.

**Note:** *Save yourself some strokes by typing **H**, the tool tip for the Hand tool.*

2. Click the left mouse button to grab the document.
3. Move the document in the direction desired.

To show the hidden tools:

1. Navigate your cursor over the Zoom-in tool.
2. Click and hold the right mouse button. You will see:

   For this tool, there is only one hidden tool, the Zoom-out tool (Z). When you hold the mouse button down, and the selection of hidden tools appears, the tool that is currently enabled is grayed out.

## Text Select Tool

When you select the Text Select tool, the cursor changes to a hairline. This particular tool is used only for selecting text. Text selected in Adobe Acrobat can be copied from a PDF file, then pasted to another part of the PDF file (by also using the TouchUp Text tool) or pasted to a document in different application.

If you want to manipulate a graphic, column, or table, you must use one of the tools hidden behind the Text Select tool. These hidden tools enable you to select other types of page elements, such as graphics, columns, and tables. The small arrow situated on the lower-right side of the Text Select tool indicates that hidden tools exist.

To display these tools:

1. Position the cursor on top of the Text Select tool.
2. Click and hold the left mouse button. The tools illustrated below appear:

In total, there are four Select tools included in Adobe Acrobat:

- Text Select tool
- Column Select tool
- Graphics Select tool
- Table/Formatted Text Select tool

One of the most common uses of the Text Select tool is to copy text from the PDF document to another part of the document or to another application.

To copy text to another part of the current PDF document when using the Text Select tool:

1. Select the Text Select tool by clicking on the toolbar or by typing **V**.
2. In your PDF document, select the text by holding the left mouse button down and dragging the cursor to the end of the desired text. When you release the mouse button, the selected text will be highlighted.
3. Copy this text by choosing **Edit | Copy**.
4. Type **T** to change the tool from the Text Select tool to the TouchUp Text tool.
5. Position the cursor at the spot where the text should be pasted.
6. Choose **Edit | Paste**.

You might, of course, want to copy a graphic image found in one of your PDF documents to another application, such as Word. Because the image you are dealing with in this instance is a graphic, you must choose the applicable tool, the Graphics Select tool. This principle applies to the other tools as well.

To choose the Graphics Select tool:

1.  While holding down the left mouse button, position your cursor on top of the Graphics Select tool.

2.  Release the mouse button. The Graphics Select tool now appears on the toolbar in the position of the original Text Select tool.

To use the Graphics Select tool:

1.  Navigate to the upper-left corner of the graphic you'd like to copy.

2.  Click the left mouse button.

3.  While holding this button down, drag the cursor to the lower-right corner of the graphic.

4.  Release the mouse button. At this point, you should see a dotted box surrounding the graphic.

5.  To copy the graphic to another application, choose **Edit | Copy**.

6.  Navigate to the destination document, such as a Word, Excel, or PowerPoint document, then choose **Edit | Paste**.

## Crop Tool

The Crop tool provides you with the ability to manipulate the page layout of the PDF document. Using the Crop tool, you can set the margins for a selected number of pages or for all of your document's pages. It is important to remember that once a page is cropped, that action cannot be undone (unless, of course, you choose not to save the altered document).

The Crop tool can be accessed from two areas in Adobe Acrobat: the toolbar and the Document | Crop Pages command on the menu bar.

To use the Crop tool found on the toolbar:

1.  Click on the **Crop** tool icon on the toolbar. At this point, the cursor will appear as a box with a dotted line running diagonally through it.

2.  Position this cursor at the upper-left side of the area you want to crop.

3. Hold the left mouse button down and drag the cursor to the lower-right side of the area you want to crop.

4. Release the mouse button. At this point, you will see a dotted box around the area you chose to crop.

5. Click the **Crop** tool button once again. Now, a Crop Pages dialog box appears on the screen. In this area, you can change the size and appearance of the borders and margins.

## Annotation Tools

Adobe Acrobat features a collection of Annotation tools that enable you to add different types of annotations to your PDF document. When the system starts up, the default Annotation tool that appears in the toolbar is the Notes tool. However, if you hold the mouse button down, the following hidden tools become visible:

■ Text Annotation tool

■ Audio Annotation tool

■ Stamp Annotation tool

■ File Annotation tool

In a workflow, where documents pass under the scrutiny of many pairs of eyes, these annotations can facilitate the process. However, there may be times when the appearance of all the annotations on the page is unnecessary or distracting. In those cases, you have the option to hide certain types of annotations.

To hide specific types of annotations:

Choose **Tools | Annotations | Filter Manager.**

OR

1. Position the cursor in the note and click the right mouse button.

2. Choose **Annotations Filter**. A list of annotation types will appear in the resulting dialog box.

3. Check the types you want to display on the PDF document.

### Notes Tool

The first visible Annotation tool is the Notes tool. This tool adds a formatted note to your document.

To add a note to your document using the Notes tool:

1. Open up a PDF document, perhaps one you created in Chapter 1.

2. Click on the **Notes** tool. At this point, the cursor will take the form of a sheet of paper.

3. Navigate to the location on the document where you want to add this note, and click (to add the standard size note).

OR

Add a custom-sized note by holding the mouse button down and dragging the box to the desired size.

At this point, you will see a sheet of paper with a small writing area, which displays your name at the top. Here, you can add a significant amount of text into the note.

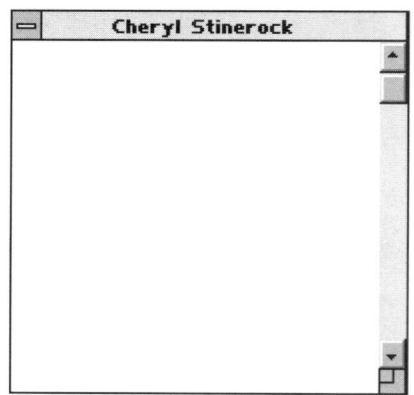

To add a message to the note:

1. Position your cursor in the writing area and click. The cursor changes to the hairline cursor (text) and the writing area becomes a text box (complete with scroll arrow), indicating that you can add text to the screen.

2. Type your message into the box.

To minimize the notes annotation:

Position the cursor inside of the note. Then, click on the minimize button which appears at the top left corner of the note.

OR

1. Navigate to the note. When the cursor is situated on top of the note, it becomes an arrow.

2. Click on the right mouse button. A number of choices are displayed.

3. Choose **Close Note**.

Notice when the note is minimized, a small icon resembling a yellow sheet of paper remains.

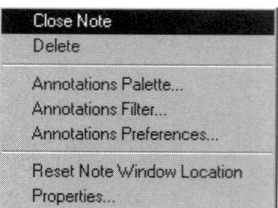

To read a closed note annotation:

Double-click on the note icon to open the annotation.

To delete a note annotation:

1. Navigate to the annotation.

**Note:** *At this point, the annotation can be opened or closed, but it cannot be in edit mode.*

2. Right-click to display a context menu.

3. Choose **Delete**.

### Text Annotation Tool  T+

This annotation tool provides you with the ability to attach annotations in the form of text only (without any type of formatted structure surrounding it).

To add a text annotation:

1. Select the **Text Annotation** tool. The cursor now resembles an open book.

2. Choose the spot on the document where you want to add the annotation, and click to initiate the annotation.

3. The cursor will change to a hairline cursor, indicating that you can now add text.

4. After you complete the text, the annotation is added to the system.

To change the appearance of the text added to a text annotation:

1. Position the cursor over the text annotation. At this point, the cursor will change to an arrow.

2. Click to display the text annotation's border.

3. Click the right mouse button.

4. A number of options will appear; choose **Properties**.

5. In the resulting dialog box, you have the ability to change the following attributes:

   ■ Font type

   ■ Font size

   ■ Text color

   ■ Background color (to show no background color, check Transparent background)

- Border
- Author

To delete a text annotation:

1. Select the text annotation.

2. Press the **Delete** key on your keyboard.

OR

1. Select the text annotation and right-click.

2. Select the **Delete** option.

3. A dialog box asking "Are you sure you want to delete this annotation?" will appear.

4. Select **OK** to delete.

### Audio Annotation Tool

By using this tool, you can easily add instructions, comments, or criticisms to a PDF document. In order to do this, your computer must have the ability to record sound and must have a sound card installed, enabling you to play back the recorded annotation.

To record a comment using the Audio Annotation tool:

1. On the toolbar, choose the **Audio Annotation** tool. The cursor now resembles a small speaker.

2. Navigate to the area on the PDF document where you want to add the annotation.

3. Click once.

4. The Audio Annotation dialog box appears.

5. Press **Start** to begin recording the message.

6. Speak into the microphone.

7. When the message is complete, end the message by pressing **Stop**. After a moment, an icon resembling a small speaker will appear on the PDF document.

To play back an audio annotation:

First, your system must be set up with an audio card. Otherwise, the audio annotations will not be heard when played back on your computer. To play the audio annotation, just click on the small speaker icon on the PDF document.

### Stamp Annotation Tool

By using the Stamp Annotation tool, you can easily stamp a document (with one of a large assortment of stamps included in the Adobe Acrobat library, such as "For Comment" or "Approved"). After the document is stamped, you can continue to add commentary to the document by adding an annotation to it.

To add a stamp annotation to the PDF document:

1. Choose the **Stamp Annotation** tool from the toolbar. The cursor will now resemble a stamp.

2. In the document, navigate to the area where you want to add the stamp.

3. Click once to add the stamp. The stamp now appears in your document.

However, the design of the stamp may not be what you need for your current purpose. Adobe Acrobat provides you with a library of stamp designs to choose from.

To change the appearance of the stamp:

1. Navigate the cursor over the stamp. When it is properly positioned, it will resemble an arrow.

2. Right-click the mouse.

3. Select **Properties** to display the Stamp Properties dialog box. Here, several different categories of stamp designs provide you with a large quantity of stamp options.

4. Select the category, then the actual stamp design from the left box.

**Note:** *The box on the right will provide a preview, eliminating the need for trial and error on the document.*

As the document is routed through an approval process, chances are that you will want to add a note of explanation to the stamp.

To add a text annotation to the stamp:

1. Position the cursor over the stamp. At this point, the cursor will change to an arrow.

2. Double-click to display the text box. Notice that the appearance of this box is very similar to the text box created by the Text Annotation tool. However, the Stamp Annotation tool controls it.

3. Type the desired comment into the text box.

4. Minimize the text box by clicking on the minimize box on the upper-left side of the text box

To display a comment associated with a stamp:

Just double-click on the stamp, and the text box will appear.

### File Annotation Tool

There are times when it is necessary to attach an external file to a PDF document. In those cases, the File Annotation tool makes it easy to attach and then launch a Word, Excel, PDF, etc., file from within the PDF document.

To attach a file to your PDF document:

1. On the toolbar, choose the **File Annotation** tool. The cursor changes to a pushpin.
2. Navigate to the area on the PDF document where you want to add the file annotation.
3. Click once.
4. A Select File to Attach dialog box appears. Choose the file you want to attach.
5. Select **Open**.
6. The File Annotation Properties dialog box appears. Here, you have the option to choose the icon that will represent the attached file on the PDF document, the description, the author, and the color.
7. Make your selections, then press **OK**.

To launch the attached file:

1. Double-click on the icon representing the attached file. A Launch File dialog box will appear, asking "Do you want to launch the attached file?"
2. Choose **OK** to launch the file.

If the file you attached is also a PDF file, you will have no problem returning to the main document. Just click on the Go to Previous View icon on the menu bar. However, if the file you attached is a non-PDF file, you need to minimize or close out of the application prior to returning to the main PDF document.

# Pencil Tool

The Pencil tool is one of the graphic markup tools that appear on the toolbar. The three additional hidden tools are: Rectangle tool, Ellipse tool, and Line tool. Each tool provides you with the flexibility to add visual marks to a PDF documents along with explanatory notes.

After a graphic is added to the PDF document, you have the option to accompany the mark with text. Additionally, all of these tools remain selected after you add the graphic to the PDF document.

The most flexible tool, regarding shape, appears to be the Pencil tool. The other tools enable you to create various sizes of one particular shape (rectangle, ellipse, line).

To create a graphic markup using the Pencil tool:

1. Open a PDF document, perhaps one you created in Chapter 1.

2. Choose the Pencil tool on the toolbar by clicking on the icon or by typing **N**. The cursor changes to a cross hair shape.

3. Navigate to the area on your document where you'd like to add the graphic markup.

4. Hold the mouse button down as you draw the graphic markup.

5. Release the mouse button when you are finished.

6. If desired, you can add additional markups to the PDF document using this tool.

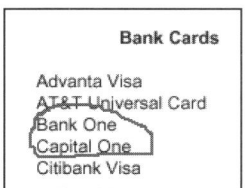

To change the appearance of the graphic markup:

1. Click on the graphic markup to display the bounding box.

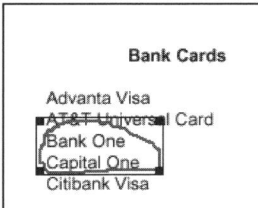

2. With the cursor situated inside of the bounding box, right-click.

3. Choose the **Properties** option. Here, you are provided with the opportunity to change the following attributes:

■ Thickness of the line

■ Color

■ Author

To attach an annotation to the graphic markup:

1. Again, click on the graphic markup to display the bounding box, then right-click.

2. Choose the **Open Note** option.

3. When the note opens, type your message into the text box.

4. To close the note, click on the minimize button on the upper left of the box.

5. To open the note, double-click on the graphic markup.

The Rectangle tool, Ellipse tool, and the Line tool function in a similar way. All provide you with the ability to add a graphic markup to your PDF document, and all enable you to attach a note annotation to the markups.

## Highlight Text Tool

The Highlight Text tool is one of the trio of text markup tools. The default tool is the Highlight Text tool. The two hidden tools are:

■ Strikethrough Text tool

■ Underline Text tool

After the text is marked up, you can add a note annotation to the text, providing the reader, during the workflow process, a valid explanation of the markup.

To mark up text using the Highlight Text tool:

**Note:** *Although this example uses the Highlight Text tool, keep in mind that these three text markup tools function essentially in the same way.*

1. Choose the Highlight Text tool by clicking on the icon found on the toolbar or by typing **U**. The cursor now appears in the shape of a hairline (the cursor usually associated with text).

2. Select the text you want to highlight. When you move the cursor to another position, you'll find the text is highlighted.

To change the appearance of highlighted text:

1. Navigate the cursor over the highlighted text until the cursor changes to an arrow, then right-click.

2. Choose the **Properties** option.

3. The resulting Highlight Properties dialog box provides you with the ability to change the color and the author.

The Strikethrough Text tool and the Underline Text tool function in the same way. Additionally, all three text markup tools enable you to associate the marked-up text with a note annotation.

To add a note annotation to the highlighted text:

1. Navigate the cursor over the highlighted text until the cursor changes to an arrow.

2. Right-click, then choose the **Open Note** option.

3. Add your explanation of the highlighted text.

4. Close the note by clicking the minimize button in the upper left corner.

| Statement Closing Date |
| 09/03/96 |
| 09/02/96 |

## Movie Tool

By using the Movie tool, you can add movie clips or sound clips for a variety of reasons, including:

- Training
- Walking users through the process of filling out certain areas of a form
- Demonstrating new products

When using a Windows-based system, there are two video file types that can be used with the Movie tool: .avi and Quicktime (.mov) files. The two sound files that can be used with a Windows-based system are: .aif and .wav.

The Movie tool adds movie and sound files to the PDF document differently. When a sound file is added to the document, the file is embedded in the document, making it essentially part of the document. If you receive that PDF document, you will automatically receive the sound file.

However, when a movie is added to a PDF document, it is not actually part of the document. The Movie tool merely adds a link to the file containing the video clip. Therefore, when a PDF file that includes links to movie clips is distributed, the file containing the movie must also be distributed.

To add a movie clip to a PDF document:

1. Prior to adding the movie clip to your document, you should have an .avi or a .mov file available on your system. If this is not the case, access your favorite search engine on the Internet and search for "AVI files" or "MOV files." Either choice will provide you with a large assortment of free .avi or QuickTime (.mov) files you can add to your PDF document.

2. Choose the Movie tool by clicking on the icon on the toolbar or typing **M**. The cursor now resembles a cross hair.

3. Navigate to the area of the PDF document where you want to add the movie clip.

4. Click once to add the default size icon, or drag the rectangle to the desired size. (When adding links to movies, it is suggested that you do not enlarge or change the size or shape of the rectangle. This may cause some type of distortion.)

5. You should now see the Open dialog box. In the Files of type area, choose **All Movies** or **QuickTime Movies**.

6. Locate the movie file you want to add to the PDF document, then press **Open**.

7. The movie is added to the selected spot on the PDF file and the Movie Properties dialog box opens.

8. Keep the default properties or enter your desired changes. In the Movie Properties dialog box, some of the attributes you can change include: Player Options, Movie Poster (the icon on the PDF file representing the movie), and Border Appearance.

9. Once you have made your choices, press **OK** or **Save Preferences**.

After a movie is added to a PDF file, you have the ability to drag the movie poster to a different location on the screen. Also, you can drag the rectangle to enlarge or shrink the size of the movie poster. As you change the size of the movie, keep in mind that the video files are saved in a format containing a fixed number of pixels. If you enlarge the movie, you may see decreased quality of the image. It is strongly suggested that the size of the movie that is added by the Movie tool is retained.

To add a sound clip to a PDF document:

1. Choose the **Movie** tool.
2. Navigate to the area of the document where you want to add the sound clip.
3. Hold the mouse button down while you create a box. When adding sound clips, it is necessary to define the active area. The rectangular area you define in this step will be the area where the sound clip can be activated.
4. When the size of the box is selected, release the mouse button.
5. The Open dialog box appears on the screen.
6. In the Files of type field, **All Files** must be selected.
7. Choose the sound file (of type .aif or .wav), then press **Open**.
8. The Movie Properties dialog box appears on the screen.
9. Choose the desired appearance of the Sound icon, then select **Save Preferences** or **OK**.

To play a movie or a sound clip:

1. Select the Hand tool by typing **H** or clicking the Hand tool on the toolbar.
2. Navigate to the movie/sound on the PDF document.
3. Click once to begin playing the movie/sound.
4. To stop the movie/sound, click again or press the **Escape** key on the keyboard.

## Link Tool

With a click, a link quickly displays another area on the same page of the document, another page of the same document, another document, or a site on the Internet. The Link tool provides you with the ability to create and manipulate links in a PDF file.

To add a link within a document:

1. Select the Link tool by clicking on the Link tool in the toolbar or by typing **L**.
2. Navigate to the text/picture/chart that will be the source of the link.
3. Hold the mouse button down, and drag to create a box around the selected area. The selected area will function as the source of the link.

4. Release the mouse button. The Create Link dialog box appears.

5. Navigate to the area of the document to which you want to link. This is the target of the link.

6. In the Create dialog box, define the appearance, action, and magnification of the link.

7. Press **Set Link** to create the link.

To use a link:

1. In order to use a link in a PDF document, you must select the Hand tool by clicking on the icon in the toolbar or by typing **H**. The cursor now appears as a hand.

2. When you navigate over the source of the link, the cursor changes to a pointing finger, indicating that a link exists.

3. Click once. Your screen will now display the target of the link.

## Article Tool

This tool gives you the ability to link together separated parts of a document. By creating this link (or "thread"), you provide the reader with an easy way to view related parts of a document in a certain sequence.

To create an article:

1. Choose the Article tool by clicking on the icon found on the toolbar or typing **A**. The cursor now appears as a cross hair.

2. Navigate to the position on the document where you want the article thread to begin.

3. Define the area by holding the mouse button down and dragging a box around the selected text. At this point, the cursor changes to the Article cursor ⬚.

4. Release the mouse button. Notice that this section now appears with an assigned number a-b, where a refers to the number of the article and b refers to the section within an article. In other words, 1-2 would mean that the section is the second section of the first article.

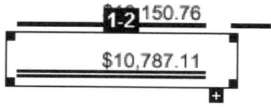

5. Navigate to the next thread in the article.

6. Hold the mouse button down and define the area you want to include in the next section.

7. Repeat the above steps until you reach the end of the article.

8. Click on any other icon to finish the article.

9. The Article Properties dialog box will appear on the screen. Here, you can define the following: title, subject, author, and keywords.

10. After you've added all desired information, press **OK**. The boxes around the chosen sections will disappear.

To navigate through an article:

1. First, choose the **Hand** tool on the toolbar. As you navigate the document, you'll notice that the Hand tool's cursor contains a downward-pointing arrow when it is situated over a defined article thread.

2. Click once to navigate to the first part of the article.

3. Click once again to navigate to the second part of the article.

4. Continue to click. When the end of the article is reached, the next click will return you to your initial position in the document.

## Form Tool

The Form tool lets you create a usable form to be accessed from your current computer system or from the World Wide Web. By using this tool, you can add a great deal of functionality to your form by using:

- Form fields
- Combo boxes
- Check boxes
- Radio buttons

To begin using the Form tool, you must begin with a form. A form is merely a PDF file which has been designed as a form. Due to the fact that the same form will be used many times, the actual design of this document is quite important.

One of the most common fields added to a form is the text field. In the following example, you will add a text field to a document to be used as a form. For more information regarding the design and creation of a form, refer to Chapter 4.

To add a text input field to a form:

1. Open the document to be used as the form. If this document is not a PDF file, convert this file to PDF format.

2. Choose the Form tool by clicking the icon on the toolbar or by typing **F**. The cursor now appears as a cross hair pointer.

3. Navigate to the position on the document where you want to add the text input field.

4. Hold the mouse button down and drag to define the input area.

5. Release the mouse button.

6. The Field Properties dialog box appears. A significant amount of information can be entered here, including the name, type, and a short description. Important to note is the fact that the type actually determines what type of information you will be able to manipulate in this dialog box.

   Add a name and a short description. Then choose **Text** in the Type field. When all information is added, press **OK**. The field is added to your form.

To enter text into the text field:

1. To add text into this field, click on the **Hand** tool.

2. Navigate to the area on the document where the text field was added.

3. The Hand tool will immediately change to a hairline, indicating that it is situated over a text input field.

4. Add your text.

## Digital Signature Tool

The Digital Signature tool enables you to sign documents digitally. While performing this process electronically, the use of this tool also provides enhanced security.

A document can be signed more than once. However, the first time the document is signed, the document is locked into an "append-only" state. This means that any information which is added to the document at a later date will appear as appended text.

Another feature of the digital signature is the fact that each signature is associated with only one version of the document. This makes it easy to determine which document each of the people in the approval process signed.

Two plug-ins included in Adobe Acrobat function as "signature handlers":

■ Acrobat Self-Sign

■ Acrobat Entrust Security

These "signature handlers" enable you to store your signature in three different formats:

■ Handwritten signature

■ Text signature

■ Graphic signature

Also, they enable you to store (along with the signature) some additional identifying information, including a password. This provides for a secure approval process.

To add a digital signature:

**Note:** *The following provides a quick and easy way to use this feature. For more in-depth coverage of this topic, refer to Chapter 5.*

1. Choose the Digital Signature tool by clicking on the icon or typing **D**. At this time, the cursor will change to a cross hair pointer.

2. Navigate to the area on your document where you want to add the signature box and the signature.

3. Hold the mouse button down and drag, creating the outline of a box, then release it.

4. The Acrobat Digital Signature Plug-in dialog box appears on the screen, giving you the ability to choose your signature handler. Acrobat Self-Sign Signatures is automatically installed. If you have not installed any other signature handler add-ins, choose **Acrobat Self-Sign**. Press **OK**.

5. If this is your first time using the Digital Signature tool, then a dialog box will appear which requests some business information (name, company, department) and requests that you set a password.

6. Next, the Acrobat Self-Sign Signatures — Sign Document dialog box will appear.

7. To view the Certificate Attributes, press **Show Certificate**. You can add the reason for signing the document and the city (optional).

8. Input your password. If you add the incorrect password, you won't be able to save the signature with this document.

9. Press **Save Document**.

10. The Save As dialog box will appear. Choose a name and storage location for the document. When the signed document has been saved, the signature box will include your name and other particulars.

> Digitally signed by Cheryl Stinerock
> cn=Cheryl Stinerock, ou=Marketing, o=CLS
> Enterprises, c=US
> Date: 2000.07.09 17:08:58 -08'00'
> Reason: I am the author of this document
> New York, NY

## Text TouchUp Tool

Keep in mind that the Text TouchUp tool (along with the hidden Object TouchUp tool — to be used when modifying images) should only be used for minor editing. Using this tool only seems beneficial if your document requires alteration of only a few characters.

The Text TouchUp tool provides you with the ability to:

- Create one line (for text input)
- Undo one level of input (e.g., if you type the word "asset," then attempt to undo, you will only be able to undo the letter "t")
- Change the text attributes
- Add characters

If a document requires a fairly substantial editing job, you should:

1. Edit the document in its original form.

2. Reconvert it to PDF format.

OR

1. Edit some of the pages of the document in their original form.

2. Reconvert them to PDF format.

3. Then insert them into the PDF document.

However, if a minute bit of editing is all your document requires, then this is a helpful tool for you to use. The following exercise will walk you through a few of the techniques available though use of the Text TouchUp tool.

To create one line of text input using the Text TouchUp tool:

1. Choose the Text TouchUp tool from the toolbar by clicking on the icon or typing **T**. The cursor will change to a hairline cursor, indicating that text manipulation is possible.

2. Position the cursor in the area where you want to add the line of text.

3. Hold down **Ctrl** and click.

4. The new line of text will begin at the cursor position. This is only one line of text. Input text will not automatically wrap around. In order to add more than one new line of text, you must repeat these steps as required.

5. Begin typing. Notice that the text appearing in the newly created line probably is not identical to the rest of the text on the document. The attributes of the text, then, should be changed.

To change text attributes using the Text TouchUp tool:

1. Using the Text TouchUp tool, highlight the text you need to change.

2. Right-click to display the pop-up menu.

3. Select **Attributes**.

4. The Font Attributes dialog box will appear on the screen and provide you with the opportunity to change font, character, and line attributes.

5. After you make the changes, click the **X** in the upper-right corner to close the dialog box.

6. Your changes will automatically be visible in the document.

# Navigation Pane

The navigation pane appears to the left of the document pane. Available on this pane are four tabs which enable you to rapidly navigate a document in this area, including:

- Bookmarks — essentially, a table of contents
- Thumbnails — screen shots which offer you quick access to certain pages
- Annotations — listing of all annotations on the document
- Signatures — listing of all signatures on the document

Choices made in the navigation pane will change your view in the document pane. In other words, the navigation pane provides you with the ability to selectively navigate the document.

To display/hide the navigation pane:

Click the **Show/Hide Navigation Pane** icon ▣ on the command bar.

OR

Click the upper-left corner of the document pane.

# Palette Menu

To access the palette menu, click the arrow on the upper-right corner of the navigation pane.

For each of the tabs, the palette menu differs. Under the Bookmarks tab, the palette menu provides you with bookmark-centered functionality, including:

- New Bookmark — Create a new bookmark.
- Show Location — Highlight in boldface the current bookmark.
- Hide After Use — After accessing a bookmark, the navigation pane will hide.
- Rename — Rename a bookmark.
- Delete — Delete a bookmark.

If you click on the Thumbnails tab, then pull up the palette menu, the options presented provide you with the ability to:

- Insert Pages — Insert pages into the document.
- Extract Pages — Extract pages from the document.
- Replace Pages — Replace a page in the document with a page from another source.
- Delete Pages — Delete pages from the document.
- Crop Pages — Choose a single page or a group of pages to crop.
- Rotate Pages — Choose a single page or a group of pages to rotate.
- Number Pages — Renumber the thumbnail pages.
- Create/Delete All Thumbnails — Auto-create thumbnails for all pages of the document or auto-delete thumbnails for all pages of the current document.

- Small/Large Thumbnails — Choose the preferred size.

The palette menu available under the Annotations tab enables you to search through the annotations added to a document and organize them in the navigation pane in a preferred manner. In this tab, the options found under the palette menu include:

- Import/Export — Provides you with the ability to use annotations from other documents or to send annotations to other documents.

- Delete — This is another way to delete an annotation.

- Find Annotation/Find Next/Find Previous — Enables you to search the content of the document's annotations using a text string.

- Type/Author/Page Number/Date — Lets you organize the annotations displayed in the navigation pane by these topics.

- Rescan Document — Allows you to rescan the document to ensure that all of the document's annotations are included on the navigation pane.

Finally, the palette menu is also available under the Signatures tab. These options give you the ability to:

- Sign and Save — To sign and save the current document, choose this option.

- Compare Pages — Choose this option to compare the PDF documents you currently have on the screen or minimized.

- Validate All Signatures — Click this option to validate the signatures on this document. If the signature is presented in the navigation pane preceded by a question mark, that signature needs to be validated.

- Sign Signature Field — When your document contains an empty signature field, you can choose the Sign Signature Field option to add a signature to the field.

- Rollback to Signature — Each signer of a document has the ability to append to the document. To view exactly what version applies to a certain signature, choose Rollback to Signature.

- Delete Signature Field — This option provides you with a method to use when deleting a signature field.

- Clear Signature Field — Choose this option to clear a signature field. Keep in mind, however, that this action creates a new version of the document with a cleared signature field. The version of the document originally containing the signature remains intact.

■ Properties — When you click on this option, various properties of the signature are displayed or are available for display (including validity information, certificate information, and the document to which the signature is applicable).

# Status Bar

By using some of the buttons on the status bar, you can easily change the display of your document in the document window and quickly navigate through the document. From left to right, these options include:

### Navigation Pane Button

This button is a toggle key. Click it to show/hide the navigation pane.

### Magnification Level

Here, the magnification level of the document currently displayed in the document pane is shown.

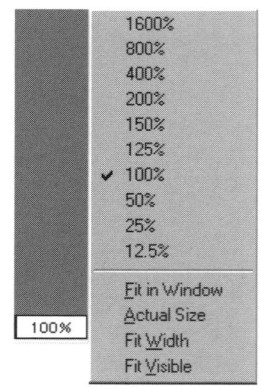

### Magnification Pop-Up Menu

This menu gives you a number of magnification sizes from which to choose.

### First Page Button

Clicking this button automatically returns the view in the document pane to the first page of the document.

### Previous Page Button

This button returns you to the previous page of the current document.

### Current Page

This area displays the number of the page currently in the document pane and the total number of pages in the document.

## Next Page Button ▶

Clicking this button will display the next page of the document in the document pane.

## Last Page Button ▶|

Click this button to display the last page of the current document in the document pane.

## Page Size  5.57 x 5.57 in

This area displays current page size of the document in the document pane.

## Page Layout Pop-Up Menu

This menu provides you with a choice of page layout.

# Document Pane

This pane is your work area. Your document appears in this area and can be revised. Through the various options located in a few areas on the screen, you have the ability to customize its appearance and control navigating through it.

# Document Pane Menu

Click on the arrow on the upper-right corner of the document pane to display the Document Pane menu.

Here, you have the ability to acquire information about the current document or to determine the appearance of the document pane.

## Document Info

Click on Document Info to display the General Info dialog box. This box contains a significant amount of historical data regarding the document. Some of these fields are editable; others are automatically generated and are not updateable.

The editable fields include: Title, Subject, Author, Keywords, and Binding. After a change is entered into one of those fields, click OK to save the change.

Some of the fixed fields include: Creator (the software that initially created the document), Created (the date/time the document was actually created), and File Size (bytes).

## Security Info

Choosing this option displays the Document Security dialog box. This box contains a listing of the existing security on the current document.

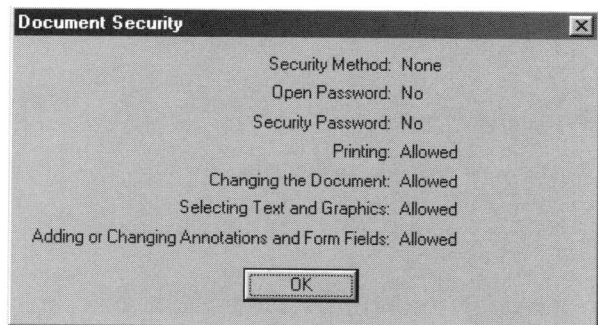

See Chapter 5 for a detailed explanation of how to set up and change document security.

## Font Info

When you click on the Font Info option, the Font Info dialog box appears on the screen. This box provides you with the history of the fonts used in this document. To view the list of all of the fonts in the current document, select the List All Fonts option.

## Preferences

Click on the Preferences option to display the General Preferences dialog box. This dialog box gives you a certain level of control regarding the appearance and the functionality of the document pane. Some of the areas you can customize include:

- Display
- Magnification

- Color
- Options (e.g., Allow background downloading, Display splash screen at startup, Open Cross-doc links in same window)

As you've most likely noticed, many of the functions are provided in more than one area of Adobe Acrobat's user interface. This gives you the ability to increase the pace at which you create and manipulate PDF documents.

The following chapters will cover many of those areas which have been briefly discussed in this chapter. The purpose of this chapter was mainly to acquaint you with the features provided by Acrobat. The following chapters will build upon that knowledge, enabling you to create documents that not only move through your workflow process, but also are actually part of the workflow.

# Chapter 3

# Enhancing PDF Files with Bookmarks, Thumbnails, and Links

PDF files provide you with many features that can expedite your processes and save time for you and your organization. When browsing through a particular document, bookmarks, thumbnails, and links provide you with the ability to jump from one part of a document to another. Although these three features are used in different ways, all of them save you a precious commodity — time!

## Bookmarks

Bookmarks are merely bits of text that are linked to specific pages within your document. They appear in a hierarchical organization, with the main bookmarks expanding to display subordinate bookmarks. One of the most common uses of bookmarks is to create a table of contents, which enables readers of the document to rapidly access selected information. To use a bookmark, a user only needs to click on the desired topic in the navigation pane to view the desired page in the document pane.

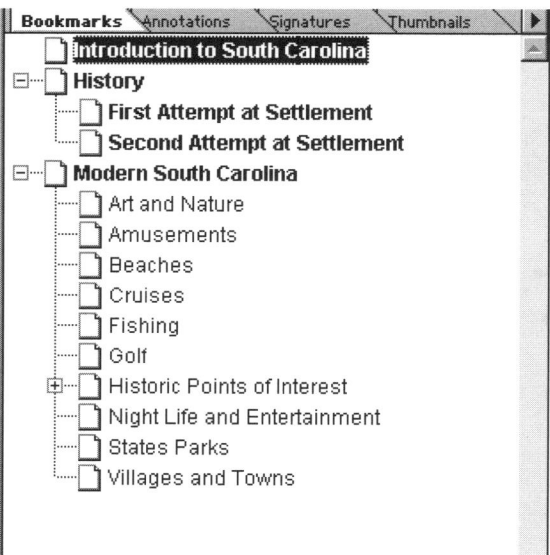

# Adding a Bookmark Automatically

Adding a bookmark to a PDF document can be done automatically with a minimum of effort. First, of course, a document must be created in an application that enables you to define text styles, headers, etc. Microsoft Word is a good example of such an application.

The following exercise will walk you through the process of formatting a Word document in a manner that will enable you to add bookmarks automatically. After the document is created, you can use Acrobat PDFMaker to convert the document to PDF format and automatically generate bookmarks.

## Required Formatting in a Word Document

1. First, create a document in Word.
2. While in Word, add section headings to the document.
3. Format the section headings by selecting the heading, then clicking **Format | Style**. The Style dialog box is displayed on the screen.

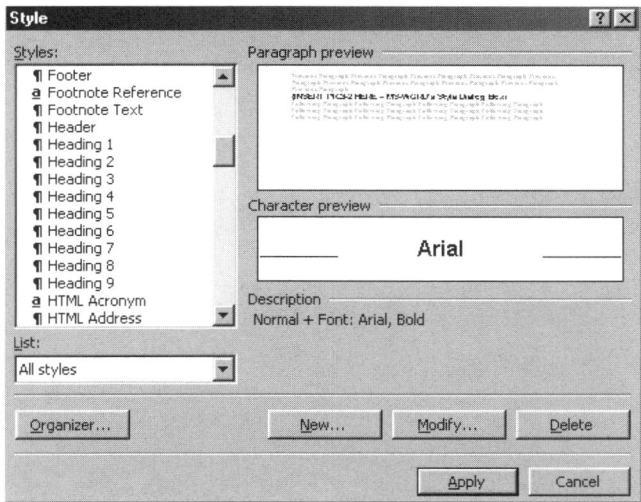

4. In the Style dialog box, choose a heading style from Heading 1 to Heading 9.

*Note: You can choose any of the other selections in this box; however, if this is done, then some of the required options during the conversion process will differ.*

As you choose the heading styles, keep in mind that Heading 1 must be followed by Heading 2, and Heading 2 must be followed by Heading 3. If this sequence is not retained, then the system will add empty levels for each missing level.

5. After the section headings are formatted, your document is ready to be converted to PDF format, complete with automatically generated bookmarks.

## Converting the Formatted Word Document to PDF Format

1. In Word, click the **Adobe PDFMaker** icon to launch the conversion process.

The Acrobat PDFMaker for Microsoft Word dialog box will appear on the screen.

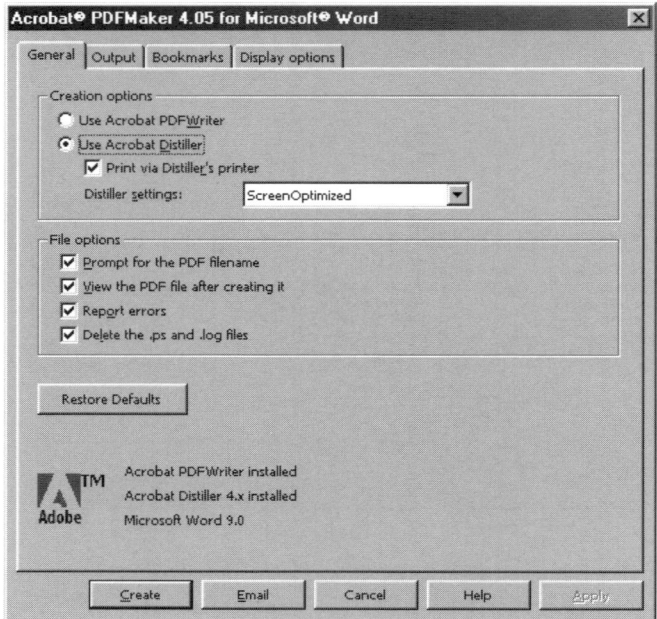

2.  On the General tab (the initial tab), choose the **Use Acrobat Distiller** option.

    ***Note:*** *PDFWriter will not automatically generate bookmarks.*

3.  Navigate to the Bookmarks tab.

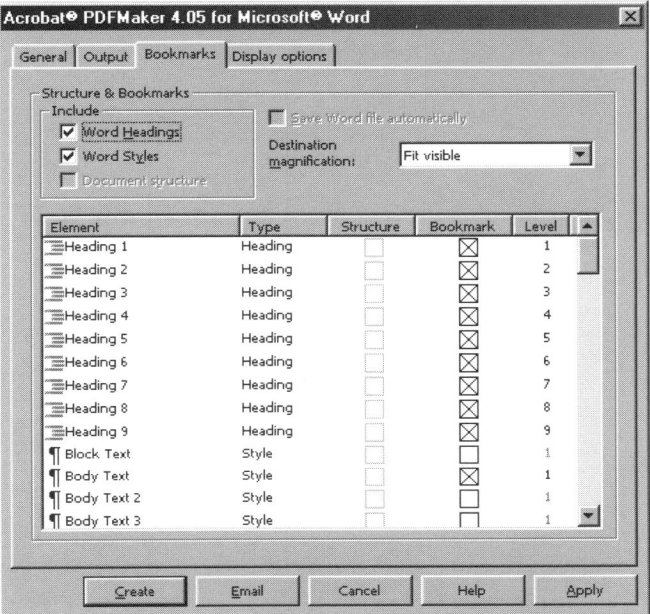

4. In the Include box, choose **Word Headings** if you formatted the document using only styles Heading 1 through Heading 9. Choose **Word Styles** if you have formatted text with any of the other available styles and if you want that text to be converted to a bookmark.

**Note:** *The style options found on the Bookmarks tab are identical to the style options found in your installed version of Word.*

If you select Word Styles, you will be provided with the ability to:

- Choose the styles that should be included when bookmarks are automatically generated. By clicking in the box appearing in the Bookmark column, the style found in the Element column is selected for inclusion as a bookmark.

- Determine at which position in the bookmark hierarchy certain style types should appear. By choosing 1, 2, 3, etc., in the Level column, you have the ability to organize a hierarchy that is specific to your project.

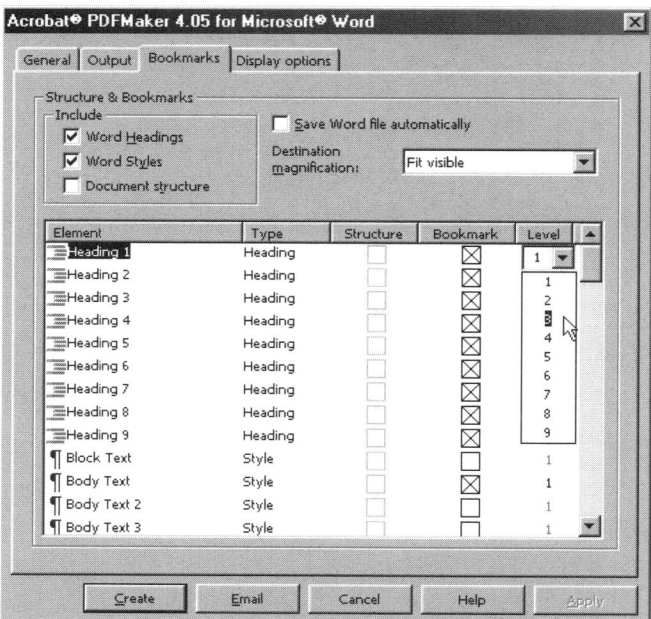

5. After all selections are made, click **Create**. The PDF file, along with bookmarks, will be automatically generated.

# Adding a Bookmark Manually

Adding bookmarks automatically is certainly the most efficient method to create a selection of bookmarks for a document. However, there is always a chance that a few desired bookmarks were not automatically created. Or, there is the possibility that you may want to include a link to a specific view that is available on the Bookmarks palette. In those cases, you may want to manually add a bookmark. To manually add a bookmark:

1. First, open the PDF document that will contain the bookmark.

2. If the navigation pane does not show, click the **Show/Hide Navigation Pane** icon ▦ (found on the command bar).

3. If the Bookmarks palette does not show on the navigation pane, click the Bookmarks tab to show it.

```
    Introduction to South Carolina
⊟   History
        First Attempt at Settlement
        Second Attempt at Settlement
⊟   Modern South Carolina
        Accommodations
        Amusements
        Art and Nature
        Beaches
        Cruises
        Fishing
        Golf
   ⊟   Historic Points of Interest
            Charlestown
            Georgetown
        Night Life and Entertainment
        States Parks
        Villages and Towns
```

4. To position the bookmark in a specific location on the Bookmarks palette, click the bookmark that is positioned above where the new
   bookmark will be added.

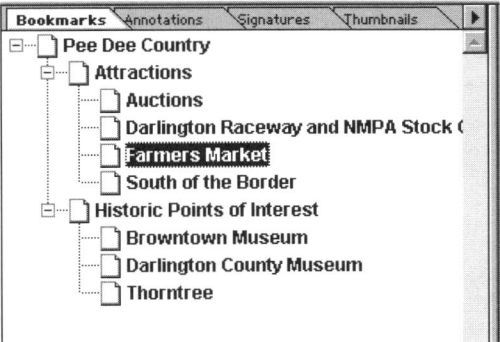

*Note:* *If you do not choose a position for the bookmark, it will automatically be added to the end of the bookmarks.*

5. In the document pane, navigate to the area within the current document to which you want the new bookmark to link.

6. Click the right-pointing arrow at the top of the navigation pane to access the Bookmarks palette menu.

7. Click the **New Bookmark** option or navigate to the bottom of the Bookmarks palette and select the **Create New Bookmark** icon.

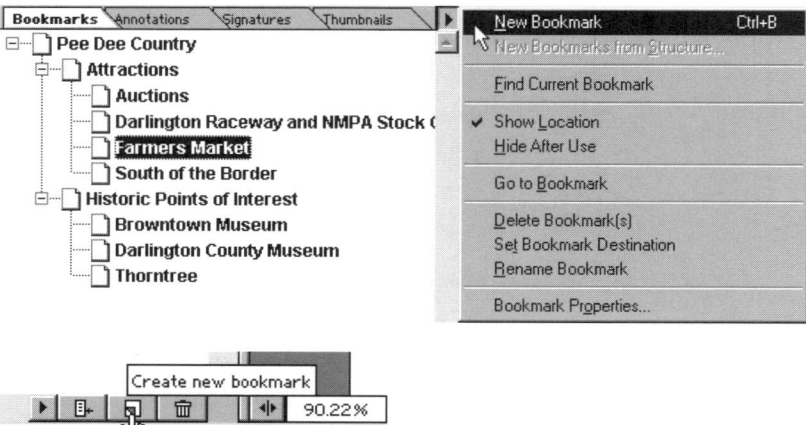

8. A bookmark named "Untitled" will appear on the Bookmarks palette. Highlight **Untitled**, then add the correct name of the bookmark.

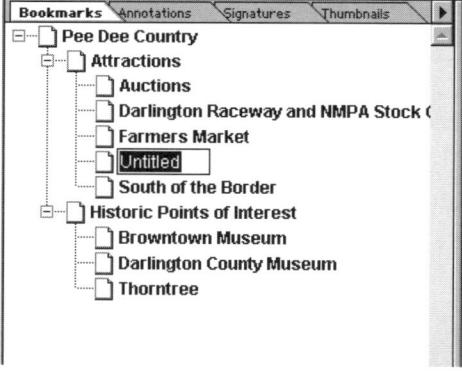

9. While the Hand tool is selected, click the new bookmark to test it.

# Adding a Bookmark Linked to Another PDF File

During the creation of a collection of bookmarks, you may want to enable the users to navigate to PDF documents other than the one in which the bookmarks reside. To link bookmarks to other PDF files:

1. Add the new bookmark into the main PDF document (please refer to the previous section, "Adding a Bookmark Manually").

2. Highlight the bookmark, then click the right mouse button to display the Bookmark menu.

3. Select **Properties**.

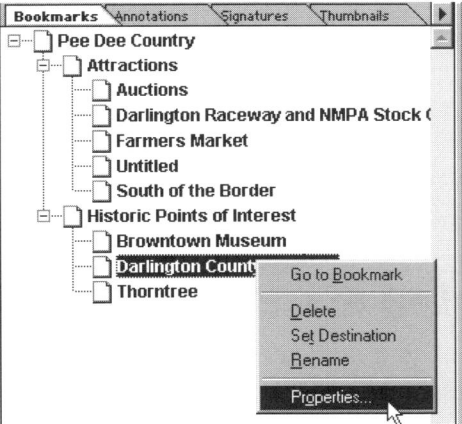

4. The Bookmark Properties dialog box appears. In the Type drop-down box, choose **Go to View**.

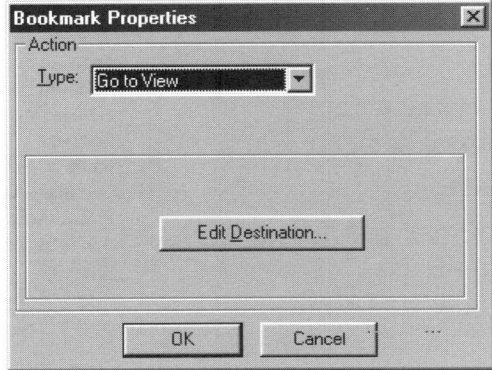

5. Press **Edit Destination**. Additional options appear in the Bookmark Properties dialog box.

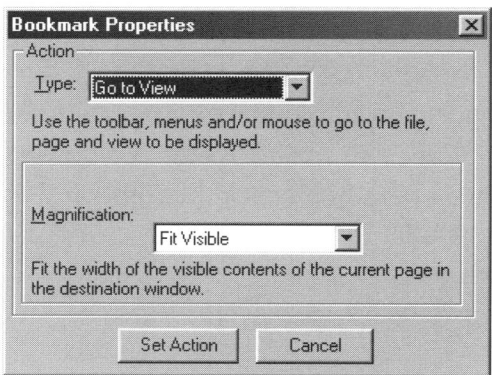

6. Navigate to the document and the view to be linked to the bookmark.
7. After the document and view are displayed, press **Set Action** to save this bookmark.

# Adding a Bookmark Linked to a Non-PDF File

As your project grows, you may need to include bookmarks linked to non-PDF files. As long as the users of your document have the application required to view the non-PDF file, they will be able to view the document linked to the bookmark. To add a bookmark that is linked to a non-PDF file:

1. Add the new bookmark to the document.
2. Highlight the bookmark, then click the right mouse button to display the Bookmark menu.
3. Select **Properties**.
4. The Bookmark Properties dialog box appears. In the Type drop-down box, select **Open File**.
5. Press **Select File**.

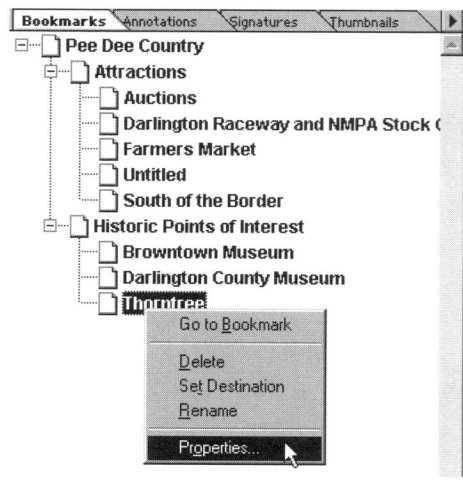

6. The Select File to Open dialog box appears. Select the file to which you want the new bookmark to link.

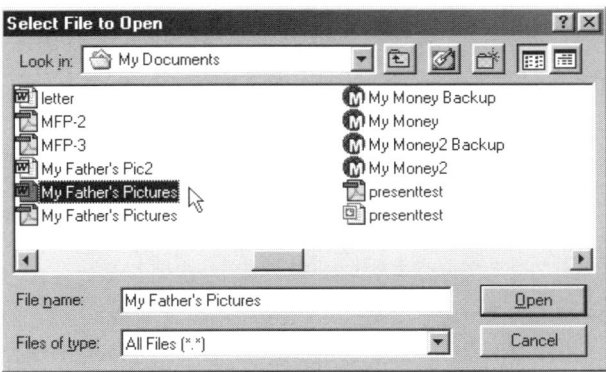

7. Notice the filename you selected appears in the Bookmark Properties dialog box. If this name is correct, click **Set Action**.

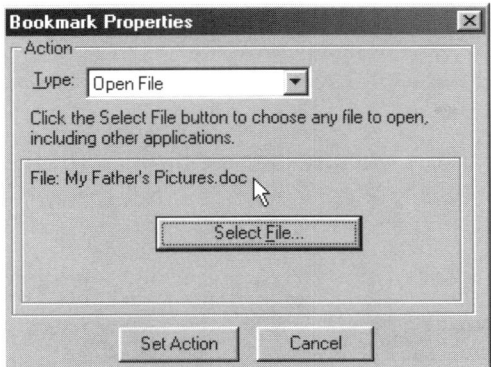

*Note: When you click on a bookmark that is linked to a non-PDF file, the following message will appear.*

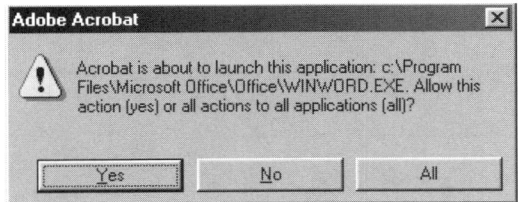

*Select **Yes** to navigate to the application and the file linked to the bookmark.*

# Adding a Bookmark Linked to a Movie

Throughout Adobe Acrobat, you can easily add movie clips to documents and configure how and when they will be accessed and played. However, if you intend to use movie clips in your final documents, you must make sure that:

■ All users of the document have Apple QuickTime (version 2.0 or later) or Microsoft Video.

**Note:** *If the users of your document use the Mac OS, they must have Apple QuickTime, version 2.0 or later, on their system.*

■ A copy of the movie is distributed along with the PDF document. (Since the movie is not embedded in the PDF document, it is always necessary to include the movie file in the document distribution package.)

## Adding a Movie to a Document

1. Choose the **Movie** tool 🎞 on the toolbar.
2. Navigate to the location in the document where you want to add the movie.
3. Click the area on the document where you want the movie to be placed. (**Note:** *Where you click will be the center of the movie.*) The Open dialog box appears.
4. Highlight the movie you want to include in the document.

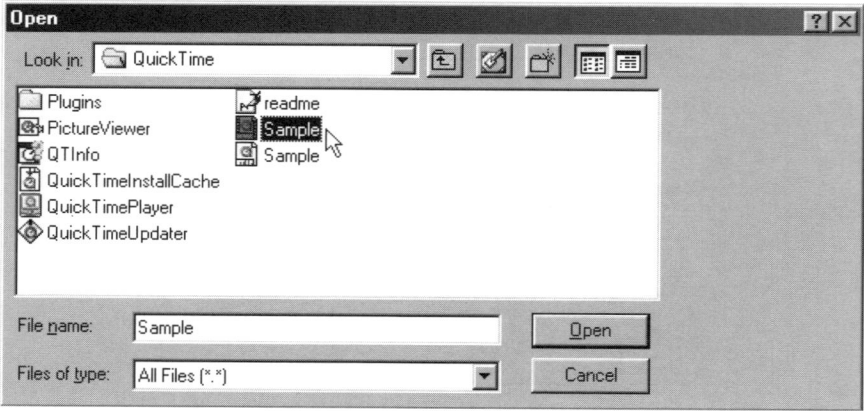

5. Click **Open**. The Movie Properties dialog box appears.

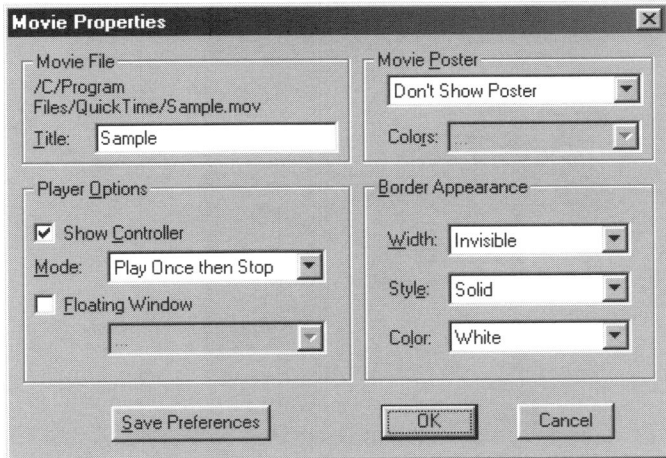

6. In the Movie Properties dialog box select all desired properties. If you want the movie to remain invisible unless the bookmark is selected, then choose:

- **Don't Show Poster** in the Movie Poster field.
- **Invisible** in the Width field.

## Creating a Bookmark to Link to the Movie

1. On the Bookmarks palette, position the cursor by clicking on the bookmark situated above where you want to add this new bookmark. Remember, when you add a new bookmark, it is automatically added beneath the cursor.

2. Click the **Create New Bookmark** icon.

3. The new bookmark will appear in the Bookmarks palette as "Untitled." To change the default name of the bookmark, highlight **Untitled** and type over it.

4. Position the cursor over the bookmark and right-click.

5. In the menu that appears, choose **Properties**. The Bookmark Properties dialog box will appear.

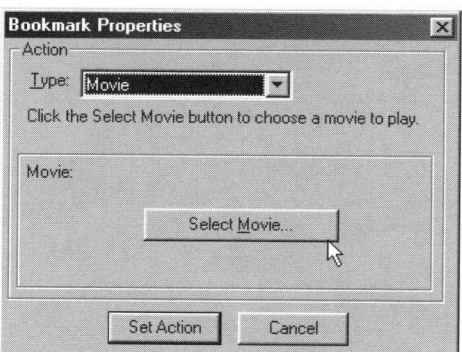

6. In the Type field, choose **Movie**.

7. Press **Select Movie** to choose the movie. Keep in mind that the movie (as demonstrated in this example) must be added to the document prior to its association with a bookmark. The Movie Action dialog box appears.

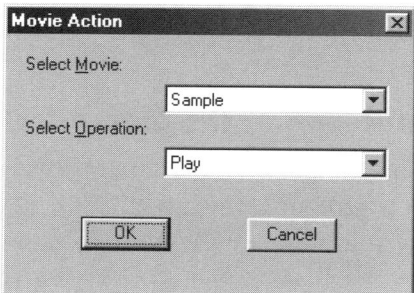

8. In the Select Movie field, the options available will include those movies that have been added to the current document and are located on the current page in the document pane. Select one of these movies to link to the bookmark.

9. In the Select Operation field, a few options are available:

   ■ Play

   ■ Stop

   ■ Pause

   ■ Resume

10. Click **OK** to close the Movie Action dialog box.

11. Click **Set Action** to close the Bookmark Properties dialog box.

To test your new bookmark, just click on the bookmark. The movie will appear in the document frame at your current position in the document. Instead of navigating from your current position to the position of the movie in the document, the movie navigates to your current location in the document. After it plays, the movie closes and disappears from your view.

## Adding a Sound to a Bookmark

When you include a sound in your PDF file, the sound file (when using the Windows OS, an .aif or a .wav file) is actually incorporated into the PDF file. Therefore, you do not need to distribute the sound file along with the PDF file; it will already be part of the package.

To add a bookmark that links to an audio file:

1. Create a new bookmark.

2. Position the cursor over the new bookmark and right-click.

3. On the menu that appears, select **Properties**. The Bookmark Properties dialog box will appear.

4. In the Type field, choose **Sound**.

5. Press **Select Sound**.

6. The Open File dialog box appears. Navigate to the desired audio file. Highlight this file, and then click **Open** to select.

7. Press **Set Action** to complete the linking process.

## Adding a Bookmark to a Web Link

To add a bookmark that is linked to a web site:

1. Add a new, untitled bookmark to the navigation pane.

2. Position the cursor over the new bookmark, then right-click. The Bookmark menu appears.

3. Select **Properties**. The Bookmark Properties dialog box appears.

4. Click on the drop-down box in the Type field and select **World Wide Web Link**.

5.  Select the **Edit URL** button. The Weblink Edit URL dialog box appears.

6.  In the field beneath Enter a Universal Resource Locator for this link type the entire URL for the web link and press **OK**.

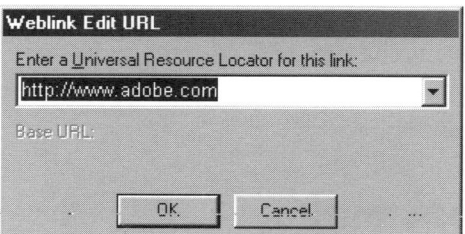

*Note:* When adding a URL, Acrobat allows http, ftp, and mailto formats.

7.  At the bottom of the Bookmark Properties dialog box, press **OK**.

Your bookmark has now been successfully linked to a URL. To use this bookmark, navigate to the new bookmark and double-click. Notice that the new bookmark does not exhibit any external indication that it is linked to a URL.

If you are connected to the Internet, the system will automatically take you to the site that was linked to your bookmark.

# Changing the Location a Bookmark is Linked To

When preparing your document for distribution, you may want to change the actual location within the document to which an existing bookmark is linked. To do this:

1.  In the navigation pane, select the bookmark you want to modify by highlighting it.

2.  Navigate to the location in the document to which you want the bookmark to link. If desired, alter the current view of the document.

3. Click the Bookmarks palette menu or position your cursor over the highlighted bookmark, then right-click to view the Bookmarks palette menu.

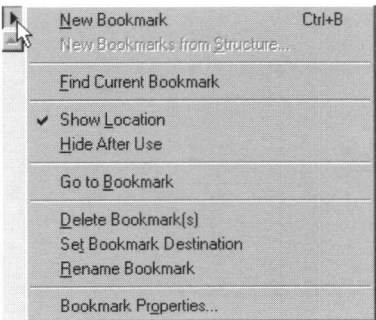

4. Select **Set Bookmark Destination**. (***Note:*** *If you right-clicked, select **Set Destination**.*)

## Adding a Section Header to a Group of Bookmarks

In the process of assembling your document's bookmarks into a more logical organization, you may need to add a section header for a group of bookmarks. To do this:

1. While in the navigation pane, position the cursor in the location where you want the section header to be added.

2. Click on the **Create New Bookmark** icon.

3. The bookmark is added with the default name "Untitled." Replace "Untitled" with the chosen name of your bookmark by highlighting and typing over the name.

4. Select the bookmark, then right-click.

5. The Bookmark menu appears. From this menu, select **Properties**.

6. In the Bookmark Properties dialog box, select **None** in the Type field.

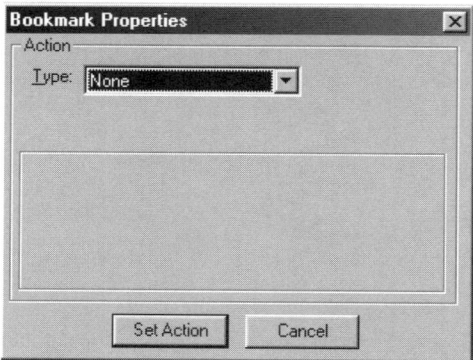

You have now successfully added a section header.

# Nesting Bookmarks

When finalizing your bookmarks, the addition of section headers is one way to better organize the structure. During the process of reorganization, you may need to nest subheadings and realign other subheadings. For the most part, nesting bookmarks is merely a drag-and-drop process.

## Nesting One Bookmark Underneath Another

1. Highlight the bookmark you intend to nest underneath another bookmark.

2. With the left mouse button held down, drag this bookmark to the destination bookmark (the bookmark to be nested under).

3. When an underscore appears beneath the name of the destination bookmark, release the left mouse button to drop the bookmark into its new nested position.

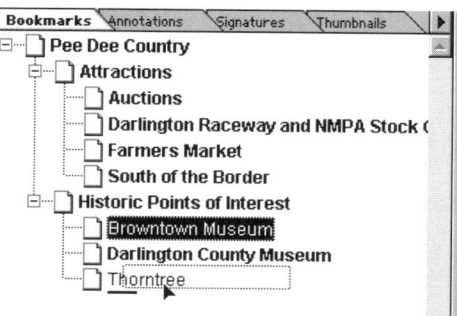

4. An Adobe Acrobat dialog box appears and asks you if you are sure that you want to move the bookmark. Click **OK**.

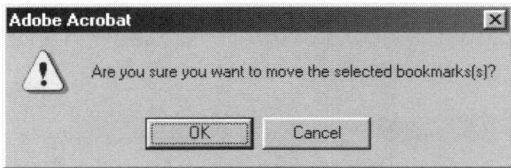

Finally, the bookmark is dropped into its new position.

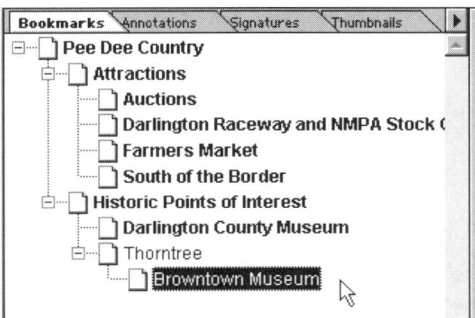

## Removing a Bookmark from a Nested Position

1. Highlight the bookmark you want to remove from a nested position.
2. With the left mouse button held down, drag this bookmark to the intended location on the Bookmark palette.
3. Position the selected bookmark below the bookmark it should appear under. (***Note:*** *This is not a nested position.*) The positioning horizontal bar must appear under the bookmark icon, not under the text of the preceding bookmark.

4. When an underscore appears beneath the icon in front of the destination bookmark, release the left mouse button to drop the bookmark into its new position.

5. An Adobe Acrobat dialog box appears, asking if you are sure you want to move this bookmark. Click **OK**.

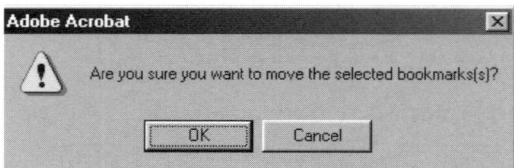

The bookmark is dropped into its new position.

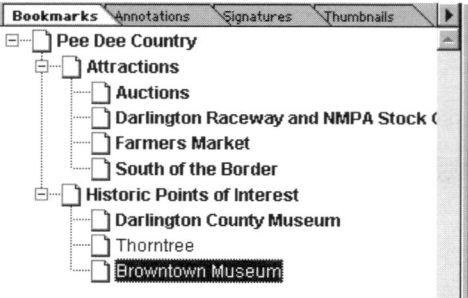

# Deleting Bookmarks

As you refine your document and prepare it for final distribution, you may need to delete a bookmark or two that do not add any value to the document. To do this:

1. Highlight the bookmark to be deleted.

2. Right-click to display the Bookmark menu.

3. Next, select **Delete**.

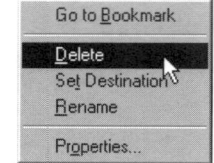

   A warning message appears asking, "Are you sure you want to delete the bookmark(s) from this document?"

4. Press **OK**.

# Expanding and Collapsing Bookmarks

A bookmark that is followed by a collapsed group of nested bookmarks is preceded by a plus sign (+). When you click on a plus sign, it converts to a minus sign and that group of bookmarks expands.

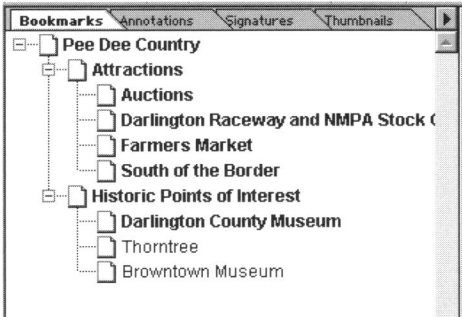

To collapse a group of bookmarks, just click on the minus sign.

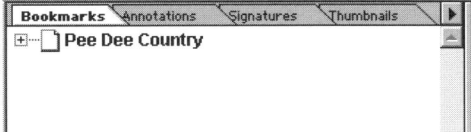

# Creating a Floating Bookmarks Palette

If you want your Bookmarks palette to appear in another part of the page, or to "float over" a different area, you want to create a floating Bookmarks palette. To do this:

1. Position your cursor over the Bookmarks tab.

2. While holding the left mouse button down, drag the Bookmarks tab to the chosen location.

3. By expanding or contracting the borders, you have the ability to size the Bookmarks palette appropriately.

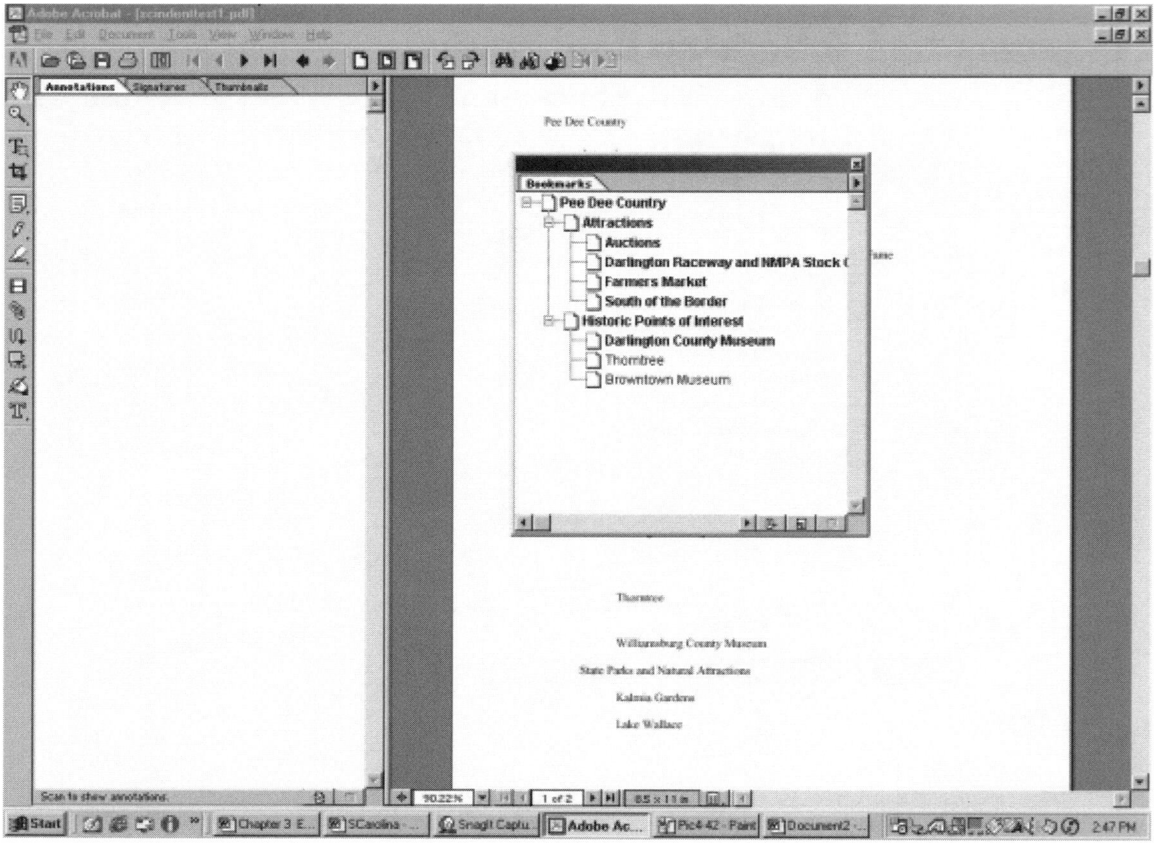

*Note: If you hide the navigation pane (click the **Show/Hide Naviga-tion Pane** button), the floating Bookmarks palette will still be visible.*

To return the Bookmarks palette from a floating position to its original position:

1. If the navigation pane is not visible, click the **Show/Hide Navigation Pane** button.

2. Position the cursor on the floating Bookmarks palette tab. Hold the left mouse button down and drag the tab to the navigation pane.

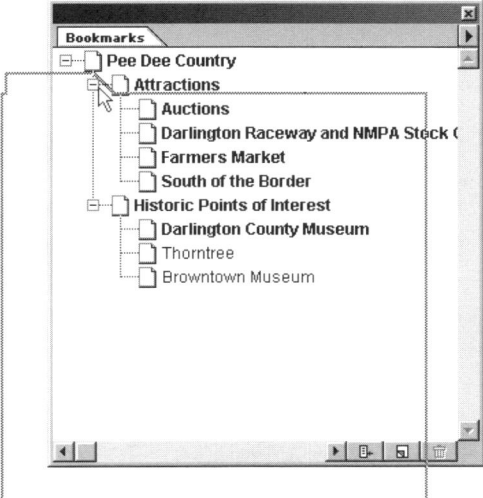

3. Position the Bookmarks tab over the other tabs on the navigation pane and release the mouse button.

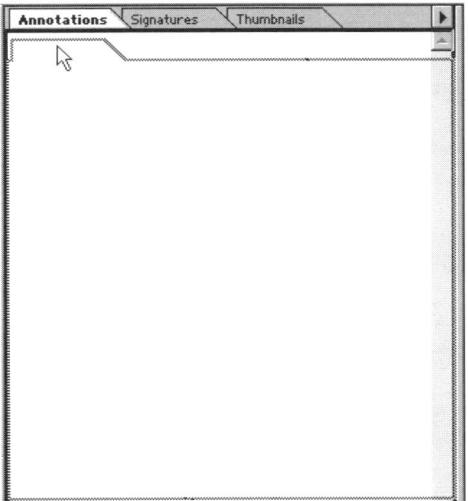

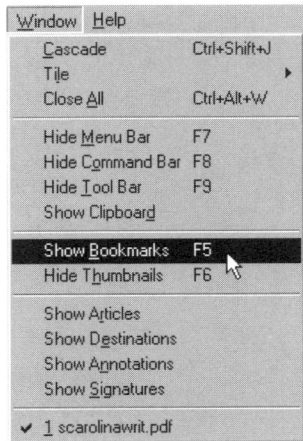

At this point, the Bookmarks tab will return to its original position.

***Note:*** *If for any reason the Bookmarks tab disappears, click on* **Window | Show/Hide Bookmarks** *on the menu bar.*

# Thumbnails

Thumbnails are small icons that represent pages in a PDF document. Found in the Thumbnails palette of the navigation pane, they provide you with the ability to navigate quickly through a document or to rapidly change the order of pages within one or more documents.

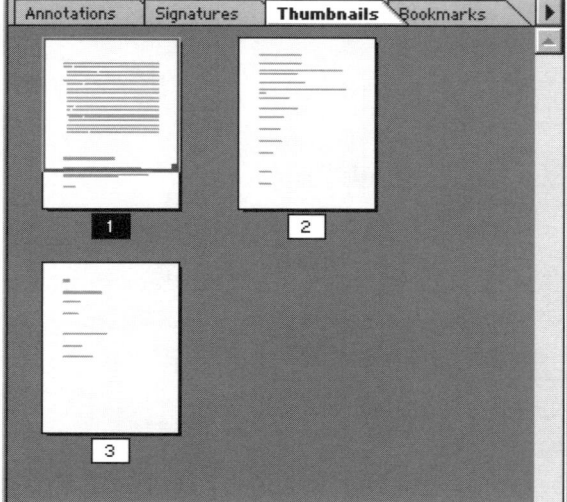

To begin this discussion of thumbnails, first open a PDF file and open the Thumbnails palette by:

Clicking on the **Thumbnails** tab in the navigation pane. (***Note:*** *If the navigation pane is not visible, click on the **Show/Hide Navigation Pane** icon* 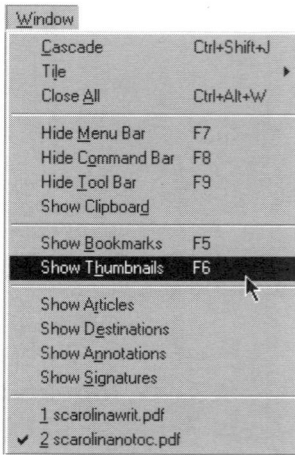 *on the command bar.*)

OR

Choosing the **Window** option on the menu bar, then selecting **Show Thumbnails**.

When the Thumbnails palette is visible, it initially displays a number of blank thumbnails equal to the number of pages in the current PDF document. Although these thumbnails are blank, they are functional. For example, if you double-click on any one of the blank thumbnails, you will automatically navigate to the corresponding page in the document pane.

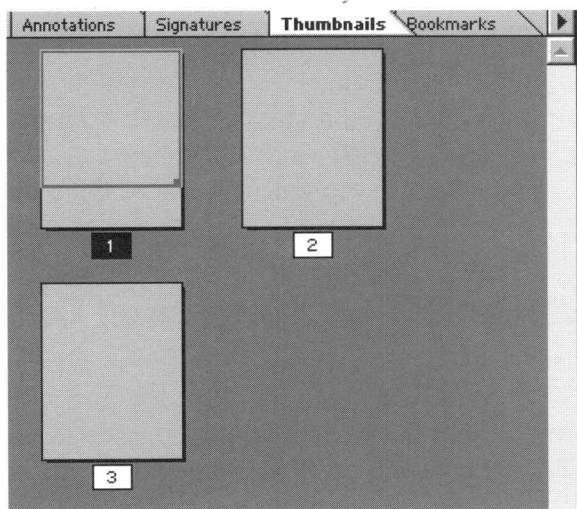

When the thumbnails are generated, a miniature visual representation of the corresponding page is added to each previously blank thumbnail. According to Adobe, this means an additional 3K per thumbnail is added to the size of the document. Due to the increased file size, thumbnails are frequently added during the development phase of a document or group of documents and then removed at the time of distribution.

# Adding/Deleting a Thumbnail

To add or delete thumbnails to/from your document:

1. If the navigation pane is not visible, click the **Show/Hide Naviga-tion Bar** button.

2. Open a PDF document.

3. On the Thumbnails palette menu, select **Create All Thumbnails** or **Delete All Thumbnails**.

If you decided to create thumbnails, thumbnails of the default size (76 x 98 pixels) for each page of the document are created.

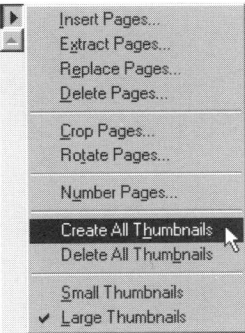

**Note:** *If you decide that smaller thumbnails are required, choose the* **Small Thumbnails** *(38 x 48 pixels) option on the Thumbnails palette menu.*

However, if you choose to delete all thumbnails, all of the thumbnails in the Thumbnails palette appear blank. Although they no longer visually represent the actual document page, these thumbnails still retain their links to the corresponding pages. In other words, if you click a particular thumbnail that is blank, you will still link to the corresponding page.

# Creating/Deleting Thumbnails in a Document Collection

A document collection is merely a group, containing more than one PDF document, which is typically stored in a folder. If you want to add thumbnails to the entire group of documents at once, Adobe Acrobat provides you with a type of "batch processing." By using batch processing, you can save yourself time.

To follow along with this exercise, create a folder and add more than one PDF document to it. To automatically add thumbnails to this group of documents:

1. Select **File | Batch Process** from the menu bar. The Select Folder To Process dialog box appears.

2. In the Selected folder and the Drives fields, choose the folder you intend to batch process.

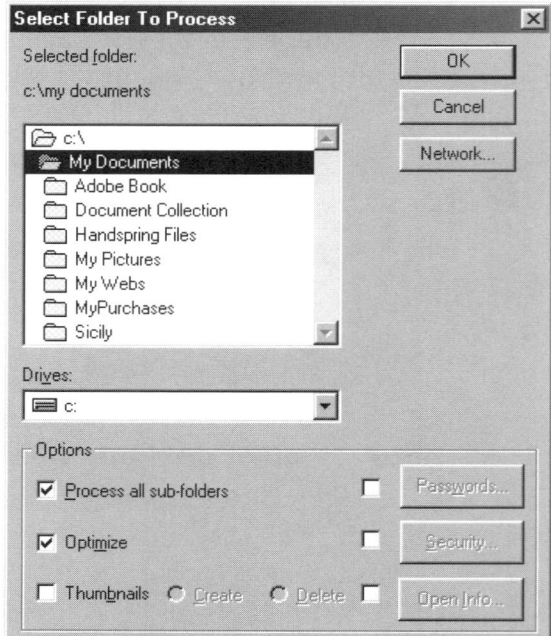

3. Under Options, select:

- **Process all sub-folders** to process all folders and files within the chosen folder.

- **Optimize** to significantly reduce the resulting file size.

*Note:* *The issue of optimization can become quite important when dealing with files on the Internet. Consider this: How long do you really want to wait while a file downloads?*

- **Thumbnails** and **Create** or **Delete** to process thumbnails in each document within the collection.

- The **Passwords** button to input the current password of the files. If the file is password protected, this is necessary to enable the system to access, then process the file. If passwords are not entered here for password-protected documents, the batch process will fail. If you intend to change any security options (e.g., the current password, the ability to change the document, the ability to print the document) you must enter this password too.

- The **Security** button to initially set passwords, to change passwords, and to set/change other security options.

*Note:* *For more detailed information, refer to Chapter 5 — Security and PDF Files.*

- The **Open Info** button to set the initial appearance and functionality of the PDF file when it is first opened. Here, you can set the initial view of the file, the window options, and the user interface options.

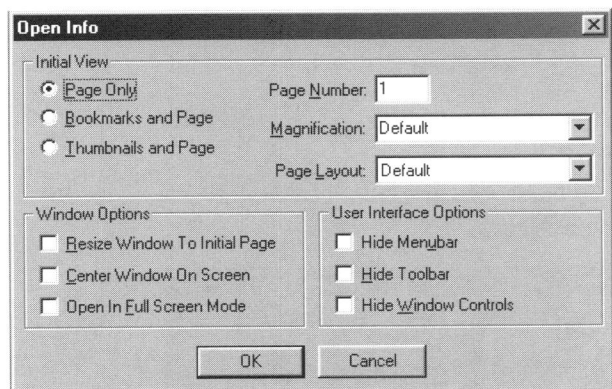

■ To show the thumbnails along with the PDF file when the document is initially opened, choose **Thumbnails and Page**, found in the Initial View area.

After all choices are made, click **OK**.

4. Click **OK** again to initiate the batch process. A Batch Processor Progress box appears, detailing the processing of each PDF file.

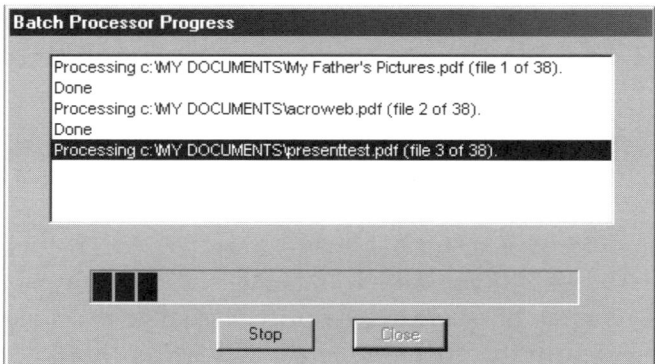

When the word "done" appears in that dialog box, the process has completed.

# Deleting a Page with a Thumbnail

Whether the thumbnail is blank or displays a picture of the actual page it represents, you can delete the linked page by deleting the thumbnail. To delete a page by using a thumbnail:

1. In the Thumbnails palette, highlight the thumbnail which is linked to the page you want to delete.

2. Right-click to display the Thumbnails palette menu.

3. Select **Delete Pages**. The Delete Pages dialog box appears.

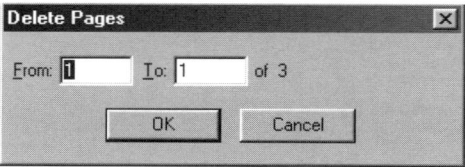

4. Here, you have the option to delete one page or a range of pages. Make your choice, then click **OK**.

# Reordering Pages within the Same Document Using Thumbnails

By simply dragging and dropping thumbnails, you can easily reorder the pages of your document. To reposition a page using thumbnails:

1. Select the thumbnail corresponding to the page you want to reposition.

2. Press the left mouse button as you drag the thumbnail from the old position to the new position.

At this point, you will notice a small icon resembling a page to the lower right of the cursor:

The appearance of this icon indicates that you are in the process of moving a page to a new position. Also, as you move the cursor, a vertical blue bar appears on the Thumbnails palette. Used to assist users when repositioning pages, the blue bar will always appear to the left of the current position of the thumbnail (page).

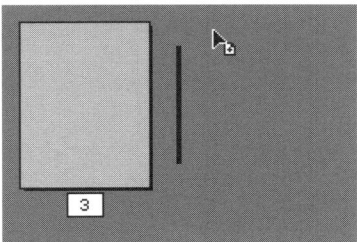

3. Once the blue bar appears to the left of the correct new location on the page, release the mouse button to drop the page. The pages of your document have been repositioned.

# Copying Thumbnails (Pages) Between Different Documents

By using the drag-and-drop feature, you can copy pages from one document to another. To do this:

1. Open two documents.

2. To position the two documents side by side, click (on the menu bar) **Window | Tile | Vertically**. At this point, only the Thumbnails palette portion of these two documents are displayed.

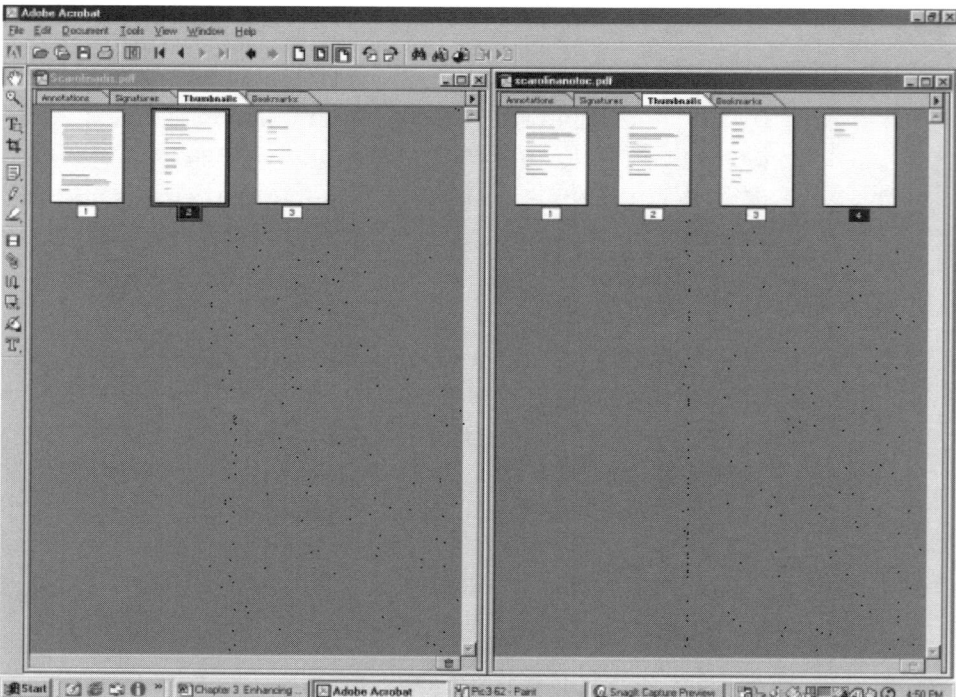

3. Navigate to the Thumbnails palette on the first document.
4. Left-click the thumbnail you want to copy to another document. When you select this thumbnail, a blue border appears around it. Drag the thumbnail to its new position on the second document's Thumbnails palette.
5. Once the blue bar appears to the left of the new location of the page, release the mouse button to drop the page.

Copies of the selected pages from the first document have now been added to the second document.

# Moving Thumbnails (Pages) Between Different Documents

By using the drag-and-drop feature, you also have the ability to move pages from one document to another. To do this:

1. Open two documents.

2. To position the two documents side by side on the screen, select (on the menu bar) **Window | Tile | Vertically**. At this point, only the Thumbnails palette from each of the documents will display on the screen.

3. Select the thumbnail that is linked to the page you want to move. When you select the thumbnail, a blue border appears around the thumbnail.

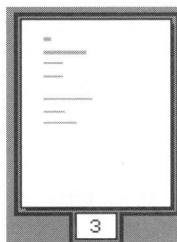

4. Click **Ctrl** and press the left mouse button. Drag the thumbnail to its new position on a different document. At this point, you will see a small plus sign to the lower right of the cursor.

5. Once the blue bar appears to the left of the page's new location, release the mouse button and the **Ctrl** key to drop the page. At this point, the selected page has been moved to the new document and deleted from the original document.

# Creating a Floating Thumbnails Palette

If you want your Thumbnails palette to appear in another part of the page, create a floating Thumbnails palette. To do this:

1. Position your cursor over the Thumbnails tab.

2. While holding down the left mouse button, drag the Thumbnails tab to the chosen location.

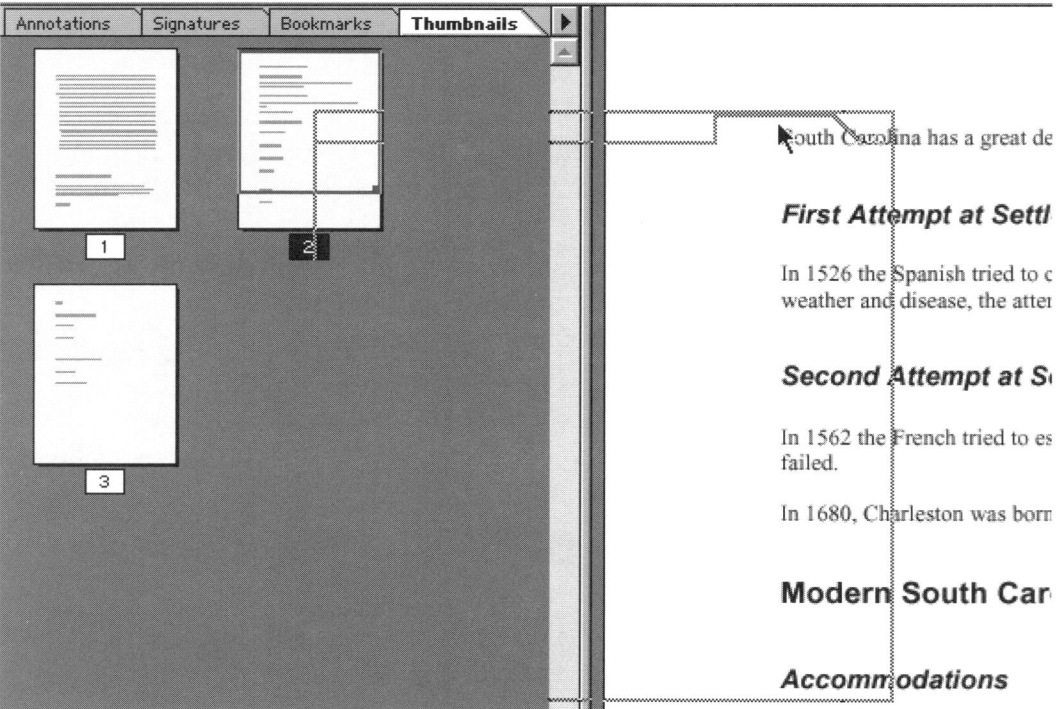

3. Expand or contract the borders of the Thumbnails palette to size it appropriately.

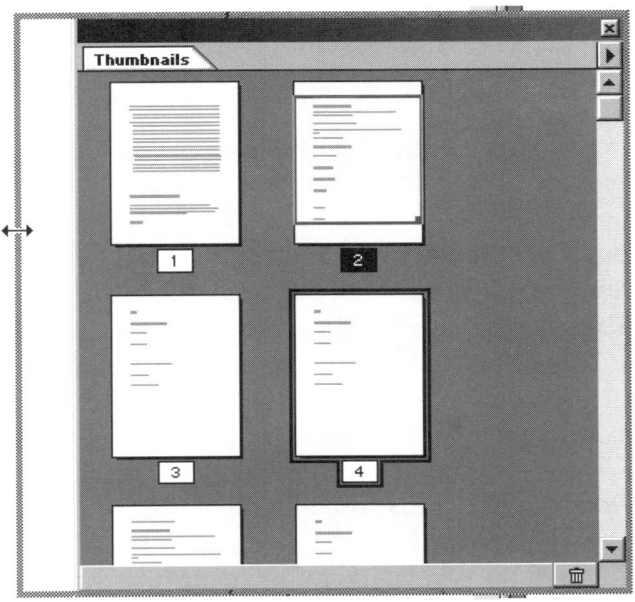

*Note:* *If you hide the navigation pane (click the **Show/Hide Navigation Pane** button), the floating Thumbnails tab will still be visible.*

To return the floating Thumbnails palette to its original position:

1. If the navigation pane is not visible, click the **Show/Hide Navigation Pane** button.

2. Position the cursor on the floating Thumbnails palette's tab.

3. Left-click and drag the Thumbnails palette to the navigation pane.

4. Position the Thumbnails palette's tab over the other tabs on the navigation pane.

5. Drop the Thumbnails palette by releasing the mouse button. The Thumbnails tab will return to its original position.

# Links

Links provide you with a method to convert simple documents into multimedia events. When links are added to a PDF document, linear navigation is no longer the only way to review a document. Basically, a link is a connection to another area of the document, a different document, or a different file. Clicking on an area defined as the source of a link automatically displays the destination of the link.

Links provide creators of documents the ability to easily add value to a PDF file. For example, links enable a user to jump from a quoted passage to a biography regarding the author of the quote. From there, a link might allow a user to jump into a short movie about the life of the author. Later in the document, words could link to definitions and percentages could link to calculations. The list of interesting possibilities goes on and on.

Although the availability of links provides creators of documents with a variety of options, one aspect of the link is clear: It creates an efficient method for readers of the document to quickly obtain relevant information concerning a topic.

## Adding a Link within a Document

The most common type of link is one in which the source (the area where the link originates) is in the same document as the destination (the area to which the link jumps). To create such a link:

1. Open the document into which you want to insert the link.

2. On the toolbar, choose the **Link** tool 🖘 .

3. Navigate to the area or text you want to define as the source of the link. (**Note:** *After the link is set up, when you click in this area, you will automatically navigate to the spot in the document to which it is linked.*) At this point, the cursor changes to a cross hair.

   ■ To define an area as the source of the link:

   Click and hold the left mouse button.

   By moving the cursor, draw a box around the area you want to define as the source of the link.

   Release the mouse button.

- To define a specific line of text as the source of the link:

  Hold the **Ctrl** key and the left mouse button.

  Select the portion of the document you want to define as the source of the link.

  Release the Ctrl key and the mouse button.

4. The Create Link dialog box appears.

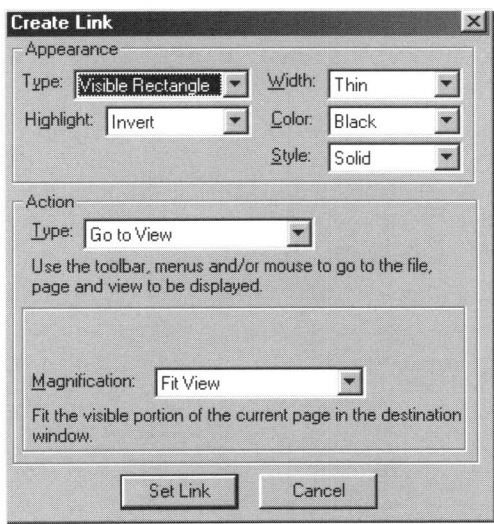

Within this dialog box are three separate areas: Appearance, Action, and Magnification. By using the options of these areas, you can define the appearance of your link.

5. In the Appearance section, you have the ability to select options which will affect the appearance of the link, including:

- Type: Here, select **Invisible Rectangle** to hide the box around the source of the link or choose **Visible Rectangle** to display this box.

- Highlight: The choices in this drop-down box refer to the appearance of the source area/text after it has been selected.

- Width: Here, you can define the width of the rectangle.

- Color: Use this option to select the color of the rectangle.

■ Style: If the rectangle is visible, you can define the style of the line, either dashed or solid, in this area.

6. In the Action section, select **Go to View**. In this field, you can define what type of link you are creating (e.g., a link to a World Wide Web URL, a movie, a sound, or a paragraph within the document). Whenever the link is to another portion of the same document, select Go to View.

7. Navigate to the area of the document you want to define as the destination of the link.

8. In the Magnification field in the Create Link dialog box, choose the desired magnification.

9. Click **Set Link**.

10. To test this link, click on the **Hand** tool found on the toolbar, then click on the area defined as the source of the link.

# Adding a Link to Other PDF Documents

When refining your document, you may need to create links from one document to another. To do this:

1. Open the document in which the source link will reside.

2. Open the document in which the destination link will reside.

3. On the toolbar, choose the **Link** tool .

4. Navigate to the area or text you want to define as the source of the link.

5. Define the area you want to designate as the source of the link by drawing a rectangle around the section or select the text you want to designate as the source of the link by pressing the Ctrl key and the left mouse button simultaneously. The Create Link dialog box appears on the screen.

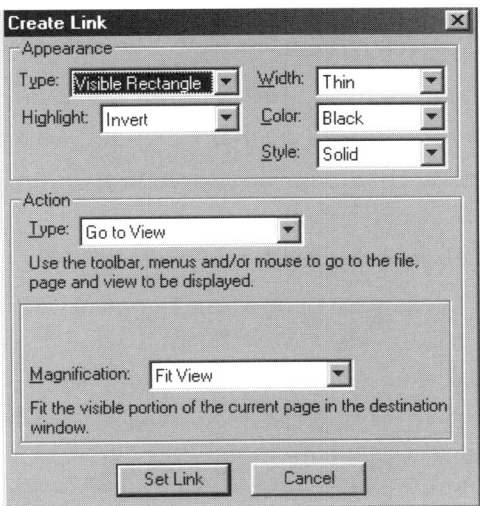

6. Choose the properties for the source link in the Appearance section.

7. In the Action section, choose **Go to View**. (***Note:*** *Be careful when choosing the Action type. Some of the selections in this drop-down box require that the destination of the action reside in the same PDF file as the source.*)

8. Navigate to the decided-upon destination document. (***Note:*** *Try using the Window menu option to toggle between the two documents.*)

9. Choose the magnification level. (***Note:*** *To view the different magnification levels on the screen, use the Actual Size, Fit in Window, or Fit Width options found on the command bar.*)

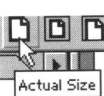 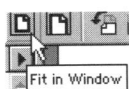 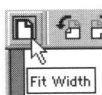

10. Choose **Set Link** to set the link.

11. Before using the link, remember to click on the **Hand** tool, found on the toolbar.

# Adding a Link to a Non-PDF Document

Within Adobe Acrobat you have the ability to add a link to a non-PDF document, such as a Word or Excel document. To link to a non-PDF file:

1. Open the document in which the source link will reside. This document, of course, is a PDF document.

2. On the toolbar, choose the **Link** tool.

3. Navigate to the area or text you want to define as the source of the link.

4. Define the area you want to designate as the source of the link by drawing a rectangle around the section or select the text you want to designate as the source of the link by pressing the Ctrl key and the left mouse button simultaneously. The Create Link dialog box appears on the screen.

5. In the Action Type field, select **Open File**.

6. Click **Select File**. The Select File to Open dialog box appears.

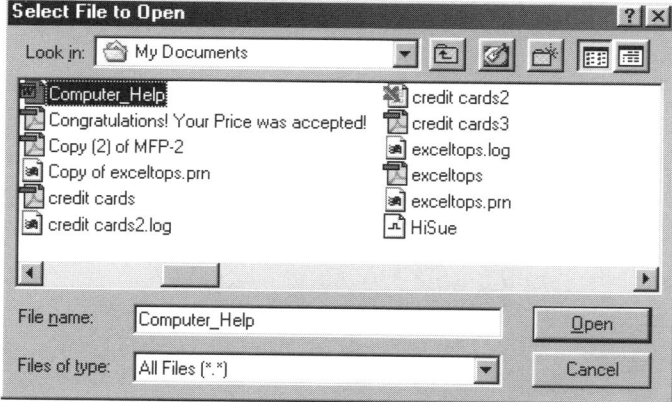

7. Choose the destination file, and then click **Open**.

8. In the Create Link dialog box, select **Set Link**.

## Using a Link to a Non-PDF Document

When you actually click on the link you've just added, an Adobe Acrobat warning box appears informing you another application will be opened to access the destination file.

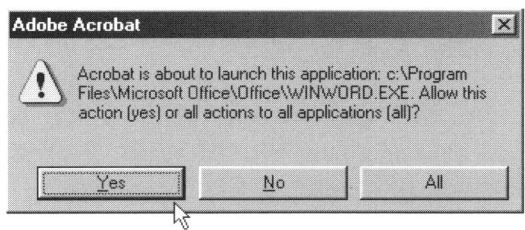

Select **Yes** to access the requested application. If you have many similar links to the same file format in the current PDF document, choose **All**. The required application, along with the file, is opened.

# Adding a Link to a URL

Taking into consideration the importance of the Internet in today's business environment, document links to Internet sites are a necessity. To link a document to a specific URL:

1.  Open the document in which the source of the link will reside.

2.  Click on the **Link** tool found on the toolbar.

3.  Define the area you want to designate as the source of the link by drawing a rectangle around the section, or select the text you want to designate as the source of the link by pressing the Ctrl key and the mouse button simultaneously. The Create Link dialog box appears on the screen.

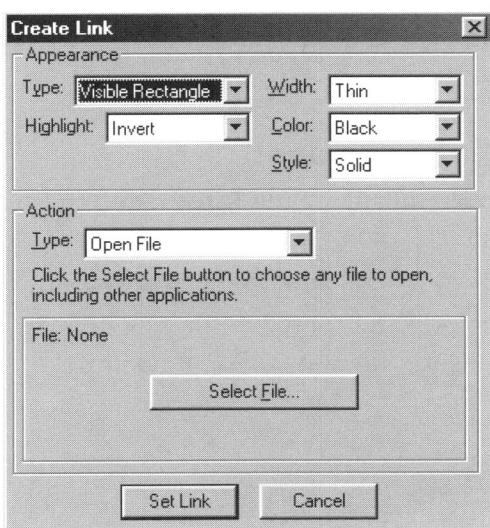

4. In the Appearance section, choose the general appearance of the source of the link.

5. In the Action section, click the arrow in the Type field to display the drop-down list. In that list, select **World Wide Web Link**. The Edit URL button appears on the Create Link dialog box.

6. Press **Edit URL** to select the URL that is the destination of the link. The Weblink Edit URL dialog box appears.

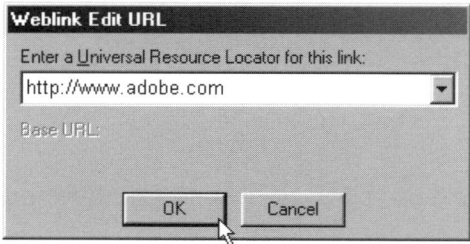

7. In the Enter a Universal Resource Locator for this link field, enter the address of the web site. (***Note:** The Universal Resource Locator (URL) must appear in its entirety; e.g., http://www.abcd.com.*)

8. Click **OK**.

9. In the Create Link dialog box, click **Set Link**.

After the web link is created, there are two distinct ways to view the contents of the web site. The first method is from within Adobe Acrobat. In this case, the web site is downloaded to your system and viewed. The second method is from your chosen browser. Here, the web page is viewed, as usual, from your browser.

## Opening a Web Link in Acrobat

1. First, create a web link using the **Link** tool from the toolbar. (Please refer to the section "Adding a Link to a URL.")

2. After the link is complete, choose the **Hand** tool from the toolbar.

3. As you navigate over the source of the link, the Hand tool will change to a pointing finger with a plus sign to its lower right.

**Note:** *The plus sign indicates that the web site is not currently part of the document.*

4. Click once on the link. The Download Status box appears.

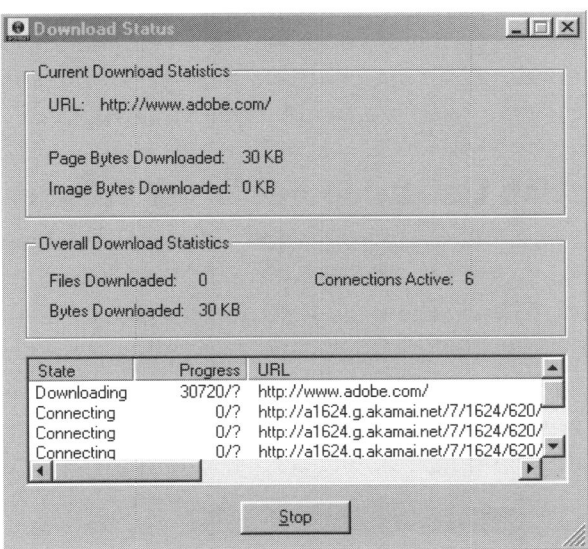

5. If you are not currently connected to the Internet, the login dialog box for your Internet Service Provider (ISP) will also appear. After you successfully log in, the Download Status dialog box becomes active.

**Note:** *If you want to discontinue the current download, click **Stop***.

6. At this point, the home page of the URL you defined as the destination link is downloaded and appended to the end of the PDF document. To download pages linked to that home page, just click on the link and the additional pages will be appended to the end of your PDF document.

As the web pages are downloaded into Adobe Acrobat, they are appended to the end of the current document. Since the web page was copied into the source PDF document after the download, the Hand tool no longer displays a plus sign when you navigate over the link. However, if there are links contained on the web page that were not downloaded, the plus sign appears as you navigate over them. When you click on these links, you will be prompted again to download the page into the PDF file.

If you need web pages contained in a PDF file for, perhaps, a presentation, downloading and appending web pages to the end of the PDF file is the perfect way to simulate to an audience navigation through a web site.

## Opening a Web Link Using a Selected Browser

You may choose not to download the additional web page onto your system, however. After all, the size of the PDF file would increase significantly. To view the page linked to the home page through a selected browser (without downloading and appending it to your current page):

1. First, define the browser in Adobe Acrobat by navigating to **File | Preferences | Weblink** and adding the required information. The Weblink Preferences dialog box is displayed.

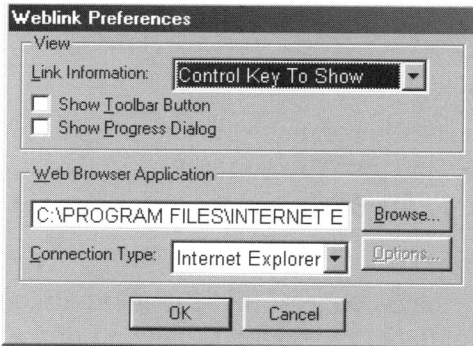

2. In the Connection Type field, choose the type of browser you want Adobe Acrobat to use when displaying web pages that are not downloaded.

3. In the Web Browser Application field, add the name of the chosen browser's executable file.

4. Click **OK**.

5. Navigate to the web link.

6. Press the **Shift** key and left-click simultaneously on the source of the link. The cursor displays a "W" on the lower right.

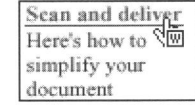

*Note:* *You can achieve the same result by right-clicking on a hyperlink, then choosing **Open Weblink in Browser** from the menu.*

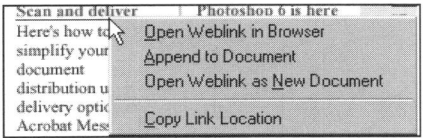

7. Once you are logged on to your ISP, your view will navigate to the chosen browser and display the web link.

## Defining the Default Browser

As mentioned in the previous section, when you open a web link using Adobe Acrobat as the browser, the web page is downloaded and appended to the end of the current PDF document. Since this action increases the size of the PDF file, you may want to view a web link using a browser such as Internet Explorer or Netscape.

Of course, if your system is set up to use Adobe Acrobat as the default browser (please refer to "Opening a Web Link in Acrobat") you need only to press the Shift key and left-click in order to view the web link in a browser external to Adobe Acrobat. However, it is possible to set up the system to default to a chosen browser. To ensure that Acrobat will reference the correct browser, you must complete the following two-step process:

### Define Default Browser in Web Capture

First, choose the settings in Adobe Acrobat that will force an external browser to be used each time a web link is clicked. To do this:

1. In Adobe Acrobat, select **File | Preferences | Web Capture**. The Web Capture Preferences dialog box appears on the screen.

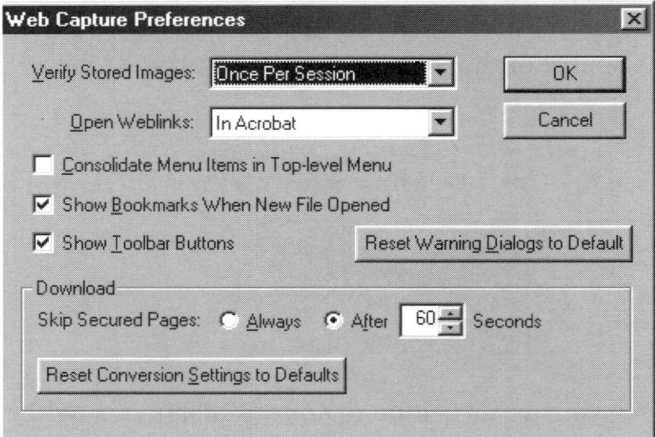

2. In the Open Weblinks field, click on the drop-down box and choose **In Web Browser**. By filling out this field, you have changed the default to the web browser. Therefore, when a web link is clicked, the system will automatically open the defined web browser and find the requested URL.

### Define Default Browser in Weblink

The second step is to define the actual browser that will be used. To do this:

1. On the menu bar, select **File | Preferences | Weblink**. The Weblink Preferences dialog box appears.

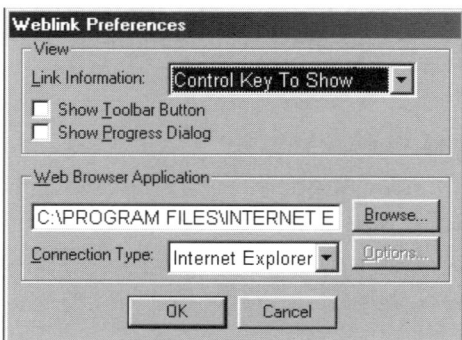

2. In the Link Information field choose **Control Key To Show** to display the name of the URL each time you press Ctrl as you navigate over it.

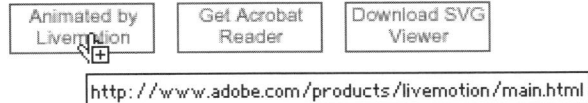

Choose **Never Show** to never show the name of the URL.

3. Select **Show Toolbar Button** to add the Open Web Browser button in the command bar. When clicked, this button will automatically open the browser that has been defined to Adobe Acrobat.

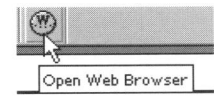

4. Select **Show Progress Dialog** to ensure that the Download Status dialog box shows when a web site is being downloaded to Adobe Acrobat.

5. In the Web Browser Application section, click **Browse** to select the browser software. In the Connection Type field, choose the connection type your browser uses. If your connection type is not listed among the choices found in the drop-down box, select **Standard**.

### Open a Web Link in the Default Browser

After the default browser has been defined in Web Capture and Weblink, each time you click on a link to the Internet, the selected browser will be used to view the site. To view a web link using the default browser:

1. First, create a web link using the Link tool from the toolbar.

2. After the link is complete, choose the **Hand** tool from the toolbar.

3. As you navigate over the source of the link, the Hand tool will change to a pointing finger with a "W" to its lower right.

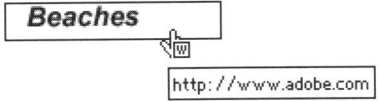

**Note:** *The "W" indicates that the web link will be opened in the browser, as selected in Web Capture.*

4. Click once on the link.

5. If you are not currently connected to the Internet, the login dialog box for your Internet Service Provider (ISP) will appear. After you

successfully log on, the current view on the screen will change to the selected browser.

However, after viewing it, you may choose to download the web page and append it to the end of the current PDF document. To do this:

Press the **Shift** key and left-click on the source of the link. The cursor immediately displays a plus sign (+) on the lower right.

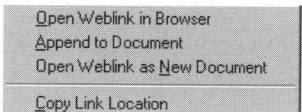

*Note:* You can achieve the same result by right-clicking, then choosing **Append to Document** from the menu.

> Open Weblink in Browser
> Append to Document
> Open Weblink as New Document
>
> Copy Link Location

Once the web page has been appended to the current PDF document, the link changes to a link to a page (as opposed to a link to a URL). Therefore, to access that particular page, it will no longer be necessary to access the Internet.

# Changing the Appearance of a Link

After the link has been added to the document, you may find it necessary to change its appearance. A number of properties define the appearance of the link, including the size, color, and visibility of the rectangle that defines the boundaries of the link and the characteristics of the rectangle after the link has been selected. Changing any of these properties takes very little time.

## Changing the Size of the Link

1. On the toolbar, select the **Link** tool .
2. Click once on the rectangle surrounding the link. Handles will appear on the four corners of the box.

> Modern South Carolina

3. Using your cursor, grab onto one of the handles and drag the rectangle to the desired size and position.

4. Release the mouse button to drop the rectangle and define a new link size.

## Changing the Appearance of the Border

1. On the toolbar, click on the **Link** tool.

2. Double-click on the link to display the Link Properties dialog box.

3. In the Type field, using the drop-down arrow, choose **Visible Rectangle** or **Invisible Rectangle**. This selection determines if the rectangle will be visible before it is clicked.

4. In the Highlight field, using the drop-down arrow, choose the rectangle's appearance after it is clicked. Specifically:

- Select **Invert** to highlight the entire link.

- Select **Outline** to outline the entire link.

- Select **Inset** to give the link a 3D look.

- Select **None** if you want nothing to appear when the link is clicked.

5. If Visible Rectangle was chosen in the Type field, you will also have the capability to select the following properties to further define the appearance of the rectangle:

- **Width** (Thin, Medium, Thick)
- **Color** (Black, Red, Blue, Custom, etc.)
- **Style** (Solid, Dashed)

# Editing a Link to a Document

As you're revising your PDF document, you may need to edit the destination of a link.

To edit the link:

1. On the toolbar, click on the **Link** tool.
2. Double-click on the link to display the Link Properties dialog box.
3. Click on **Edit Destination**. Your view moves to the page where the destination of the link resides. Additionally, the Link Properties dialog box displays the Magnification field.
4. Navigate to the area of this document or another document that you want to define as the destination of the link.
5. In the Magnification field, use the drop-down box to determine the size of the link's destination.
6. When all changes are complete, click **Set Link**.

# Editing a Link to a URL

Frequently, the need arises to change the URL to which a PDF document was initially linked. To edit a link to a URL:

1. On the toolbar, select the **Link** tool.
2. Navigate to the source of the link and double-click to display the Link Properties dialog box.

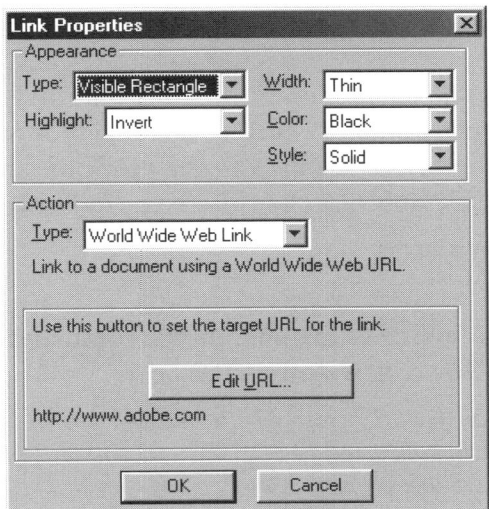

3. Click **Edit URL**. The Weblink Edit URL dialog box appears.

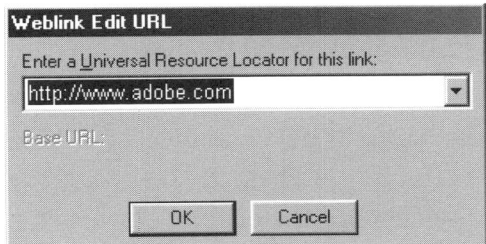

4. Click on the drop-down box to choose a different URL. If the intended URL is not available in that link, type over the current URL to change the destination of the link.

5. Click **OK** on the Weblink Edit URL dialog box.

6. Click **OK** on the Link Properties dialog box.

7. Next time you click on this link, you will navigate to the newly selected URL.

# Using a Link

One problem with using some links is the fact that they leave you in the middle of another portion of the current document or another document (or URL) altogether. Navigating back to the previous page, though, is just a matter of using the Adobe Acrobat interface. To illustrate:

1. Open a PDF document.

2. Click on a link.

3. To return to the source of the link, on the command bar, select the **Go to Previous View** icon.

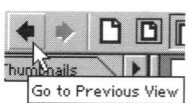

**Note:** *This feature only works from within Adobe Acrobat. If you link to a file which has not been converted to PDF format, you will not have this navigational tool available to you.*

# Deleting a Link

There are a few options available when deleting a link:

1. First, choose the **Link** tool on the toolbar.

2. Click on the link you want to delete.

3. Choose one of the methods below to delete the link:

   ▪ Right-click on the source of the link to display the Link menu, then choose **Delete**.

   ▪ Press the **Delete** key on the keyboard.

   ▪ On the menu bar, choose **Edit | Delete**.

4. The Adobe Acrobat warning message appears asking, "Are you sure you want to delete the link from the document?" Click **OK** to delete the link.

## Chapter 4

# The Power of PDF Forms

One of the outstanding benefits of using the PDF file format is the ease of form design and creation. Whether you place the form on a web site and electronically accumulate reader responses, or you distribute forms and collect user responses via e-mail, PDF forms provide you with the functionality to easily distribute the forms and efficiently accumulate the response data.

Before you begin this walk-through of form creation, grab an existing form or create one of your own. By doing this, you will have the opportunity to try some of the form functionality as it's discussed while you navigate the sections of this chapter.

## Creating Forms Using MS Word

Sometimes, the easiest way to create a PDF form is to initially create it in another application, then convert it to PDF format. Keep in mind that any application that provides you with word processing capability can be used to create the initial form. However, in order to use the form functionality available in Adobe Acrobat, the application used must provide a method that enables you to convert the form from its original format to PDF format. To determine if this is the case, check the application to ensure that it contains the PDFMaker icon, offers the PDFWriter driver, or provides the ability to create PostScript files (which can be converted to PDF format using Distiller).

To create a PDF form using Microsoft Word:

1.  Open Word and create a form. Add the required special formatting and graphics.
2.  Save the form.
3.  Click on the **Create Adobe PDF** icon.

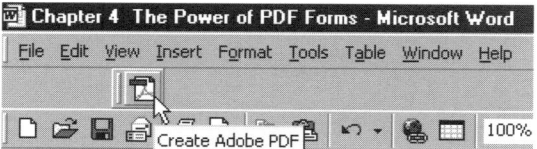

The Acrobat PDFMaker dialog box appears.

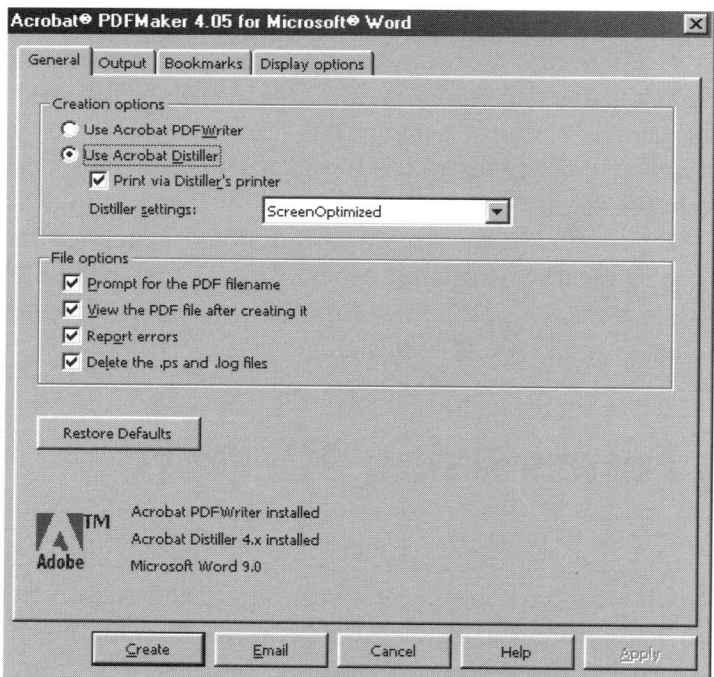

4.  Select the Creation options and the File options you need on the General tab. If necessary, make your selection of the options found on the Output, Bookmarks, and Display options tabs. Choose only the options you need from each category.
5.  Click **Create**. The conversion process begins immediately.

6.  When the file has been converted to PDF format, the Save PDF file as dialog box appears.

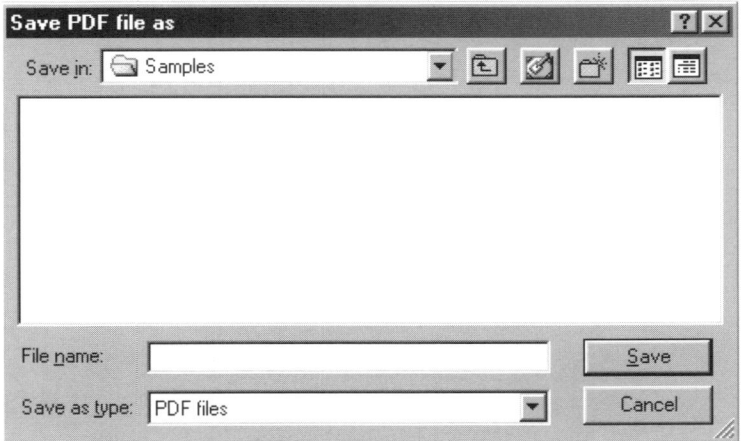

Add the name of the new PDF file and the folder it will reside in.

7.  Click **Save** to save the new PDF file.

Now you are ready to augment the PDF file by using Adobe Acrobat.

# Field Types on a Form

To enable your form to collect the appropriate information at the appropriate times, add the type of field that correctly matches the intended use of the field. For example, if you want the user to choose between options A, B, and C, choose the radio button field type. On the other hand, if one of the form's fields requires a brief description of a situation, insert a text field. To design and create a form that is accurately used by the readers, it is highly important to ensure that the function of the field matches the expected user response.

## Adding Text Boxes to a Form

One of the more common types of fields is the familiar text field. Form readers typically add names, addresses, brief descriptions, short answers, etc., to this type of field. Due to the fact that this type of field can accommodate up to 32,000 characters, form users can become quite descriptive! Because of this potentially long length, when you define the attributes of the text fields, limit the length of entries.

To add a text box to a form:

1. Navigate to the toolbar and select the **Form** tool. The cursor immediately becomes a cross hair.

2. Create the field by pressing the left mouse button and dragging down and to the right to define the height and width of the field.

3. When the rectangle representing the field has been completed, release the mouse button. The Field Properties dialog box appears on the screen.

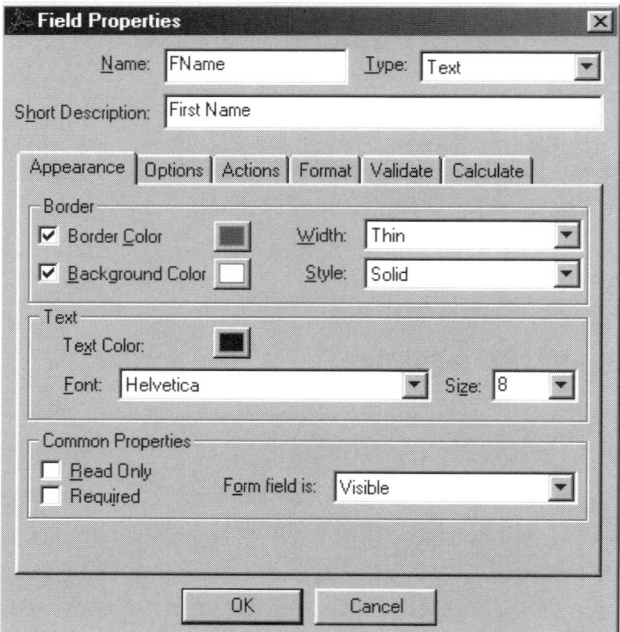

4. At the top of the dialog box is the required Name field. Select a unique name and enter it into this field.

5. If desired, add a description of the field to the Short Description field.

6. Also appearing at the top of the dialog box is the Type field. Click on the drop-down arrow and select **Text**.

Underneath the upper part of the dialog box are six tabs that enable you to define the appearance, actions, and defaults of the field.

## Adding a Text Box — The Appearance Tab

The Appearance tab provides you with the ability to define the basic appearance of the form field. To define the appearance of the form field:

1. In the Border section, define the basic appearance of the form field's border (border color, background color, width, and style).

2. In the Text section, define the font type, size, and color to appear within the form field.

3. In the Common Properties section:

   ■ Select **Read Only** to prohibit data input.

   ■ Select **Required** to indicate that the user must enter data into this field prior to clicking on the Submit button.

   ■ Click on the drop-down arrow in the Form field is area to determine if the field is:

      ■ Visible

      ■ Hidden

      ■ Visible but doesn't print

      ■ Hidden but printable

## Adding a Text Box — The Options Tab

When all choices are made on the Appearance tab, click on the **Options** tab.

1. In the Default field, enter the default text for this field.
2. Click on the drop-down arrow in the Alignment field to select the positioning of the text (left, right, or center).

**Note:** *The position chosen is the position that the text will be entered from. For example, if Right is chosen, the text will be typed into the field from right to left.*

3. Select **Multi-line** to allow users to press Enter, and then move to the next line within the field. If this option is not chosen, all text will appear on one single line. However, if this option is chosen, the Password option will not be enabled.
4. Select the **Limit of ___ characters** option if you want to limit the amount of text a user can enter into this field. The text boxes can accept a significant amount of information — up to 32,000 characters. If space is an issue, this option should be chosen.
5. Select **Password** to define the field as a password field. Text entered in a password field appears as "***."

**E-mail Address**      `********************`

## Adding a Text Box — The Actions Tab

When all choices are made on the Options tab, click on the **Actions** tab.

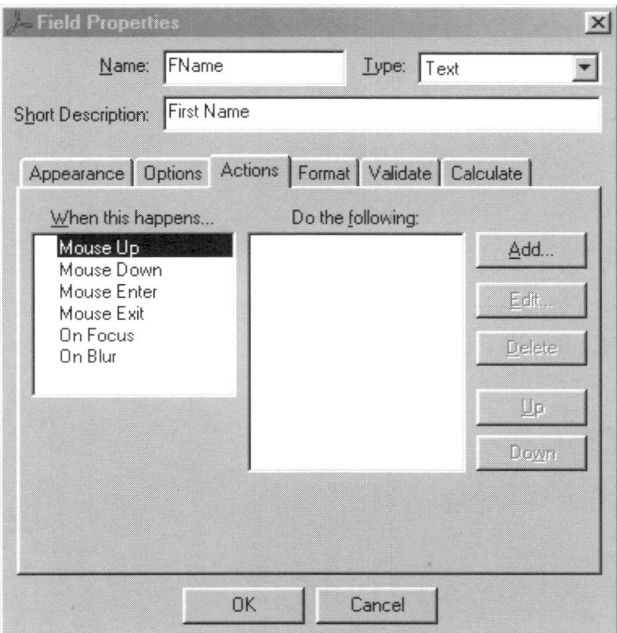

1.  On this tab there are two fields: When this happens... and Do the following. Under When this happens... the following list of mouse actions appears:

    ■ *Mouse Up* — Releasing the mouse button.

    ■ *Mouse Down* — Pressing the mouse button.

    ■ *Mouse Enter* — Navigating the mouse over the form button.

    ■ *Mouse Exit* — Navigating the mouse off of the form button.

    ■ *On Focus* — Occurring after Mouse Down, but before Mouse Up.

    ■ *On Blur* — Occuring after all other mouse actions, as the field "loses focus."

    To link a mouse action to another action, highlight the mouse action and click **Add**. The Add an Action dialog box appears.

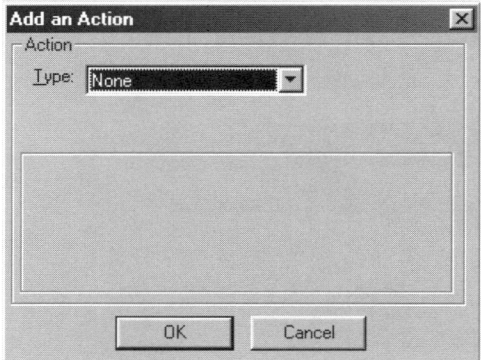

2. Click the drop-down arrow in the Type field to link the mouse action to another action. Depending on the type selected, you may be prompted to fill out other fields.

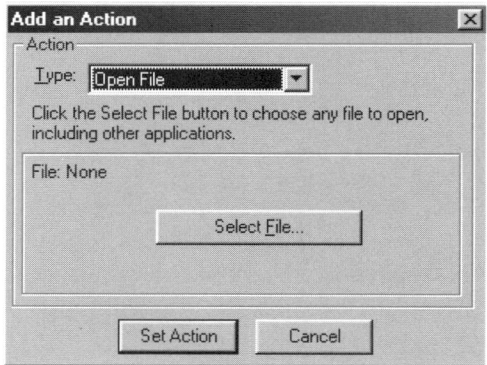

3. Once an action is chosen and suitably defined, click **Set Action**.

## Adding a Text Box — The Format Tab

When all choices are made on the Actions tab, click on the **Format** tab. These selections determine the formatting the data entered will acquire.

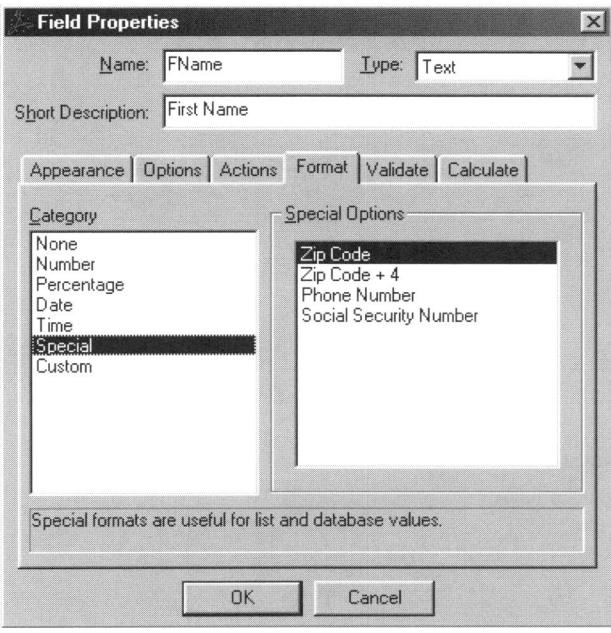

1. Two areas appear on this tab: Category and Options. (**Note:** *The options available depend on the category selected.*) The available categories include:

   ■ None
   ■ Number
   ■ Percentage
   ■ Date
   ■ Time
   ■ Special
   ■ Custom

2. Select a category, and enter the requested information in the Options area.

## Adding a Text Box — The Validate Tab

When all choices are made on the Format tab, click on the **Validate** tab.

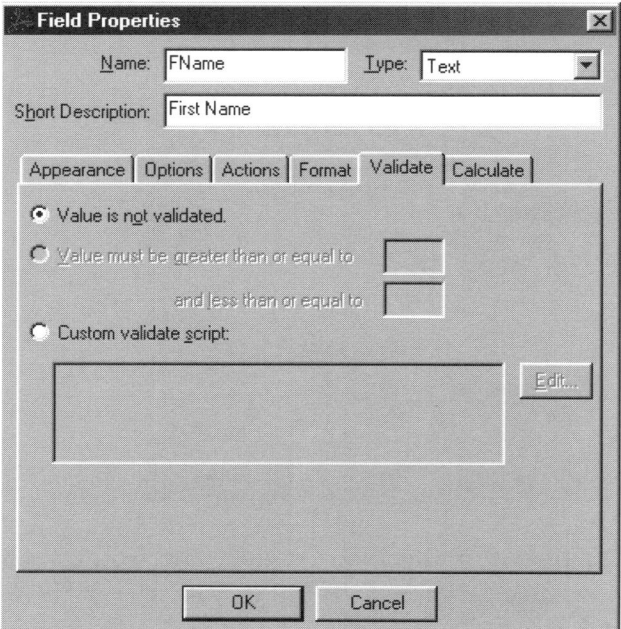

This tab offers three choices. You have the option to retain the defaulted selection, or define one of your own. The choices are:

- *Value is not validated* — This is the default.
- *Value must be greater than or equal to; and less than or equal to* — This option is only available when Number or Percentage is chosen on the Format tab.
- *Custom validate script* — Add JavaScript here to customize a field's validation.

## Adding a Text Box — The Calculate Tab

When all choices are made on the Validate tab, click on the **Calculate** tab.

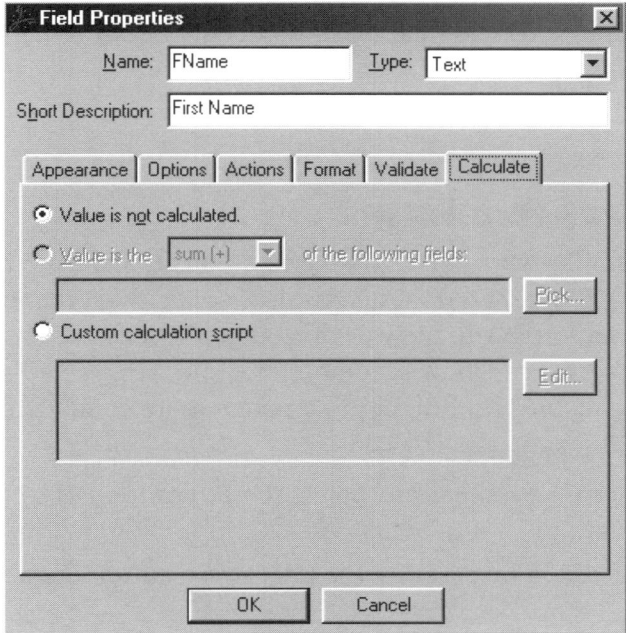

This tab contains three calculation choices. As found on the Validate tab, you can retain the default selection or add your own calculation. These choices include:

- *Value is not calculated* — This option is the default.
- *Value is the sum/product/etc. of the following fields* — This choice is only enabled if Number or Percentage is selected on the Format tab. The actual calculation and the fields involved in this calculation are defined in this area.
- *Custom calculation script* — If required, add JavaScript here to drive the calculation.

## Completing the Addition of a Text Box

When all required options in the six tabs are chosen, click **OK** to complete the definition of the text field.

First Name

To test the new text field, leave edit mode and click on the Hand tool (found on the toolbar).

First Name

# Adding Combo Boxes to a Form

If you are familiar with Windows-based applications, you are, by default, familiar with combo boxes. When using a combo box, the user can click on a drop-down arrow to view a "drop-down" list of possible field entries. In this way, a user can view a number of choices in a small space. Combo boxes, then, enable the designer to create a more compact form.

To create a combo box on a form:

1. Navigate to the toolbar and select the **Form** tool. The cursor becomes a cross hair.

2. Create the field by pressing the left mouse button and dragging to the right.

3. When the rectangle representing the field has been completed, release the mouse button. The Field Properties dialog box appears on the screen.

4. Add the name of this field to the Name field.

5. In the Type field, click on the drop-down arrow and select **Combo Box**.

6. In the Short Description field, add a brief description.

The lower portion of the dialog box contains six tabs where you can define the field's appearance and actions. Only one tab, the Options tab, requires an entry when creating a combo box. The other five tabs initially contain field defaults, which can, of course, be customized later.

## Adding a Combo Box — The Appearance Tab

The Appearance tab provides you with the ability to define the basic appearance of the form field. To define the appearance of the form field:

1. In the Border section, define the basic appearance of the form field's border (border color, background color, width, and style).

2. In the Text section, define the font type, size, and color to appear within the form field.

3. In the Common Properties section:

   ■ Select **Read Only** to prohibit data input.

   ■ Select **Required** to ensure that the user enters data into this field prior to clicking on the Submit button.

   ■ Click on the drop-down arrow in the Form field is area to define if the field is:

      ■ Visible

      ■ Hidden

      ■ Visible but doesn't print

      ■ Hidden but printable

## Adding a Combo Box — The Options Tab

When all choices are made on the Appearance tab, click on the **Options** tab.

**Field Properties** ☒

Name: Location     Type: Combo Box ▼

Short Description: Location of Office

| Appearance | Options | Actions | Format | Validate | Calculate |

Item: Southeast     Add

Export Value:     Delete

East Coast
MidWest
West Coast

Up

☑ Sort Items     Down

☑ Editable     Selected item is default

OK     Cancel

Complete the definition of the combo box by entering the following information:

1. Type each combo box entry into the Item field.

2. Click **Add** to add the entry to the combo box.

*Note: The combo box can contain a maximum of 50 entries.*

3. Enter an Export Value for the entry only if the entries will be exported to a CGI application. If that is not the case, leave the field blank. Blank fields default to the name appearing in the Item field.

4. Select **Sort Items** to sort the selection list in alphabetical sort order.

5. Select **Editable** to enable users to add choices not appearing in the selection list.

6. Highlight the entry in the selection list that will appear as the default choice in the combo box.

## Adding a Combo Box — The Actions Tab

When all choices are made on the Options tab, click on the **Actions** tab.

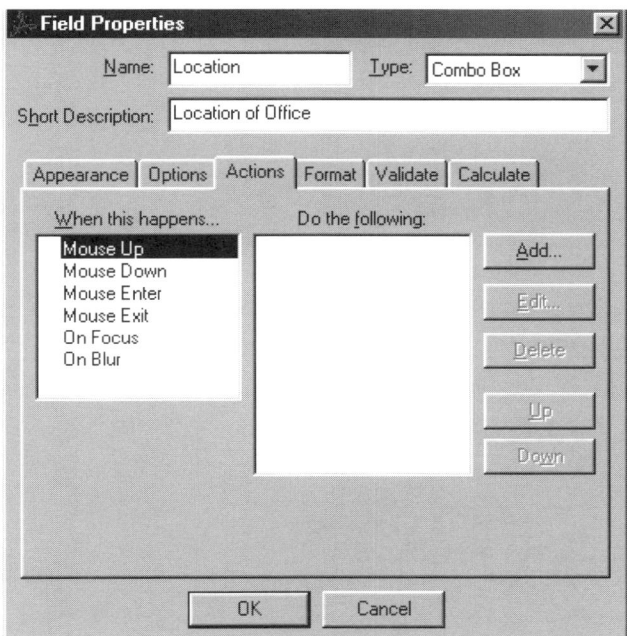

On this tab, there are two fields: When this happens… and Do the following. Under When this happens… appears the following list of mouse actions:

- *Mouse Up* — Releasing the mouse button.

- *Mouse Down* — Pressing the mouse button.

- *Mouse Enter* — Navigating the mouse over the form button.

- *Mouse Exit* — Navigating the mouse off of the form button.

- *On Focus* — Occurring after Mouse Down, but before Mouse Up.

- *On Blur* — Occurring after all other mouse actions, as the field "loses focus."

Define the actions of this combo box by entering the following:

1. Choose one of the mouse actions to define the trigger and click **Add**. The Add an Action dialog box appears.

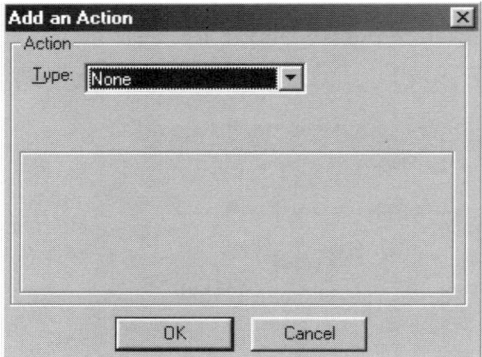

2.  Click the drop-down arrow in the Type field to choose the action that will occur once the mouse action (trigger) occurs. Depending on the chosen type, you may be prompted to fill out other fields.

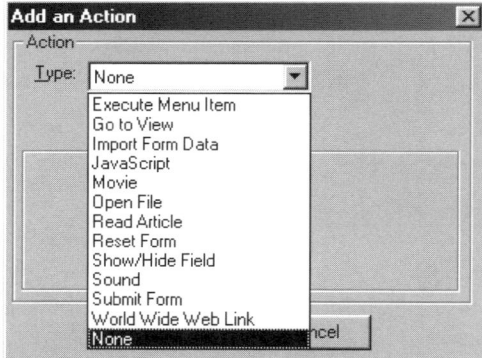

3.  Once a suitable action is chosen and defined, click **Set Action**.

## Adding a Combo Box — The Format Tab

When all choices are made on the Actions tab, click on the **Format** tab. The choices made in this area determine the formatting of the data entered into the field.

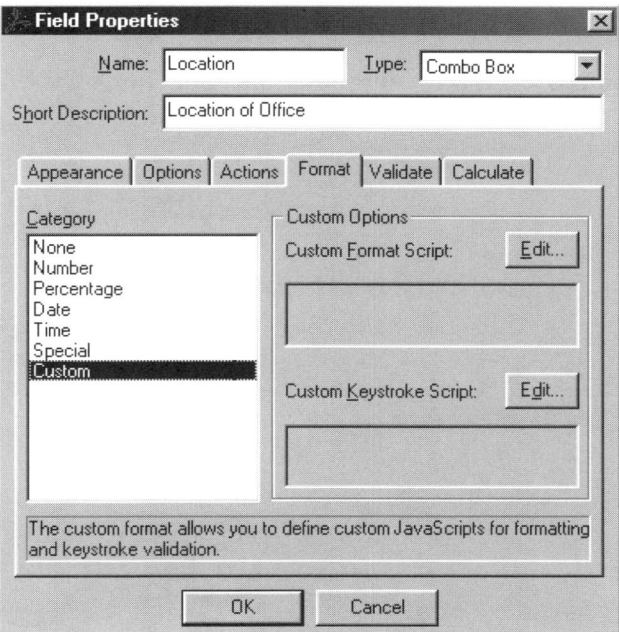

Two areas appear on this tab: Category and Options.

**Note:** *The actual options available will differ, depending on the category selected.*

The available categories include:

■ None

■ Number

■ Percentage

■ Date

■ Time

■ Special

■ Custom

To add formatting to the combo box, select a category. The Options area will change accordingly. Enter the requested information in the Options area.

## Adding a Combo Box — The Validate Tab

When all choices are made on the Format tab, click on the **Validate** tab.

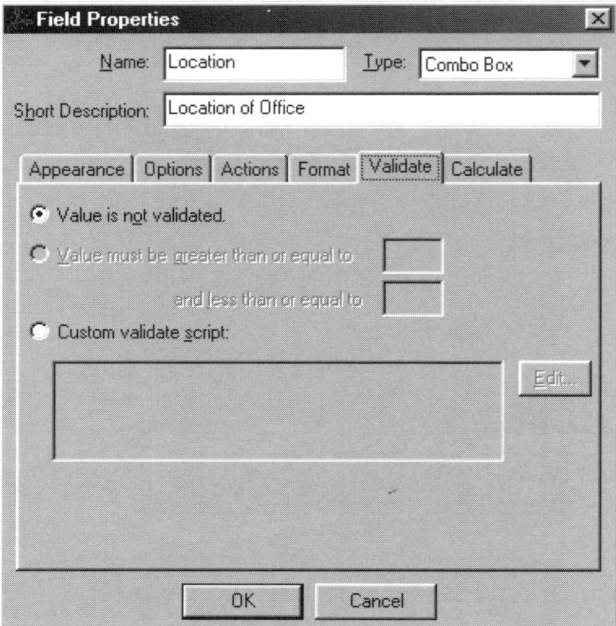

On this tab there are three choices:

- *Value is not validated* — This is the default.
- *Value must be greater than or equal to; and less than or equal to* — This option is only available when Number or Percentage is selected on the Format tab.
- *Custom validate script* — Here, add simple JavaScript to customize the validation required for a specific field.

## Adding a Combo Box — The Calculate Tab

When all choices are made on the Validate tab, click on the **Calculate** tab.

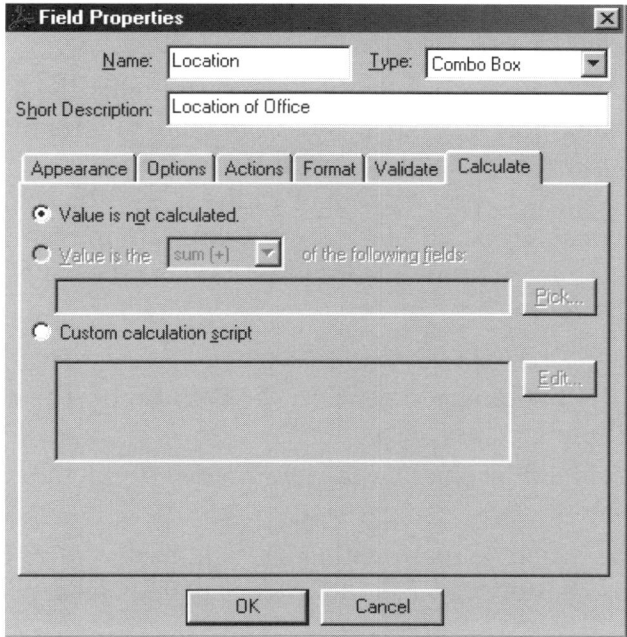

This tab contains three calculation choices:

■ *Value is not calculated* — This option is the default.

■ *Value is the sum/product/etc. of the following fields* — This choice is only enabled when Number or Percentage is selected on the Format tab. Here, define this field's calculation and any other fields involved in the calculation.

■ *Custom calculation script* — Add any JavaScript that will control the calculation here.

## Completing the Addition of a Combo Box

After the Options tab is filled out, and any required additional information has been added to the other tabs:

1. Click **OK** to save the form field.

2. To test the form field, leave edit mode and choose the **Hand** tool on the toolbar.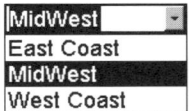

# Adding List Boxes to a Form

List boxes and combo boxes appear to be very similar fields. Although they have similarities, these fields function quite differently. The list box provides users with the ability to scroll through a list of selections and ultimately make a choice. Depending on the size of the box, one or more of the selections may be visible while scrolling. On the other hand, the combo box displays a drop-down selection box of the list of choices. All choices in the combo box can be viewed in one glance.

To add a list box form field:

1.  Navigate to the toolbar and select the **Form** tool. The cursor immediately becomes a cross hair.

2.  Create the field by pressing the left mouse button and dragging to the right.

3.  When the rectangle representing the field has been completed, release the mouse button. The Field Properties dialog box appears on the screen.

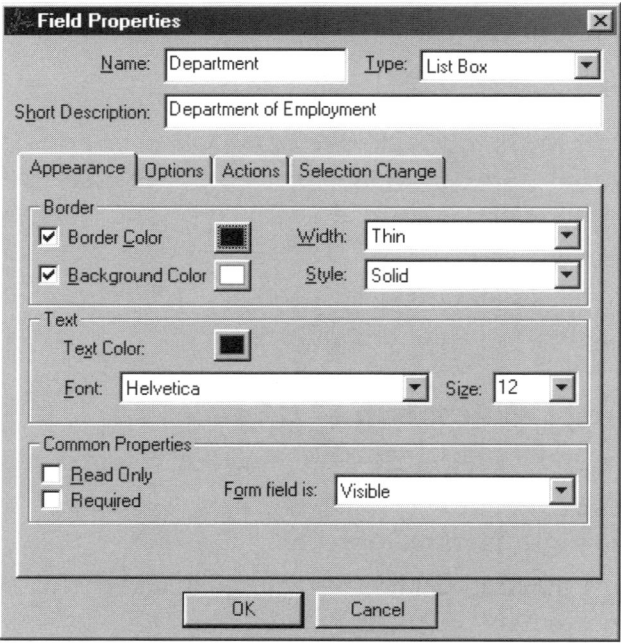

4.  Add the name of this field to the Name field.

5. In the Type field, click on the drop-down arrow and select **List Box**.

6. In the Short Description field, add a brief description of the field.

The lower portion of the dialog box contains four tabs that enable you to define the appearance of the field and a few of the actions of the field. When creating list boxes, only one tab, the Options tab, requires entry. The other three tabs initially contain defaults that can be changed later to customize the field.

## Adding a List Box — The Appearance Tab

The Appearance tab provides you with the ability to define the basic appearance of the form field. To define the appearance of the form field:

1. In the Border section, define the basic appearance of the form field's border (border color, background color, width, and style).

2. In the Text section, define the font type, size, and color to appear within the form field.

3. In the Common Properties section:

   ■ Select **Read Only** to prohibit data input.

   ■ Select **Required** to indicate that the user must enter data into this field prior to clicking on the Submit button.

   ■ Click on the drop-down arrow in the Form field is area to define if the field is:

      ■ Visible

      ■ Hidden

      ■ Visible but doesn't print

      ■ Hidden but printable

## Adding a List Box — The Options Tab

When all choices are made on the Appearance tab, click on the **Options** tab and add the following options:

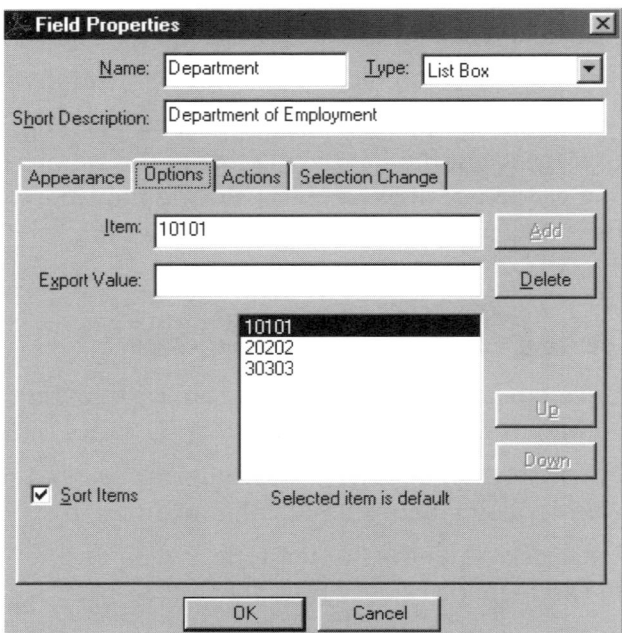

1. Type each list box entry in the Item field. Click **Add** to add each entry to the list box.

**Note:** *The list box can contain a maximum of 50 entries, where the name of each entry is no longer than 50 characters.*

2. Enter an Export Value for the entry only if it will be exported to a CGI application. If that is not the case, leave the field blank. If the field is blank, it will default to the name appearing in the Item field.

3. Select **Sort Items** if you want the selection list to appear in alphabetical order.

4. Highlight the entry in the selection list that will be the default choice in the list box.

## Adding a List Box — The Actions Tab

When all choices are made on the Options tab, click on the **Actions** tab.

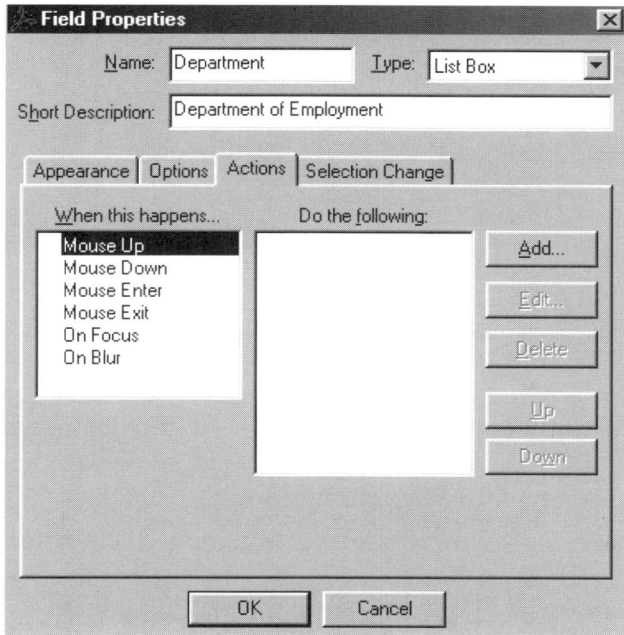

On this tab, there are two fields: When this happens… and Do the following. Under When this happens… appears a list of mouse actions:

■ *Mouse Up* — Releasing the mouse button.

■ *Mouse Down* — Pressing the mouse button.

■ *Mouse Enter* — Navigating the mouse over the form button.

■ *Mouse Exit* — Navigating the mouse off of the form button.

■ *On Focus* — Occurring after Mouse Down, but before Mouse Up.

■ *On Blur* — Occurring after all other mouse actions, as the field "loses focus."

To select all required actions for the list box field:

1. Choose one of the mouse actions to define the trigger and click **Add**. The Add an Action dialog box appears.

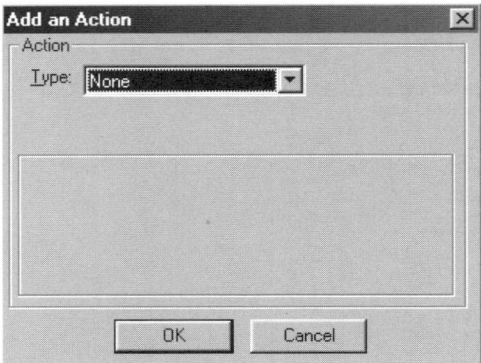

2. Click the drop-down arrow in the Type field to choose the action that is triggered by the mouse action. Depending on the chosen action, you may be prompted to fill out other fields.

3. Once a suitable action is selected and defined, click **Set Action**.

## Adding a List Box — The Selection Change Tab

When all choices are made on the Actions tab, click the **Selection Change** tab.

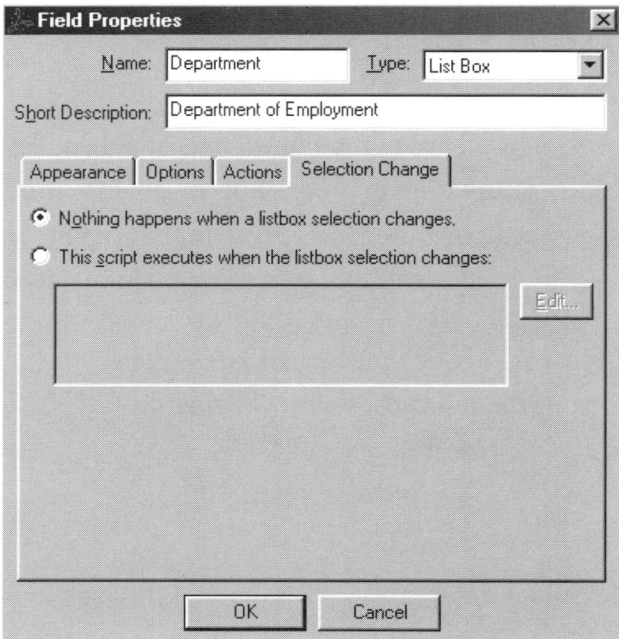

Two choices are found on this tab:

- *Nothing happens when a listbox selection changes* — This option (the default) causes nothing to happen when the list box selection is changed.

- *This script executes when the listbox selection changes* — If you choose this option, the added JavaScript will execute once the list box selection is changed.

If This script executes when the listbox selection changes is chosen:

1. Click **Edit** to display the Acrobat Forms dialog box.

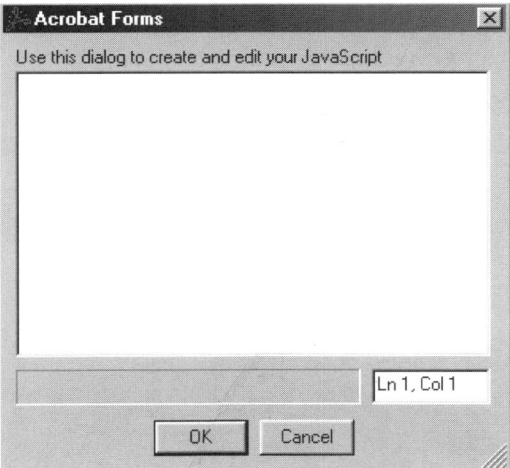

2. Enter JavaScript code that will execute once the list box selection is changed.

3. Click **OK**.

## Completing the Addition of a List Box

After the Options tab is filled out, and all additional information has been added to the other tabs:

1. Click **OK** to save the list box form field.

2. To test this form field, leave edit mode by choosing the **Hand** tool on the toolbar.

Department

# Adding Check Boxes to a Form

Many forms contain areas that prompt users to select zero or more field options (e.g., Check all that apply). To provide the form's users with the ability to select zero or more options, use a series of check boxes. However, if only one selection from a group should be chosen, a series of radio buttons is the better choice.

**Note:** *For additional information, please refer to "Adding Radio Buttons to a Form."*

Check boxes are generally used when forms request users to "Check areas of interest" or "Check those items you own." By using a check box, more than one response to a request is possible.

To add a check box form field:

1. Navigate to the toolbar and select the **Form** tool. The cursor immediately becomes a cross hair.

2. Create the field by pressing the left mouse button and dragging to the right to define the height and width of the field.

3. When the rectangle representing the field is complete, release the mouse button. The Field Properties dialog box appears on the screen.

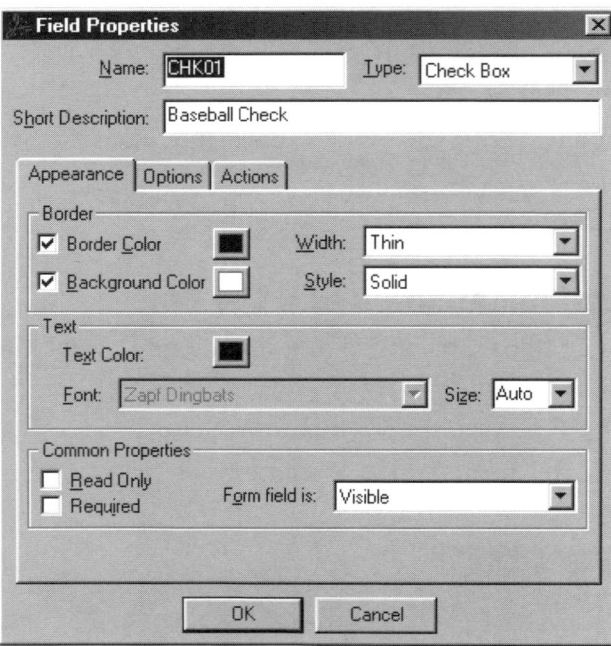

4. Add the name of this field to the Name field.

5. In the Type field, click on the drop-down arrow and select **Check Box**.

6. In the Short Description field, add a brief description of the field.

The lower portion of the dialog box contains three tabs, which enable you to define the field's appearance and actions. When creating check boxes, only one tab, the Options tab, requires entry. The other two tabs initially contain defaults that can be changed later to customize the field.

## Adding a Check Box — The Appearance Tab

The Appearance tab provides you with the ability to define the basic appearance of the form field. To define the appearance of the form field:

1. In the Border section, define the basic appearance of the form field's border (border color, background color, width, and style).

2. In the Text section, define the font type, size, and color to appear within the form field.

3. Since the options in the Common Properties section do not make sense when defining the appearance/functionality of a check box, they are not necessary when defining a check box. However, if the fields are selected:

   ■ **Read Only** prohibits data input.

   ■ **Required** indicates that the user must enter data into this field prior to clicking on the Submit button.

   ■ The choices available in the Form field is area define if the field is:

      ■ Visible

      ■ Hidden

      ■ Visible but doesn't print

      ■ Hidden but printable

## Adding a Check Box — The Options Tab

When all selections are made on the Appearance tab, click on the
**Options** tab.

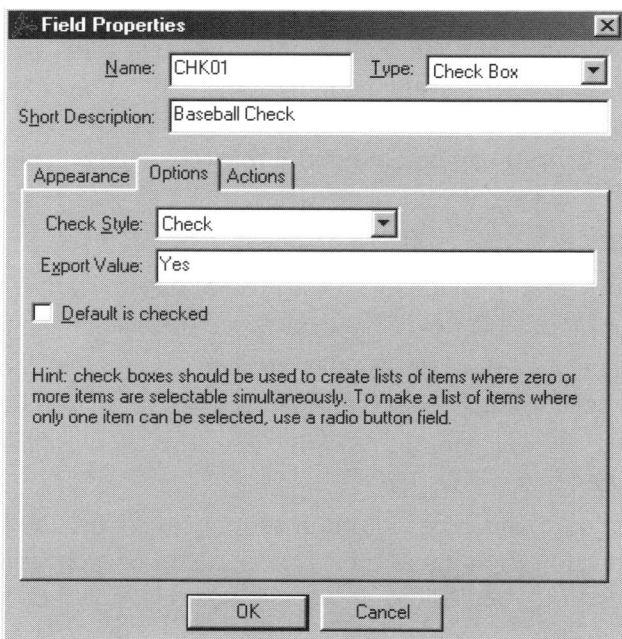

On this tab, make the following choices:

1.  In the Check Style field, click the drop-down arrow to choose the type
    of character that will appear in a selected check box.

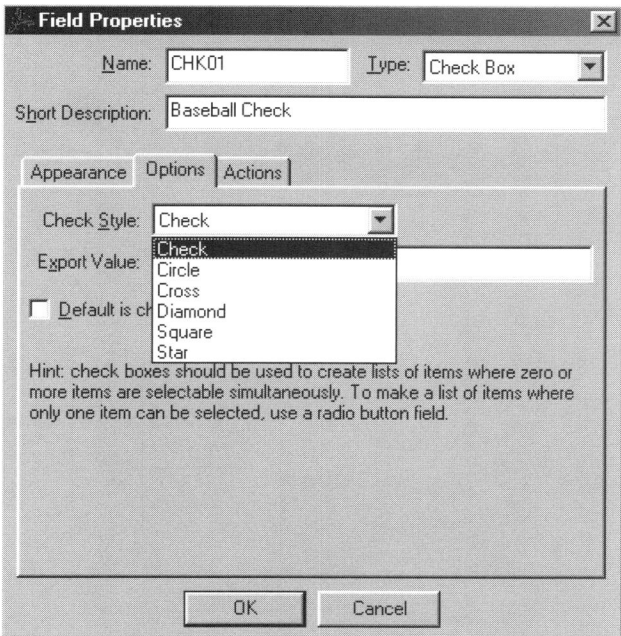

2. Leave the default Yes in the Export Value field to indicate to the CGI application that a certain check box was selected.

***Note:*** *The Export Value field contains information sent to a CGI application to identify selected form fields.*

3. Click **Default is checked** to initially populate the check box with a check (or another character).

## Adding a Check Box — The Actions Tab

When all choices are made on the Options tab, click the **Actions** tab.

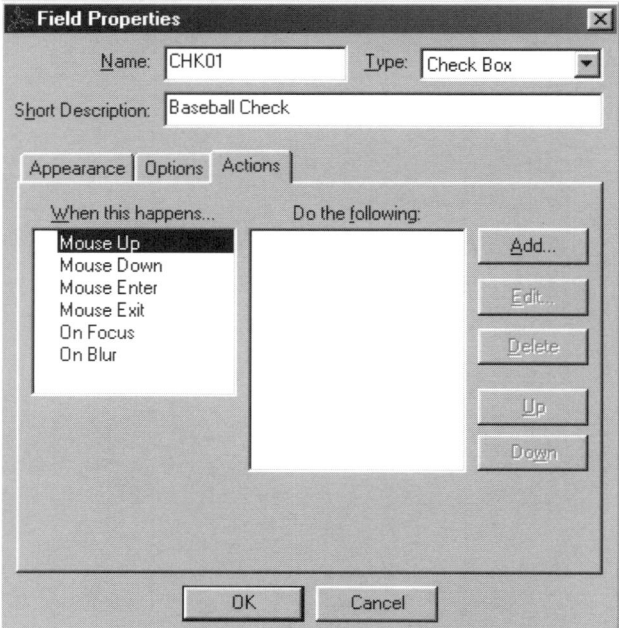

On this tab there are two fields: When this happens... and Do the following. Under When this happens... the following list of mouse actions appears:

■ *Mouse Up* — Releasing the mouse button.

■ *Mouse Down* — Pressing the mouse button.

■ *Mouse Enter* — Navigating the mouse over the form button.

■ *Mouse Exit* — Navigating the mouse off of the form button.

■ *On Focus* — Occurring after Mouse Down, but before Mouse Up.

■ *On Blur* — Occurring after all other mouse actions, as the field "loses focus."

To complete the Actions tab:

1. Choose the mouse actions that will be linked to an action, then click **Add**. The Add an Action dialog box appears.

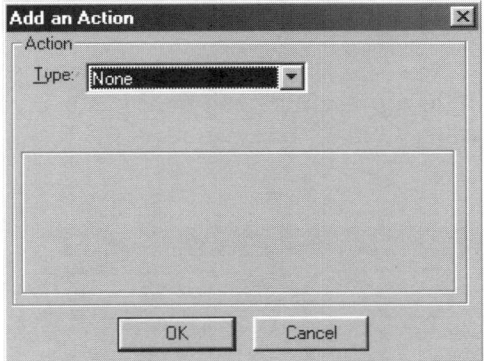

2. Click the drop-down arrow in the Type field to choose the action to link to the mouse action. Depending on the chosen type, you may be prompted to fill out other fields.

3. Once a suitable action is chosen and defined, click **Set Action**.

### Completing the Addition of a Check Box

To finally add the check box to the form:

1. After all desired information is entered into the tabs, click **OK** to save the form field.

2. To test the form field, leave edit mode and choose the **Hand** tool on the toolbar.

3. Repeat the steps in this section for each check box added to the current form.

Sports Interests:

Baseball ☑

Football ☐

Hockey ☐

Tennis ☑

## Adding Radio Buttons to a Form

When you want the user of the form to select only one option, use a radio button form field. To provide the user with the ability to choose zero to many selections, the check box is the preferred choice.

Radio buttons are generally used when the directions to the form's users are something like "Check your age range," "Check your salary range," or any question where only one answer is allowable. To add a radio button form field:

1. Navigate to the toolbar and select the **Form** tool. The cursor immediately becomes a cross hair.

2. Create the field by pressing the left mouse button and dragging to the right.

3. When the rectangle representing the field has been completed, release the mouse button. The Field Properties dialog box appears on the screen.

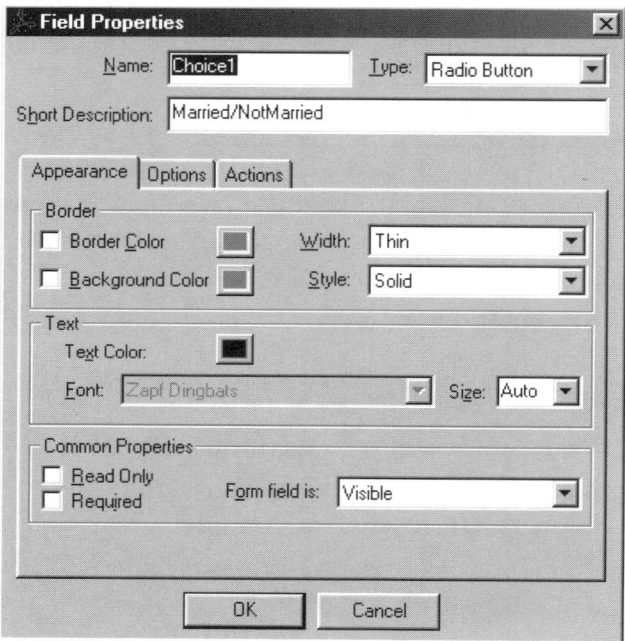

4. Add the name of this field to the Name field.

*Note:* *Radio buttons that function together must have the identical name.*

5. In the Type field, click on the drop-down arrow and select **Radio Button**.

6. In the Short Description field, add a brief description of the field.

The lower portion of the dialog box contains three tabs that enable you to define the appearance of the field and a few of the actions of the field. When creating radio buttons, only one tab, the Options tab, requires entry. The other two tabs initially contain defaults that can be changed later to customize the field.

## Adding a Radio Button — The Appearance Tab

The Appearance tab provides you with the ability to define the basic appearance of the form field. To define the appearance of the form field:

1. In the Border section, define the basic appearance of the form field's border (border color, background color, width, and style).

2. In the Text section, define the font type, size, and color to appear within the form field.

3. Although the options in the Common Properties section do not make sense when defining the appearance/functionality of a radio button (after all, why would one add a read-only radio button?), you still do have the ability to define the fields as follows:

   ■ Select **Read Only** to prohibit data input.

   ■ Select **Required** to indicated that the user must enter data into this field prior to clicking on the Submit button

   ■ Click on the drop-down arrow in the Form field is area to define if the field is:

      ■ Visible

      ■ Hidden

      ■ Visible but doesn't print

      ■ Hidden but printable

## Adding a Radio Button — The Options Tab

When all choices are made on the Appearance tab, click on the **Options** tab.

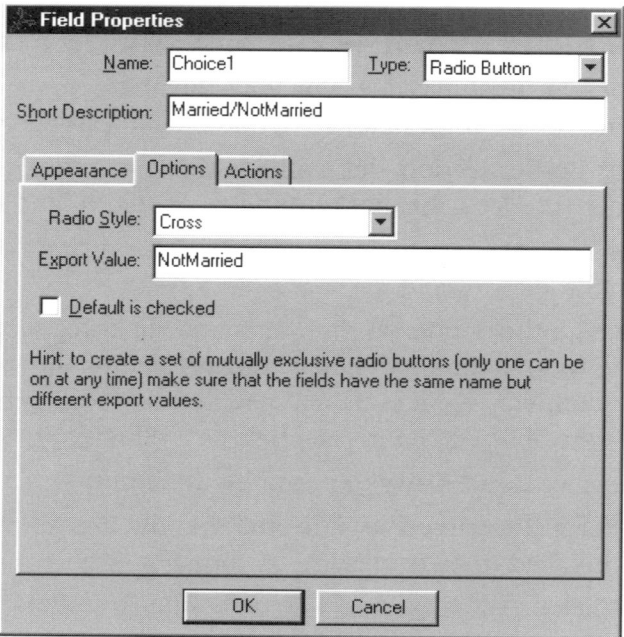

To define the options available on this radio button:

1. Click on the Radio Style drop-down list to choose the appearance of the selection character and the actual radio button.

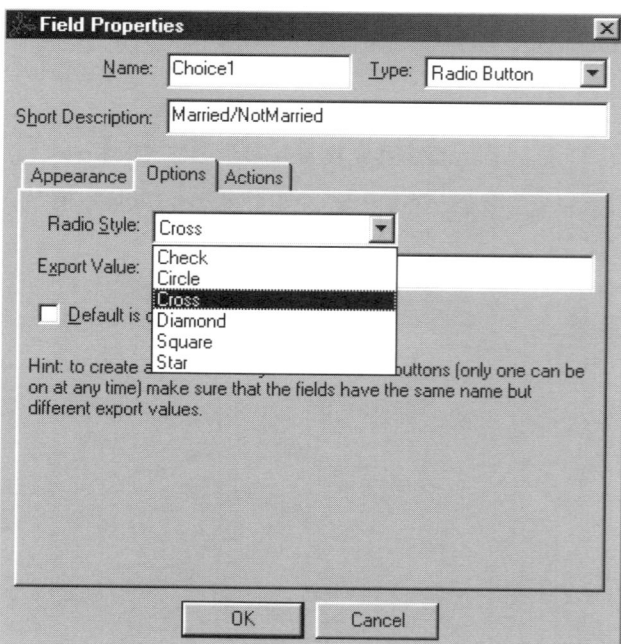

2. The Export Value field is where differentiation between the radio buttons functioning together appears. Here, enter different values for each radio button that will function together.

3. Select **Default is checked** if you want a specific radio button to initially appear as checked.

## Adding a Radio Button — The Actions Tab

When all choices are made on the Options tab, click on the **Actions** tab.

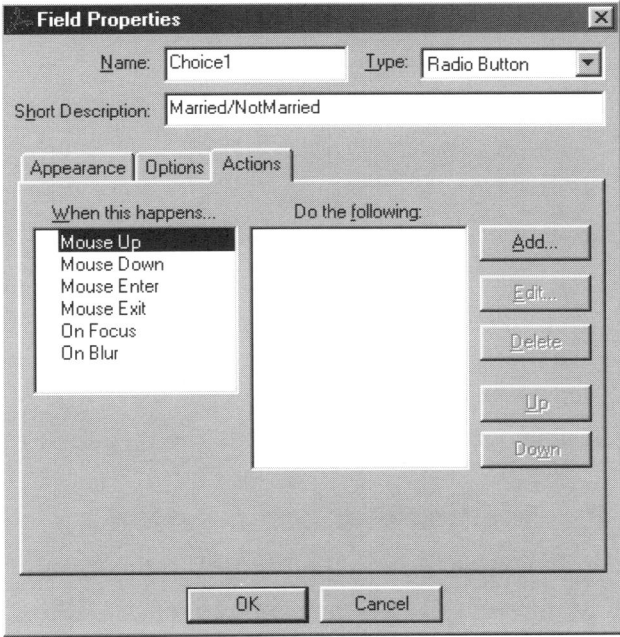

On this tab there are two fields: When this happens... and Do the following. Under When this happens... the following list of mouse actions appears:

- *Mouse Up* — Releasing the mouse button.
- *Mouse Down* — Pressing the mouse button.
- *Mouse Enter* — Navigating the mouse over the form button.
- *Mouse Exit* — Navigating the mouse off of the form button.
- *On Focus* — Occurring after Mouse Down, but before Mouse Up.

■   *On Blur* — Occurring after all other mouse actions, as the field "loses focus."

To complete this tab:

1.  Choose one of the mouse actions to link to an action and click **Add**. The Add an Action dialog box appears.

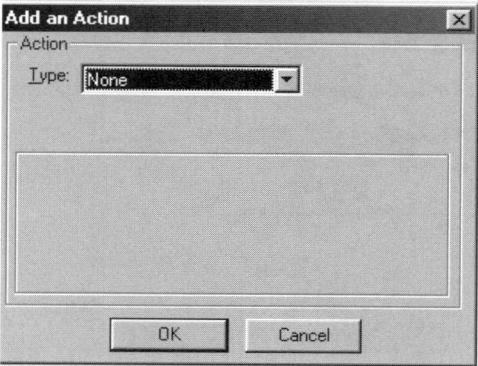

2.  Click the drop-down arrow in the Type field to choose the action linked to the mouse action. Depending on the chosen type, you may be prompted to fill out other fields.

3.  Once a suitable action is chosen and defined, click **Set Action**.

## Completing the Addition of a Radio Button

To finally add the completed radio button(s) to the form:

1.  When all required information is entered, click **OK** to save the form field.

2.  To test the form field, click the **Hand** tool on the toolbar to leave edit mode.

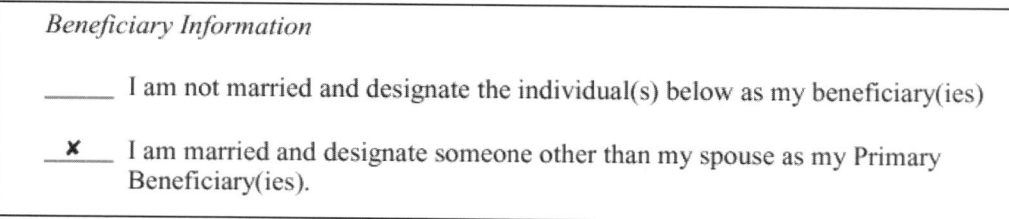

# Adding Signature Fields to a Form

If your form must travel across the desks of a number of different people, including signature fields is a good idea. Signature fields provide users with the ability to verify that the form has navigated through a number of steps in the approval process or to "lock" the document.

Adobe Acrobat provides you with the functionality to add electronic signatures, instead of manually written signatures. Electronic signatures are fortified with password protection that enables only the entitled person to sign a document. To add a signature field to a form:

1. Navigate to the toolbar and select the **Form** tool. The cursor immediately becomes a cross hair.

2. Create the field by pressing the left mouse button and dragging to the right to define the height and width of the field.

3. When the rectangle representing the field is complete, release the mouse button. The Field Properties dialog box appears on the screen.

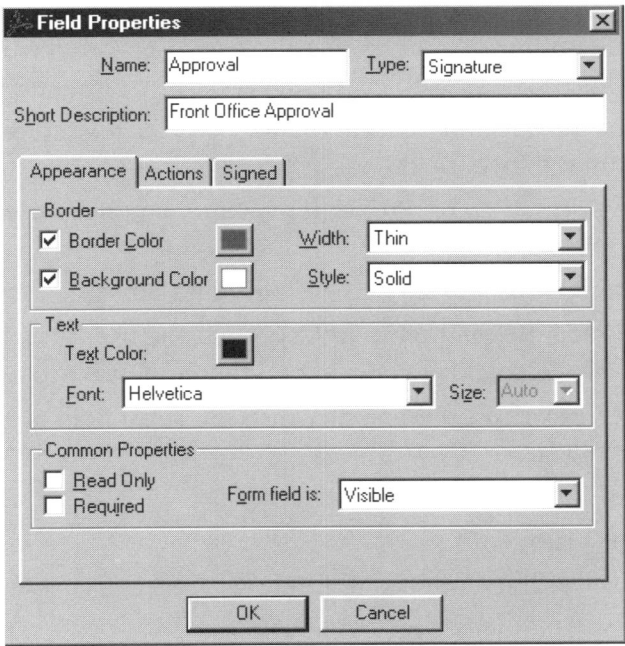

4. Add the name of this field to the Name field.

5. In the Type field, click on the drop-down arrow and select **Signature**.

6. In the Short Description field, add a brief description. The short description will appear in an information box when you move the cursor across the field.

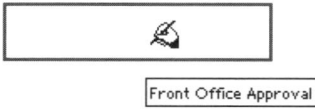

The lower portion of the dialog box contains three tabs that enable you to define the appearance and a few of the actions of the field. When creating signature fields, the three tabs initially contain defaults that can be changed later to customize the field.

## Adding a Signature Field — The Appearance Tab

The Appearance tab provides you with the ability to define the basic appearance of the form field. To define the appearance of the signature field:

1. In the Border section, define the basic appearance of the form field's border (border color, background color, width, and style).

2. In the Text section, define the font type, size, and color to appear within the form field.

3. Using the Common Properties section, you have the ability to define the following:

   ■ Select **Read Only** to prohibit data input.

   ■ Select **Required** to indicate that the user must enter data into this field prior to clicking on the Submit button.

   ■ Click the drop-down arrow in the Form field is area to define if the field is:

      ■ Visible

      ■ Hidden

      ■ Visible but doesn't print

      ■ Hidden but printable

## Adding a Signature Field — The Actions Tab

When all choices are made on the Options tab, click on the **Actions** tab.

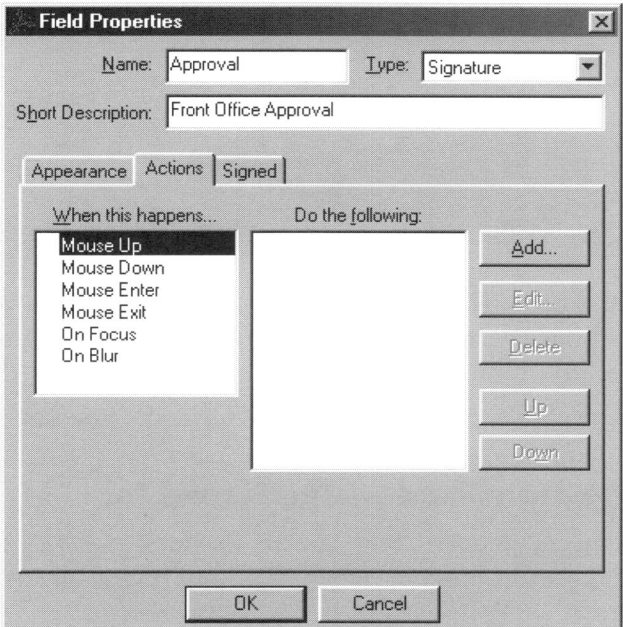

On this tab there are two fields: When this happens… and Do the following. Under When this happens… the following list of mouse actions appears:

■ *Mouse Up* — Releasing the mouse button.

■ *Mouse Down* — Pressing the mouse button.

■ *Mouse Enter* — Navigating the mouse over the form button.

■ *Mouse Exit* — Navigating the mouse off of the form button.

■ *On Focus* — Occurring after Mouse Down, but before Mouse Up.

■ *On Blur* — Occurring after all other mouse actions, as the field "loses focus."

1. Select one of the mouse actions to define the trigger.

2. Click **Add**. The Add an Action dialog box appears.

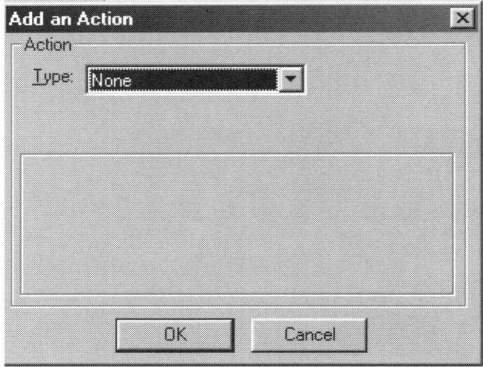

3. Click the drop-down arrow in the Type field to choose which action to link the mouse action to. Depending on the chosen type, you may be prompted to fill out other fields.

4. Once a suitable action is chosen and defined, click **Set Action**.

## Adding a Signature Field — The Signed Tab

When defining a Signature field, specify in the Signed tab area exactly how this field should function when/if a signature is electronically entered.

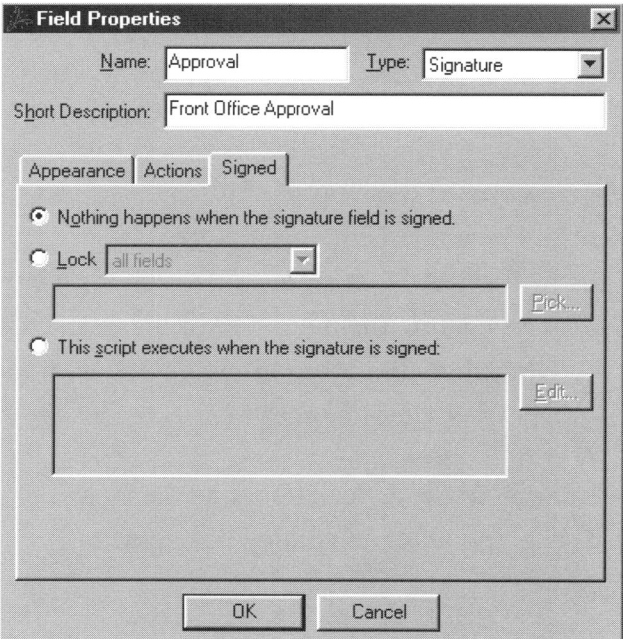

To complete the definition of the Signature field, select one of the options on the signed tab:

■ Select **Nothing happens when the signature field is signed** to indicate, as the request states, that if signed, the signature field doesn't trigger another action.

■ Or, select **Lock** to lock certain fields when the signature field is filled.

   Click the drop-down arrow next to the Lock selection to choose the fields to lock when the signature field is signed. Notice that the default is all fields.

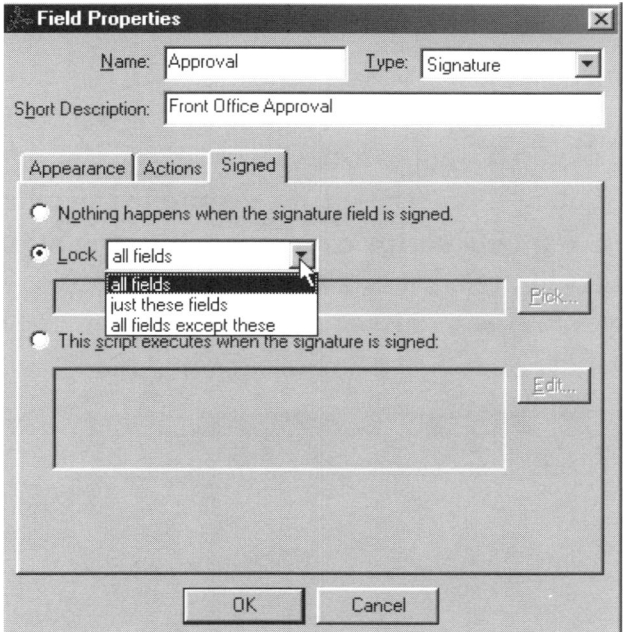

If you choose just these fields or all fields except these, the Pick button becomes enabled.

Click **Pick** to select the fields to be included or excluded. The Select a Field dialog box appears on the screen.

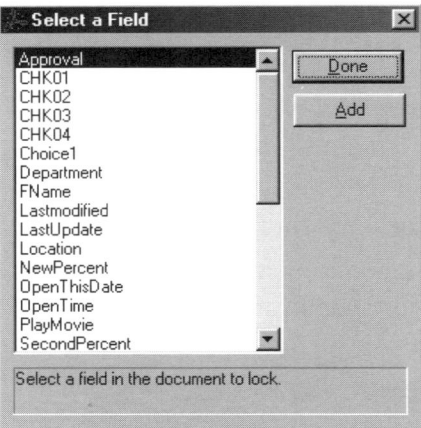

Highlight a field, and then click **Add** to select it. Repeat this step for each field you want to lock.

When all fields are chosen, click **Done** to close this dialog box.

■ Or, choose **This script executes when the signature is signed** to add an action that executes when the signature field is signed.

When you choose this option, the Edit button becomes enabled.

Click **Edit** to display the Acrobat Forms dialog box.

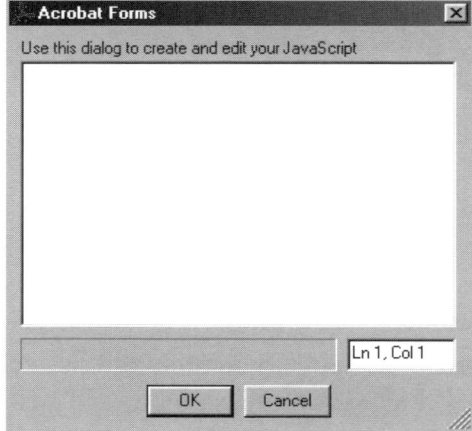

Add your JavaScript into this box, then click **OK** to close the box.

## Completing the Addition of a Signature Field

After all desired information is entered into the tabs, click **OK** to save the form field. To test the signature field, leave edit mode by selecting the **Hand** tool on the toolbar and then add a signature to the signature field.

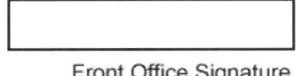

Front Office Signature

## Adding a Signature to a Signature Field

1. Navigate across the Signature field. Immediately, the cursor changes to the Signature cursor.

2. Click once on the Signature field. The Acrobat Digital Signature Plug-in dialog box appears on the screen.

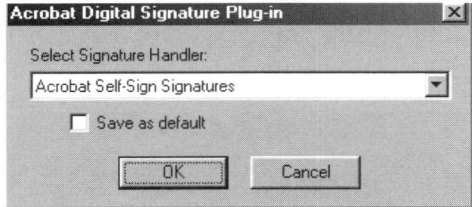

3. In the Select Signature Handler field, choose **Acrobat Self-Sign Signatures**.

4. Select **OK**. The Acrobat Self-Sign Signatures — Log In dialog box appears. Prior to signing, enter your user password.

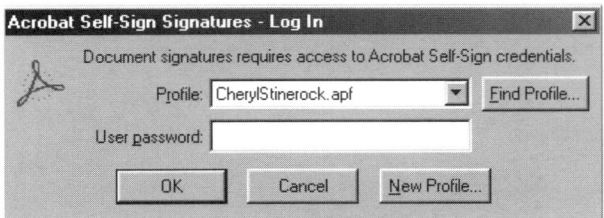

5. After you successfully log in, the Acrobat Self-Sign Signatures — Sign Document dialog box appears on the screen.

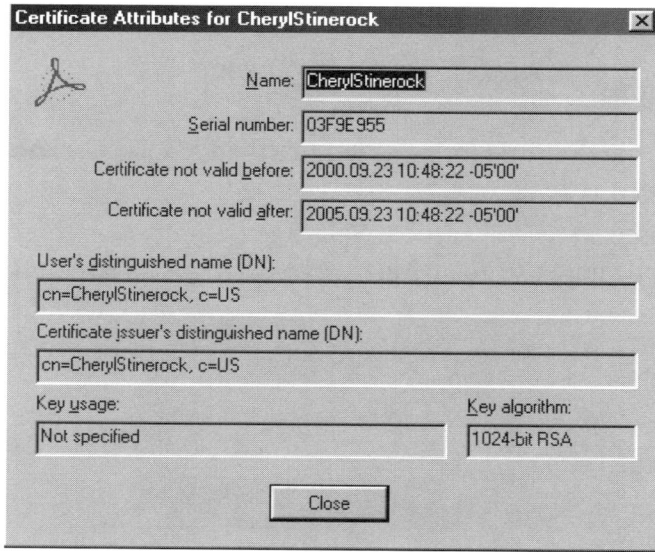

In the Document signed with certificate issued to field, the name of the current person logged in to the system appears. To display details regarding that person, click **Show Certificate**. The Certificate Attributes for... dialog box appears, displaying specific information about the signer of the document.

6. Click **Close** to return to the Acrobat Self-Sign Signature — Sign Document dialog box.

7.  Define the exact content of the signature in the Additional Signing Information section of this dialog box.

**Note:** *The signature only needs to be defined when it is initially added.*

■ In the Reason for signing document field, click on the drop-down arrow and select one of the provided choices, or supply a reason of your own.

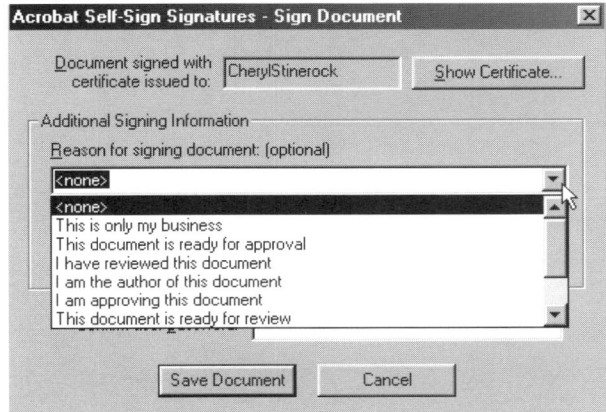

■ In the Location field, enter the name of the location to include in the signature.

8.  At the bottom of the dialog box, enter your password (for additional setup information regarding signature and passwords, please refer to Chapter 5 — Security and PDF Files).

9.  Click **Save Document** to save this signature.

10. As soon as the signature is saved, all the signature information is added to the field.

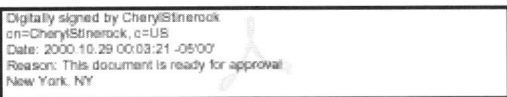

Front Office Signature

### Re-Signing the Signature Field

If the signature information needs to be changed for any reason, it is possible to re-sign the signature field. To re-sign the field:

1. Double-click the signature field. An Acrobat Digital Signature dialog box appears.

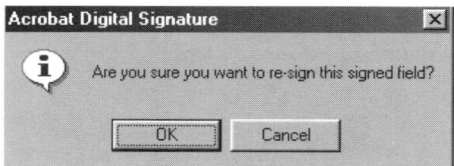

2. Click **OK**. The Acrobat Self-Sign Signatures — Sign Document dialog box appears.

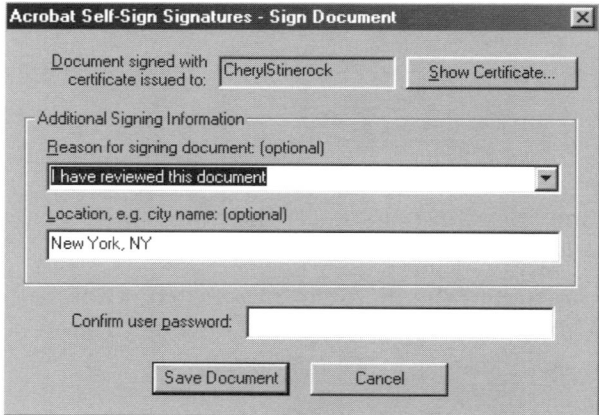

3. Enter all changed signature information into this dialog box.
4. Enter your password into the Confirm user password field.
5. Click **Save Document**.

# Adding Interactive Buttons to a Form

The addition of interactive buttons to a form, on the web, or merely on your desktop, provides a great deal of functionality. Acrobat provides you with the ability to place buttons onto your form that control the launching of multimedia presentations (movies or PowerPoint presentations), pre-populate fields, submit fields to other applications, refresh the fields on the form, and help you navigate through a multi-page form.

**Note:** *Some of this functionality is available when forms are available on web sites. Those topics will be covered in Chapter 6.*

With a minimal effort, interactive buttons provide your form with increased functionality.

To create an interactive button:

1. Navigate to the toolbar and select the **Form** tool. The cursor immediately becomes a cross hair.

2. Create the field by pressing the left mouse button and dragging to the right to define the height and width of the field.

3. When the rectangle representing the field has been completed, release the mouse button. The Field Properties dialog box appears on the screen.

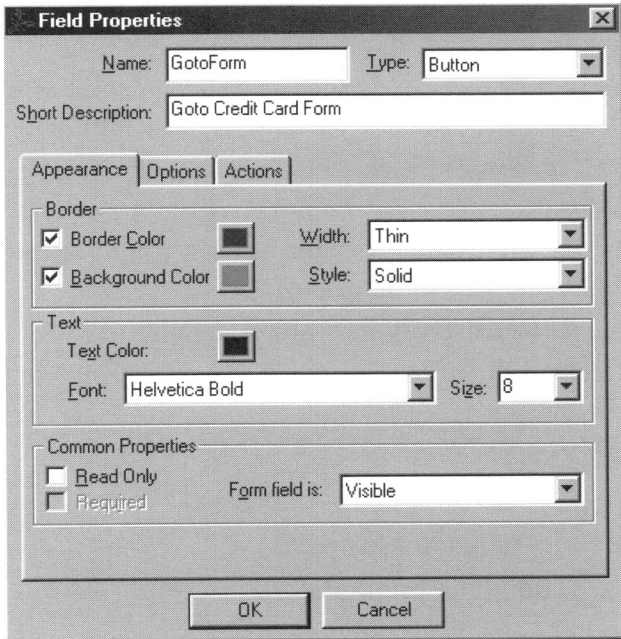

4. Add the name of this field to the Name field.

5. In the Type field, click on the drop-down arrow and select **Button.**

6. In the Short Description field, add a brief description. The short description will appear in an information box when you move the cursor across the interactive button.

The lower portion of the dialog box contains three tabs that help you to define the appearance of the button and a few of the button's actions. By adding appropriate information into the following tabs, you can easily control the actions of the button.

## Adding an Interactive Button — The Appearance Tab

The Appearance tab provides you with the ability to define the appearance of the button's border and the text appearing on the button. To complete the Appearance tab:

1. In the Border section, define the basic appearance of the form field's border (border color, background color, width, and style).

2. In the Text section, define the font type, size, and color to appear on the button.

3. Using the Common Properties section, you have the ability to define the fields in the following ways:

   ■ Select **Read Only** to prohibit data input.

   ■ Click on the drop-down arrow in the Form field is area to define if the button is:

      ■ Visible

      ■ Hidden

      ■ Visible but doesn't print

      ■ Hidden but printable

*Note:* *When Button is selected in the Type field, Required is disabled.*

## Adding an Interactive Button — The Options Tab

When all choices are made on the Appearance tab, click on the **Options** tab.

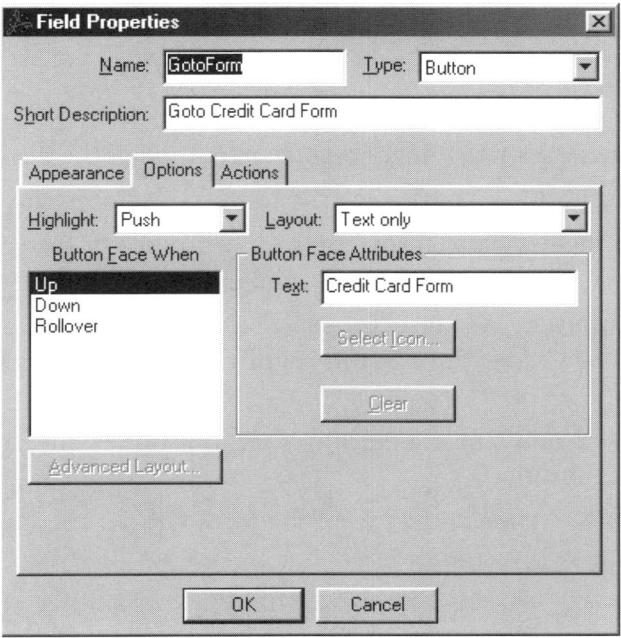

This tab enables you to choose the appearance of the button before, during, and after it is clicked. To complete the Options tab:

1. Click on the Highlight drop-down list to choose the appearance of the button after it is clicked.

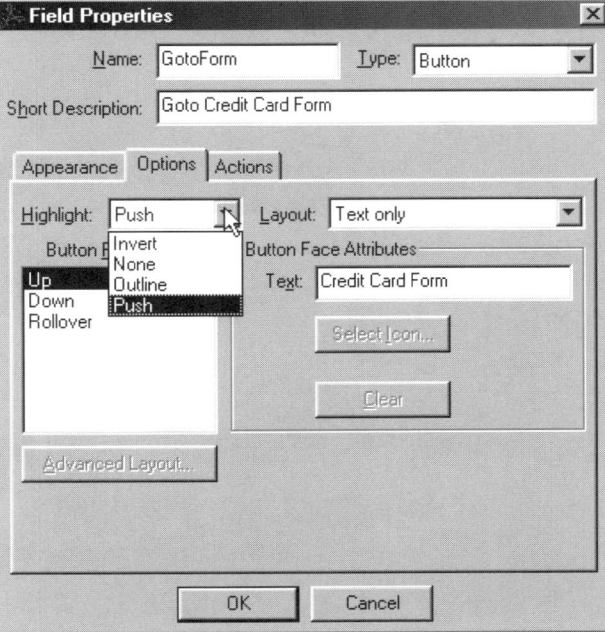

Each available option gives the button a different appearance when clicked:

■ *Invert* reverses the colors of the button when it is selected.

■ *None* causes no change in appearance when the button is pressed.

■ *Outline* adds an outline to the button when it is clicked.

■ *Push* enables you to specify the appearance of the form's button, depending on the position of the mouse button.

2. The Button Face When section is usually filled out automatically. However, if you choose Push in the Highlight box, three distinct selections appear:

■ *Up* — When a mouse button is up, it is not interacting with the form button.

■ *Down* — When you click on the form button, the mouse button is in a "down" position.

■ *Rollover* — When a mouse is "rolling over" an object, the position of the mouse button is "rollover."

3. Next, click the drop-down arrow next to the Layout field.

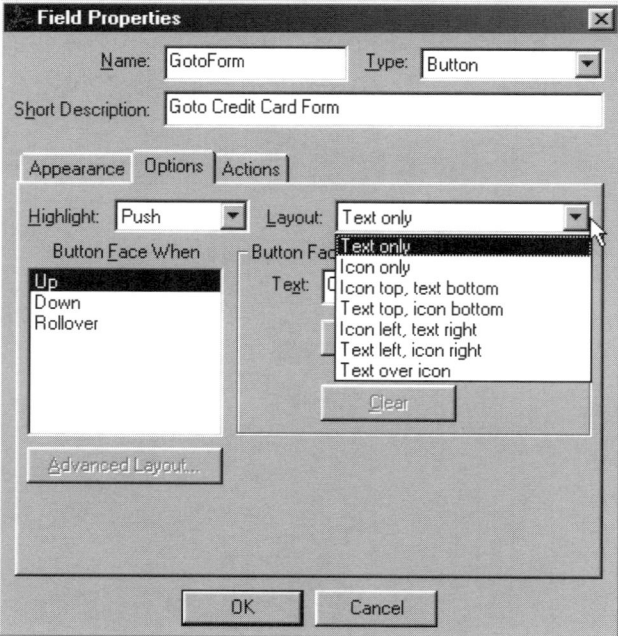

Here, you can define the appearance of the button as text only, icon only, or a combination of the two.

4. In the Text field, add the name that will appear on the button.

5. If your selection in the Layout field included the display of an icon (e.g., Icon only, Text over icon), click **Select Icon**. The Select Appearance dialog box appears.

6. Click **Browse** and select the icon to add to the button.

*Note: The icons must be in PDF format.*

7. Click **OK**.

8. To change the icon settings/selection, click **Clear** to clear the Button Face Attributes.

## Adding an Interactive Button — The Actions Tab

When all choices are made on the Options tab, click on the **Actions** tab.

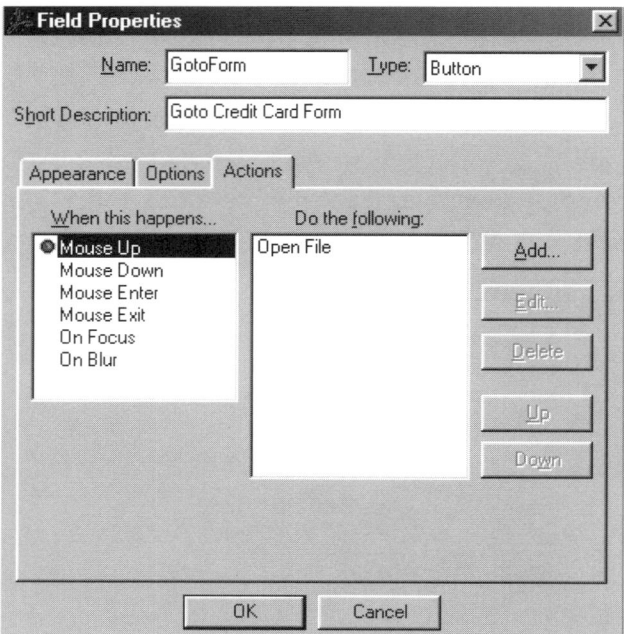

The Actions tab is where the real functionality of the button is defined. Here, you can choose one of the action options available in a selection list, or you can define a very specific action.

The two fields on this tab are: When this happens... and Do the following. Under When this happens... is the following list of mouse actions:

- *Mouse Up* — Releasing the mouse button.
- *Mouse Down* — Pressing the mouse button.
- *Mouse Enter* — Navigating the mouse over the form button.
- *Mouse Exit* — Navigating the mouse off of the form button.
- *On Focus* — Occurring after Mouse Down, but before Mouse Up.
- *On Blur* — Occurring after all other mouse actions, as the field "loses focus."

To complete this tab:

1. Choose one of the mouse actions to define the trigger, and click **Add**. The Add an Action dialog box appears.

2. Click the drop-down arrow in the Type field to choose the action that is linked to the mouse action. Depending on the chosen type, you may be prompted to fill out other fields.

3. Once a suitable action is chosen and defined, click **Set Action**. Repeat these steps for each action required.

**Note:** *No more than 10 actions in one field is Adobe's recommendation.*

### Completing the Addition of an Interactive Button

To finalize the addition of an interactive button:

1. When all field properties have been selected, click **OK**.

2. To test the button, leave edit mode and choose the **Hand** tool on the toolbar.

# Design Considerations When Creating Forms

When creating a form, there are a few aspects regarding its design that you should consider prior to electronic distribution or placement on a web site.

## Aligning Fields Using Gridlines

When eyes navigate across and up and down a form, they seek symmetry. If fields are lined up evenly, then the form appears well designed. On the other hand, if the fields appear unaligned and haphazardly arranged, then the form gives the impression of "amateur night."

To assist you when aligning fields, Adobe Acrobat provides you with a Grid tool. To display the grid:

1. Open your document.

2. Choose **View | Show Forms Grid** on the menu bar.

   A grid is displayed covering the entire PDF form.

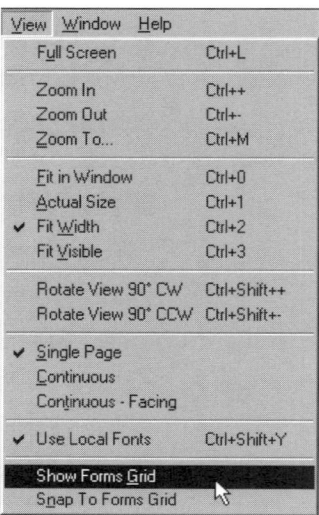

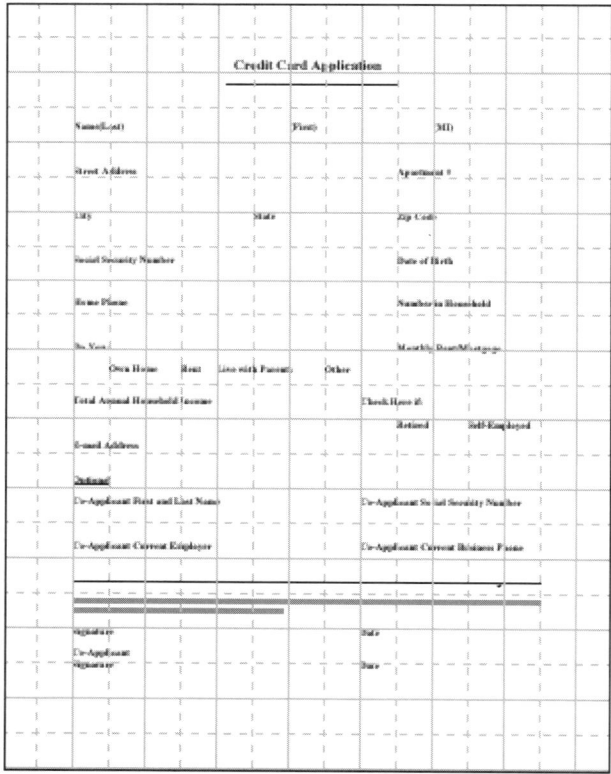

# Changing the Appearance of the Gridlines

When you initially display the gridlines, they default to solid gray lines. These gridlines are 72 points apart and are subdivided by eight gridlines (indicated by dotted lines). To change any of these defaults:

1. On the menu bar, choose **File | Preferences | Forms Grid**. The Grid Settings dialog box appears.

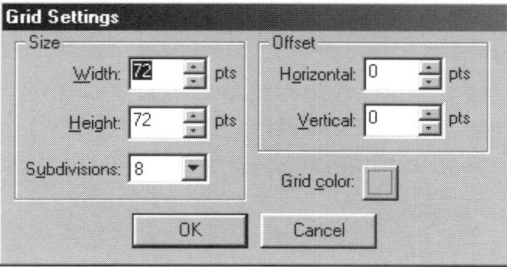

2. Complete this dialog box by entering the following:

   ■ In the Size section, change the size of the main gridlines by indicating (in points) the desired size in the Width and Height fields.

   ■ Also in the Size section, change the number of subdivisions (indicated by the dotted lines) inside of the main gridlines by changing the number in the Subdivisions field.

   ■ In the Offset section, change the offset by entering new values in the Horizontal and Vertical fields.

   ■ Click on the **Grid color** button to select a new color for the gridlines.

3. When all changes have been made, click **OK** to accept the changes. The grid appearing on the screen will change to reflect the setting updates.

# Aligning Fields Using the Snap to Forms Grid Option

While editing the form, you may find it tedious to align the sides of the form fields within the grid. To force the vertical sides of the form fields to align with the vertical gridlines:

1. Choose **View | Show Forms Grid** from the menu bar to display the forms grid.

2. Choose **View | Snap To Forms Grid**. The form fields on your form may appear unaligned with the vertical gridline, as illustrated below:

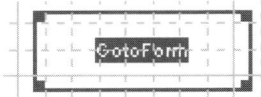

3. Click on the **Forms** tool on the toolbar to edit the form fields.

4. Click on the form field you want to align with the vertical lines. As you grab one of the handles and drag, the vertical side of the field automatically snaps into alignment with the nearest vertical gridline.

**Note:** *This action does not cause any of the fields to automatically change size. If the field is unaligned due to size, it will remain that way when this option is chosen.*

# Setting Tab Order

The Tab key is frequently used to navigate from one form field to another. Efficient forms provide users with a logical tab order. However, when a form is initially created in Adobe Acrobat, the tab sequence follows the order in which the form fields were created. A good rule of thumb is to always check the tab order of the form fields prior to distribution of the form.

To check the order of the form fields:

1. Open the form.

2. Click on the **Form** tool found on the toolbar.

3. Position your cursor on one of the form fields and right-click to display the context menu.

4. Select **Set Tab Order**.

 The context menu closes and the cursor appears with a "#" next to it. In the upper-left corner of each of the form fields, a number indicating its tab order appears.

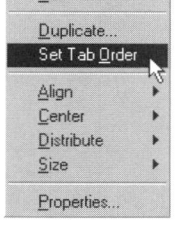

5. To change the tab order, click once on each of the form fields in the desired tab order. The number appearing on the upper left of each of the form fields automatically changes to reflect the new tab order.

6. To test the new tab order, click the **Hand** tool on the toolbar, then tab to each of the fields.

# Duplicating Form Fields

Sometimes, the only way to ensure that a few fields will be identical in size is to duplicate them. In the case of radio buttons or check boxes, duplication is probably the only way to create uniformly sized fields. There are two ways you can duplicate form fields: copy and paste and drag-and-drop.

## Copy and Paste Method of Duplicating Fields

To duplicate fields by using the copy and paste method:

1. On the toolbar, select the **Form** tool.

2. Click to highlight the form field you want to duplicate.

3. On the menu bar, select **Edit | Copy**.

4. On the menu bar, select **Edit | Paste**.

5. An identical copy of the field will appear in the center of your view of the form.

**Note:** *Everything about the copy is identical to the original, <u>including the name</u>.*

## Drag-and-Drop Method of Duplicating Fields

To duplicate fields by using the drag-and-drop method:

1. On the toolbar, select the **Form** tool.

2. Click on the form field you want to duplicate.

3. Press the **Ctrl** key and the left mouse button simultaneously. A copy of the field is automatically created.

4. Drag the new copy to reposition it. The original will
   remain in its original position.

# Adding Labels

As your eyes navigate over a form, labels provide the fields with identification. Labels inform you where to enter information and what type of
response is required. To add a label to a PDF form:

1. Create a form field.

2. In the Field Properties dialog box, select **Text** in the Type field.

3. Choose the Name and fill in the Short Description.

4. On the Appearance tab, deselect **Border Color** in the Border section
   if a border is not desired. Choose **Read Only** in the Common Properties section.

5. On the Options tab, add the text of the label in the Default field.

6. When all preferences are selected, click **OK**.

# Using JavaScript to Add Control at the Document Level

Adding JavaScript to a form enables you to add new functionality to the
document. Follow the examples below to walk through the process of adding fields that display the time and the date the document was opened.

## Adding a Time Stamp at the Document Level

To create the Time field and its label:

1. Open a PDF document.

2. Select the **Form** tool on the toolbar.

3. Create a text form field.

4. Create a duplicate of that form field.

5. Align these two fields side by side.

*Note:* One of these fields will function as the label and the other will display the time at which the document was opened.

To define the first label field:

1. Double-click the first field to display the Form Properties dialog box.
2. In the Name field, type **OpenTime**.
3. In the Type field, select **Text**.
4. On the Appearance tab, select **Read Only** in the Common Properties section.
5. Select **Visible** in the Form field is field.
6. Navigate to the Options tab and enter **Time Opened:** into the Default field.
7. On the Format tab, select **None** as the Category.
8. Click **OK** to accept the definition of this label field.

Time Opened:

To define the Time field:

1. Double-click on the second form field to display the Form Properties dialog box.
2. In the Name field, type **Time**.
3. In the Type field, select **Text**.
4. On the Appearance tab, select **Read Only** in the Common Properties section.
5. Select **Visible** in the Form field is field.
6. Choose the format this field should take. To do this, navigate to the Format tab and select **Time** from the Category list and **2:30 pm** from the Time Options list.
7. Click **OK** to save this definition.

To add the document-level JavaScript:

1. Navigate to the menu bar and select **Tools | Forms | Document JavaScripts**. The JavaScript Functions dialog box will appear on the screen.

2. In the Name field, add the name of the form field that will display the results of the JavaScript (here, that field is Time).

3. Click **Add** to display the Acrobat Forms dialog box.

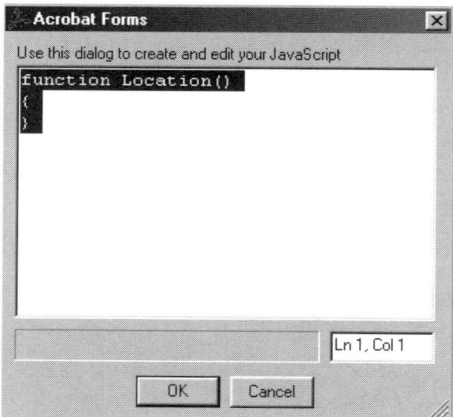

4. When it first appears, the Acrobat Forms dialog box is populated with a template for a function definition. Delete that code prior to entering your own.

5. In the space provided, type in the following JavaScript:

```
var f = this.getField("Time");
f.value = util.printd("hh:mm",new Date());
```

6. This simple piece of JavaScript will bind the Time field to this code, get the current system date when this document is initially opened, format the time, then display this information in the Time field.

**Note:** *The date includes the current time and date.*

2:10 am

## Adding a Date Stamp at the Document Level

To create the Date field and its label, copy the Time label field and the Time field created previously.

To define the second label field:

1. Double-click the first field to display the Form Properties dialog box.
2. In the Name field, type **OpenThisDate**.
3. In the Type field, select **Text**.
4. On the Appearance tab, select **Read Only** in the Common Properties section.
5. Select **Visible** in the Form field is field.
6. Navigate to the Options tab and enter **Date Opened:** into the Default field.
7. On the Format tab, select **None** as the Category.
8. Click **OK** to accept the definition of this label field.

Date Opened:

To define the Date field:

1. Double-click on the second form field to display the Form Properties dialog box.
2. In the Name field, type **ThisDate**.
3. In the Type field, select **Text**.
4. On the Appearance tab, select **Read Only** in the Common Properties section.
5. Select **Visible** in the Form field is field.
6. Navigate to the Format tab and select **Date** from the Category list and **Jan 3, 1981** (the "mmm d, yyyy" format) from the Time Options list.
7. Click **OK** to save this definition.

To add the document-level JavaScript:

1. Navigate to the menu bar and select **Tools** | **Forms** | **Document JavaScripts**.

2. The JavaScript Functions dialog box will appear on the screen. Type **ThisDate** in the Name field.

3. Click **Add** to display the Acrobat Forms dialog box.

4. Delete the code that automatically appears in the Acrobat Forms dialog box.

5. In the space provided, type in the following JavaScript:

```
var f = this.getField("ThisDate");
f.value = util.printd("mmm d, yyyy",new Date());
```

6. When the document is initially opened, the ThisDate field will be populated with the current date.

> Oct 29, 2000

To test the new fields:

1. Save and close the current form.

2. Reopen the current form. The Time and the ThisDate fields will automatically populate with the current date and time.

> | Time Opened: | 2:10 am |
> |---|---|
> | Date Opened: | Oct 29, 2000 |

# Using JavaScript to Add Control at the Field Level

By inserting JavaScript into a field definition, you can add control to the form at the field level. Control at the field level provides you with the ability to:

■ Auto-populate certain fields

■ Ensure that field entries are always within selected parameters

■ Display only required fields on the form

The following sections illustrate how some of these controls are easily added to form fields.

## Populating More Than One Field at a Time

Certain editable fields on a form, such as a Name field, may need to appear more than once on the form. To keep the amount of information a user needs to enter into the form at a minimum, add duplicate fields. By entering information into one of the fields, all of the duplicates of that field are automatically populated. This reduction of repetition saves a precious commodity — time.

To add duplicate fields to the form:

1.  Create the first field, defining all attributes of the field accurately.

2.  Create a copy of that field. Do not change any of that information.

3.  Move the copy to the desired location.

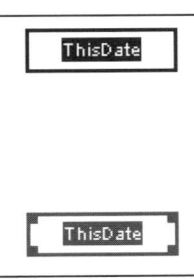

To test the field:

1.  Click on the **Hand** tool to leave edit mode.

2.  Navigate to the first field and enter some information.

3.  Notice that the second field has been populated with the identical information.

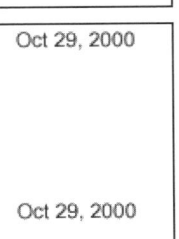

## Hiding One Field Until Information is Entered into Another Field

In some forms, you may decide not to show certain fields until other fields are populated. For example, the creator of a form may choose to display the Quantity field only when the Item Description field is used. To do this:

1.  Create a form field on a PDF form.

2.  In the Field Properties dialog box, add **Item Description** into the Name field, and select **Text** from the Type drop-down list.

3.  On the Appearance tab, choose the Border and Text attributes and Common Properties.

4.  Parallel to the Item Description form field, add a second form field.

5.  In the Field Properties dialog box, give this field the name **Quantity**. In the Type drop-down list, select **Text**.

6. On the Appearance tab, choose the desired Border and Text attributes for the Quantity field.

7. In the Common Properties section of the Appearance tab, click the Form field is drop-down list and select **Hidden**. Initially, then, this field will be hidden to the user.

8. Because this field will contain numeric data (which you may choose to use in calculations elsewhere on the form), navigate to the Format tab. In the Category column, select **Number**. A Number Options section will appear on the right side of the Format tab.

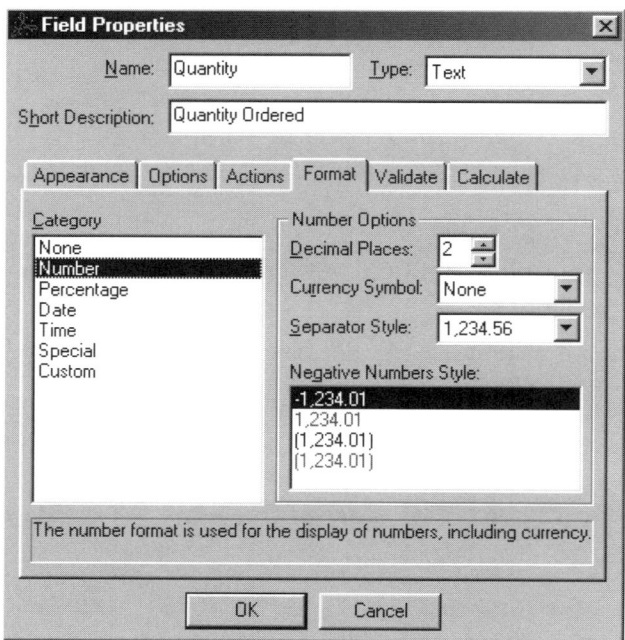

Choose:  Decimal Places = **0**

Currency Symbol = **None**

Separator Style = **1,234.56**

Negative Numbers Style = **–1,234.01**

9. When all formatting selections have been made, click **OK**.

10. Return to the Item Description field and navigate to the Actions tab. On this tab, you have the ability to define a mouse action as a trigger to a specific action (e.g., display a movie clip, play a sound, show/hide a field).

11. In the When this happens column, choose **Mouse Down**. By choosing Mouse Down, you will keep the Quantity field hidden until you actually begin typing into the Item Description field.

12. Click **Add**. The Add an Action dialog box appears.

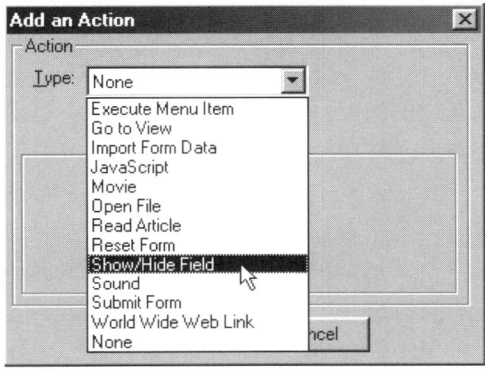

13. In the Type field, click the drop-down arrow to display the action choices.

14. Select **Show/Hide Field**.

15. An Edit button appears in the Add on Action dialog box. Click **Edit**.

16. The Show/Hide Field dialog box appears on the screen. In this dialog box, define the show/hide action the mouse action will trigger.

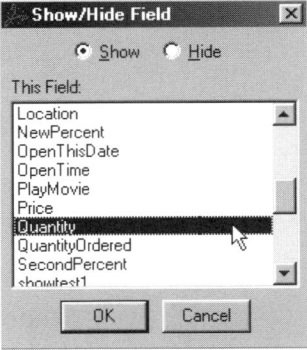

17. At the top of the box, select **Show**.

18. In the This Field list, select the **Quantity** field.

19. Click **OK**. The Show/Hide Field dialog box closes.

20. Click **Set Action**. The Add an Action dialog box closes.

21. Click **OK** to accept all changes. The Field Properties dialog box closes.

22. Select the **Hand** tool to test the functionality of these fields. After you click on the Item Description field, the Quantity field will automatically display.

# Adding More Functionality to Form Fields

The following sections describe several ways to make form fields more useful.

## Adding a Button That Displays a Completed Form

During creation of the form, you may want to provide users with an example of a form that was properly filled out. One way to do this is to add a button to the form that automatically displays the example of a correctly completed form.

To do this:

1. Click on the **Form** tool to put the form into edit mode.

2. Create a box on the form. A good idea is to place it at the top of the form, giving users the opportunity to view an example as soon as they open this form.

3. In the Field Properties dialog box, select **Button** as the Type.

4. Add a name and short description.

5. In the Border and Text sections of the Appearance tab, choose those attributes to create the desired appearance of the button.

6. In the Common Properties section, select **Read Only**.

7. On the Options tab, select:

   ■ The layout of the button

   ■ The appearance of the button when the mouse interacts with it

   ■ The text that appears on the button

   ■ The icon that appears on the button

8. After all desired options are chosen, navigate to the Actions tab.

9. Under the When this happens box, choose **Mouse Down**. (**Note:** *Mouse Down will trigger the selected mouse action.*) The Add an Action dialog box appears on the screen.

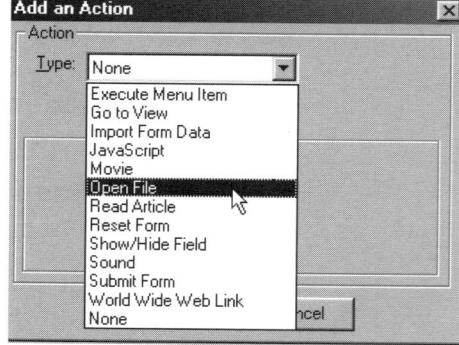

10. Select **Open File**. The dialog box changes to reflect this selection.

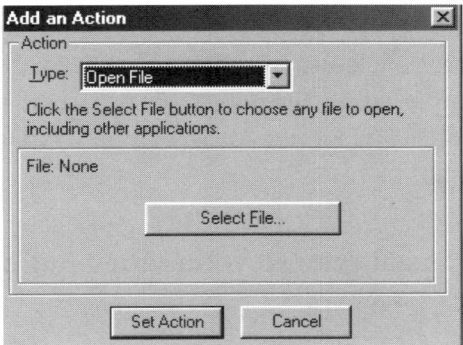

11. Click **Select File**. The Select File to Open dialog box appears.

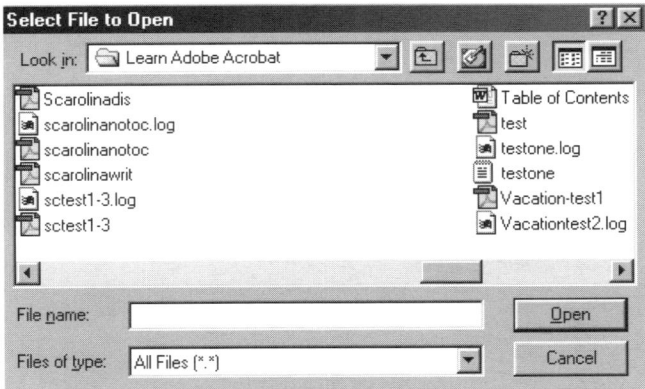

12. Choose the file in which the example of the form resides.

13. Click **Open**.

14. Click **Set Action**.

15. Click **OK** to save this new button.

16. To test the button, select the **Hand** tool and click the button.

## Adding Calculations to Form Fields — Changing the Percentage Calculation

Simple JavaScript can be used to automate a variety of functions within the form. If, for example, you want to enable a percentage field to accept 34 as 34% (instead of .34 as 34%), a few lines of JavaScript could easily make that conversion.

To add this calculation:

1. Create a form field and enter **NewPercent** in the Name field.

2. Select **Text** in the Type field.

3. Navigate to the Format tab and select the **Percentage** category. The section on the right changes to Percent Options.

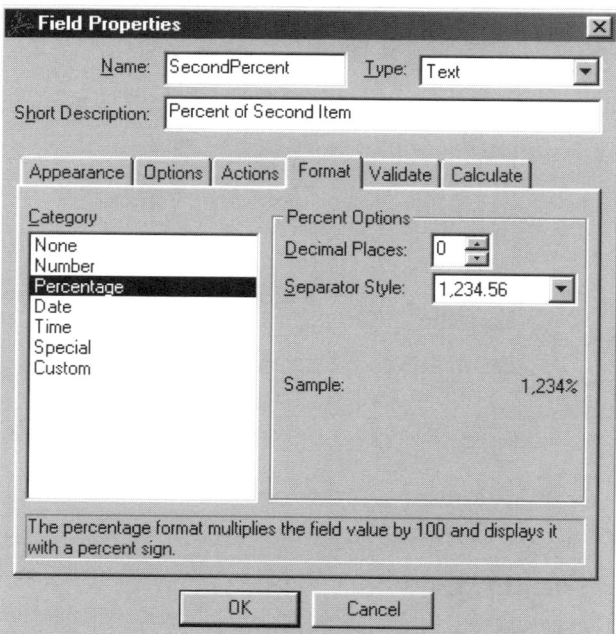

4. Set Decimal Places to **0**.

5. Navigate to the Calculate tab.

6. Select **Custom Calculation Script**. Here, you can enter your own JavaScript code.

7. Click **Edit**.

8. Enter the following Javascript:

```
var f = this.getField("NewPercent");
f.value = f.value/100;
```

By adding this code, all entries to this field (which are immediately multiplied by 100) will be divided by 100. In other words, an entry of 54 will appear in this field as 54%.

9. Click **OK**.

10. Click **OK** again to save this definition.

## Adding Customized Validation to Form Fields — Adding a Value Range Check

By using the Validate tab in the Field Properties dialog box of a text field, you can specifically define parameters for a field. For example, on an office supplies order form, a business might want to prohibit employees from ordering items that cost more than $50. If that was the case, such a form might include a quantity field that was disabled every time a price of more than $50 was entered into the Price field.

In the following example, the QuantityOrdered field is not visible if more than $50 is entered into the Price field.

1. First, create a text field.

2. Enter **Price** in the Name field.

3. Next, create a second text field.

4. Enter **QuantityOrdered** into the Name field.

5. Return to the Price field. Navigate to the Validate tab and choose **Custom validate script**.

6. Click **Edit** and add the following JavaScript:

```
var quantity = this.getField("QuantityOrdered");
quantity.hidden = (event.value > 50);
```

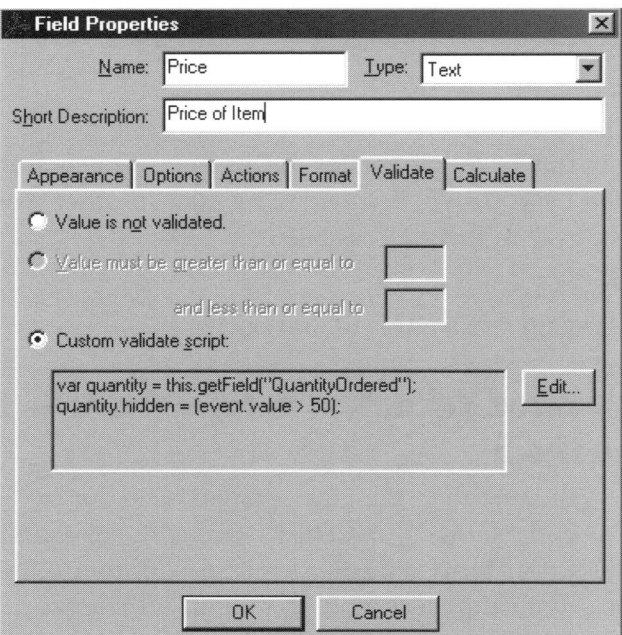

## Adding Sound to List Box Form Fields to Indicate Change of Selection

For certain types of form fields, it is sometimes desirable to audibly indicate that a change has occurred. To use a sound to indicate a selection change in a list box:

1. On a form, create a field, giving it the type **List Box**.

2. In the top portion of the Field Properties dialog box, choose a name and add a short description.

3. On the Appearance tab, choose the Border and Text attributes and the Common Properties.

4. Navigate to the Options tab and add the selections available in this list box.

5. Navigate to the Selection Change tab.

6. This tab automatically defaults to Nothing happens when a listbox selection changes. Since you want to add a sound to indicate that the list box selection has changed, select **This script executes when the listbox selection changes**.

7. Click **Edit**.

8. In the Acrobat Forms dialog box, enter the following JavaScript:

   ```
   app.beep(0);
   ```

   When adding this line of JavaScript, the one parameter required (which, in the example above, is equal to 0) determines the type of sound played when the list box selection is changed. Any of the choices below, though, can be used:

| Message Type | Value |
| --- | --- |
| "error" | 0 |
| "warning" | 1 |
| "question" | 2 |
| "status" | 3 |
| "default" | 4 |

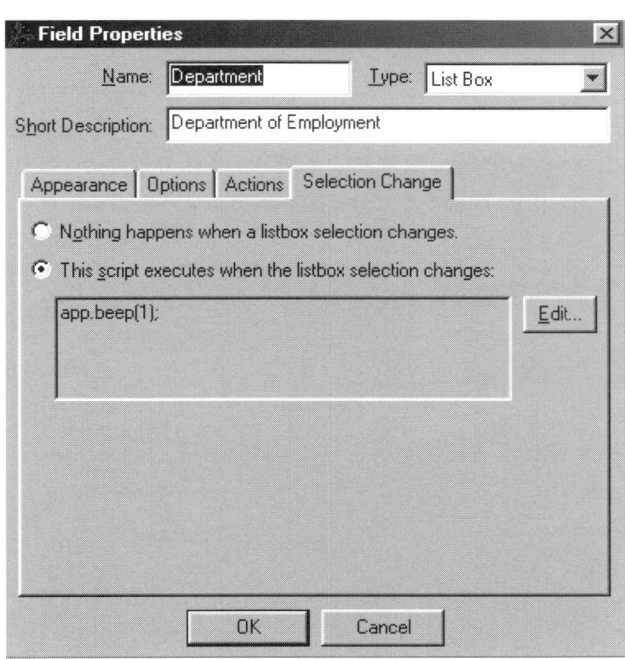

## Adding an Interactive Button to Play a Movie

Movies add significant interest to any form. Video clips can be added to provide instructions to users or to include information regarding a high-lighted subject. Interactive buttons provide you with a user-friendly way to display a movie in a form. A simple click of a button plays the linked movie.

However, the movie must be added to the form before the interactive button is provided. Links to movies only function if the movie exists on the form. To minimize the appearance of the movie when it's not being played, hide the link until a button is pressed.

To add the movie, then the interactive button, to the form:

1. Choose the **Movie** tool 🎞.

2. With the cross hair cursor, draw a small box (since it will be hidden, keep it as small as possible). The Open dialog box appears.

3. In the Open dialog box, choose the movie you want to add to the form.

4. Click **Open**. The Movie Properties dialog box appears.

5. In the Movie Poster section, click the drop-down arrow and choose **Don't Show Poster**. By selecting this option, the first frame of the movie won't display in the form field you created.

6. In the Player Options section, select **Show Controller** to show the movie controls as the movie plays. Click the drop-down arrow in the Mode field to choose how you want the movie to play (Play Once then Stop, Play Once Stay Open, Repeat Play, Back and Forth).

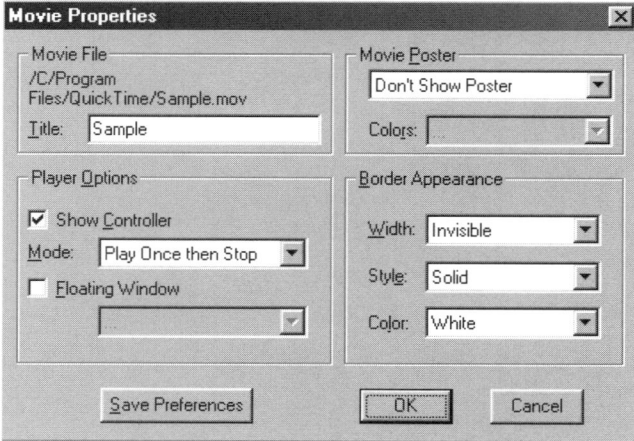

7. Click **OK** to add the movie to the form.

8. Select the **Form** tool on the toolbar and create a new form field. The Field Properties dialog box appears on the screen.

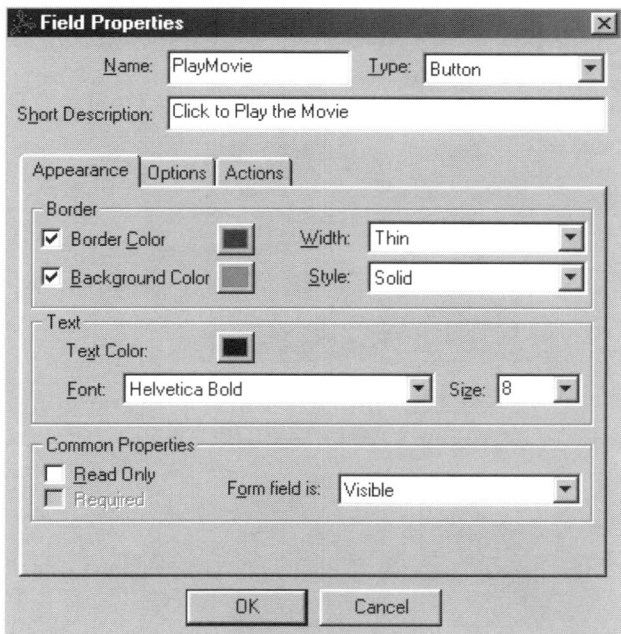

9. At the top of the Field Properties dialog box, choose **Button** as the Type and enter **PlayMovie** as the Name.

10. On the Appearance tab, select the desired attributes (Border, Text, and Common Properties).

11. On the Options tab, enter **Text Only** in the Layout field.

*Note: Of course, you can be more elaborate when designing the button. This choice was made only to make this example less complex!*

12. In the Button Face Attributes section, enter the text that will appear on the button (e.g., Play Movie) in the Text field.

13. Navigate to the Actions tab. Here, define the mouse action that will trigger the movie to play.

14. In the When this happens column, select **Mouse Down**.

15. Click **Add**. The Add an Action dialog box appears.

16. On the Add an Action dialog box, click the Type field's drop-down list, and select **Movie**.

17. Click the **Select Movie** button that appears on the dialog box. The Movie Action dialog box appears.

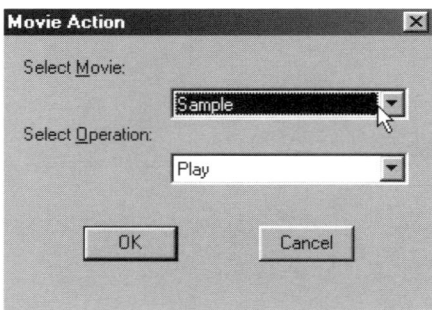

18. The drop-down list in the Select Movie field includes all movies added to the current form. To link a movie to this button, highlight it.

19. In the Select Operation field, choose **Play**. This selection causes the movie to play each time the interactive button is pressed.

20. Click **OK** to accept these options. The Movie Action dialog box closes.

21. Click **Set Action**. The Add an Action dialog box closes.

22. Click **OK**.

23. To test the new button, select the **Hand** tool on the toolbar and click the **Play Movie** button.

# Chapter 5

# Security and PDF Files

Face it. A major concern of any business operating in today's environment is security. Your information, after all, is only as valuable as it is secure. Adobe Acrobat provides you with a number of options throughout the application, ensuring that a certain level of security is maintained.

Specifically, Adobe Acrobat enables you to:

- Select the level of security added to an external link. Do you want all viewers of your document to have the ability to access links residing outside the document?

- Add password protection security to your documents.

- Define your individual signature. Since the signature is password protected, only authorized users can use it.

# Defining Link Security

When links are added to a document, the intended audience may only be a small part of the distribution list. Links to external documents or spreadsheets containing confidential information require security at the "link level." The following sections will walk you through the processes of setting up and testing link security.

## Selecting the Security Level on an External Link

When certain documents are distributed, chances are you do not want to provide all recipients with the ability to access links (such as links to Internet sites) that are external to the PDF document. One setting available in Adobe Acrobat allows you to toggle back and forth, enabling and disabling access to external links. To enable access to external links:

1. Select **File | Preferences | General**. The General Preferences dialog box appears.

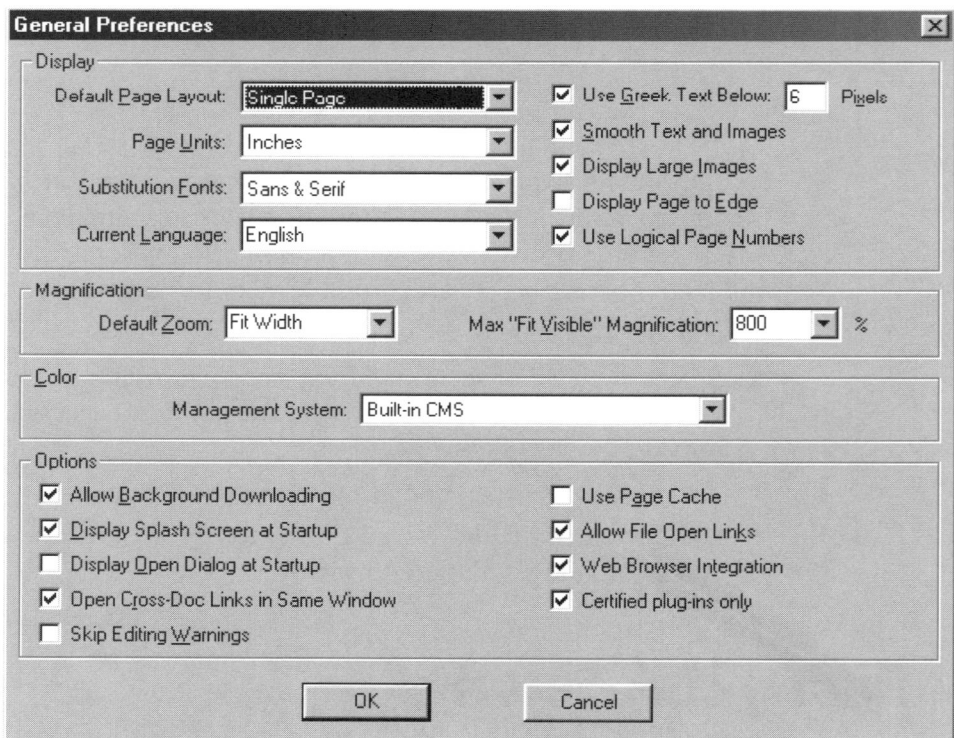

2. Select **Allow File Open Links** in the Options section.

**Note:** *By choosing this option, you now have the ability to access links that are external to the document. However, if this option is not chosen, you will not be able to access external links.*

# Testing the Chosen Security Level on an External Link

After you add new security to a document, it is always a good idea to test the security to ensure that the security selected is the security expected. To test the existing security level for external links to the document:

1. Navigate to an external link that resides within your document.

**Note:** *An external link can link to a file in another application or a URL.*

2. Double-click on the link. If the link is to an external file, an Adobe Acrobat message box will appear.

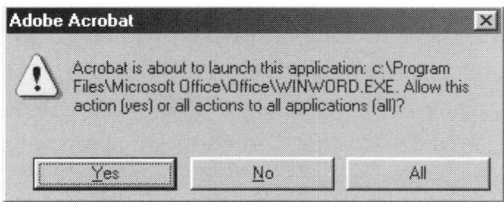

Select one of the following choices to determine if you want the external link to open:

■ Click **Yes** if you want to allow this external link to open. If the external link opens an external file, the required application will launch and the file will open.

■ Click **No** if you do not want to allow this link to open.

■ Click **All** if you want all external links found in this document to open when selected.

3. However, if the external link opens a URL, the login box for your ISP appears.

4. Log on to the ISP. The URL (the destination of the link) then opens.

# Setting Security for a PDF Document

Adobe Acrobat allows you to specifically define the type and level of security to add to a PDF document.

Two types of document-level passwords are available: a Read Access-level password and an Update-level password. The Read Access-level password enables the user to only read the PDF document. On the other hand, the Update-level password provides the user with the authority to edit, insert, or delete information found in the PDF document.

By defining the document-level password for a file, you ensure that a certain group of people will be able to view the necessary information, and only a selected few will have the capability to update the information. As covered later in this section, passwords can be added manually or through batch processing.

## Checking the Current Security of a PDF Document

All PDF files contain readily accessible information describing the current security on the document. To check the current security of a PDF document:

1. On the menu bar, select **File | Document Info | Security**. The Document Security dialog box appears.

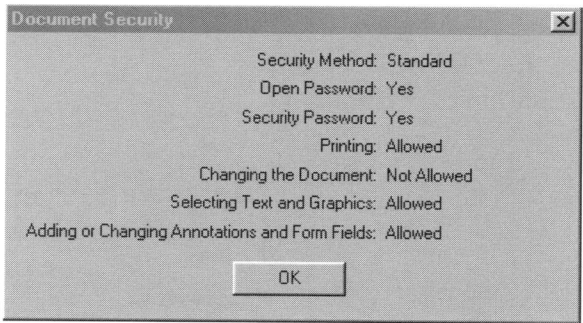

2. Click **OK** to close the dialog box after viewing the information.

# Adding Security to a PDF Document

The Read Access-level password (the Open password) provides you with access to the selected document. The Update-level password (the Change Security Options Password) gives you the ability to alter the current security set on a PDF document. If there are other security options selected (e.g., do not allow printing, do not allow changing the document), but there is no Update-level password defined, those other security options are automatically disabled when the document is accessed. In order to ensure that those options are not disabled when the Read Access-level password is used, always define an Update-level password.

To add the Read Access/Update-level passwords to an existing PDF document:

1. Open the PDF document.

2. On the menu bar, click **File | Save As**. The Save As dialog box appears.

3. Select the correct file and directory in which to save the document.

4. Expand the drop-down box found in the Security area located at the bottom of the dialog box.

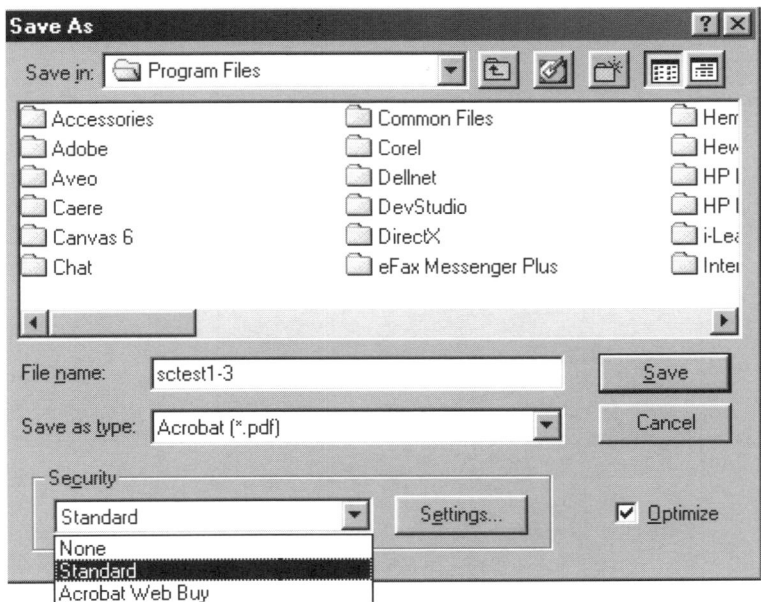

5. Choose **Standard**. The Security dialog box appears.

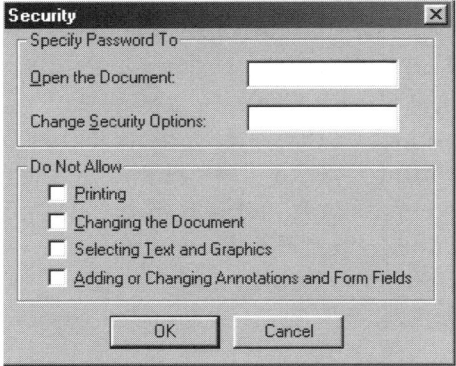

6. Add an Open the Document password.

7. Add a Change Security Options password.

8. In the Do Not Allow section, choose functions to disable in this document.

9. When all security options are selected, click **OK**. The Confirm Password To Open the Document dialog box appears.

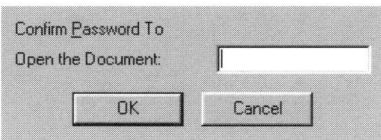

10. In the Confirm Password To Open the Document field, retype the Open the Document password.

11. Click **OK**. The Confirm Password To Change Security Options dialog box appears.

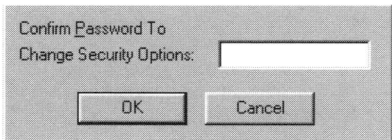

12. In the Confirm Password To Change Security Options field, retype the Change Security Options password.

13. Click **OK**. Your view returns to the Save As dialog box. The Settings button is now enabled.

14. After security has been defined for this document, click **Save** (found in the Save As dialog box).

# Adding Security to a Document When Converting to PDF Format with Distiller

Distiller enables you to automatically add security to a document when a PostScript file is converted to PDF format. Unfortunately, when Distiller is accessed through PDFMaker, the security option is not available.

When Distiller is used during the conversion processes, the PDF file's security must be defined before the file is converted to a PDF file. To add security to a document when converting with Distiller:

1. Open Distiller. The Acrobat Distiller dialog box appears.

2. Click on the **Settings | Security** option found on the menu bar.

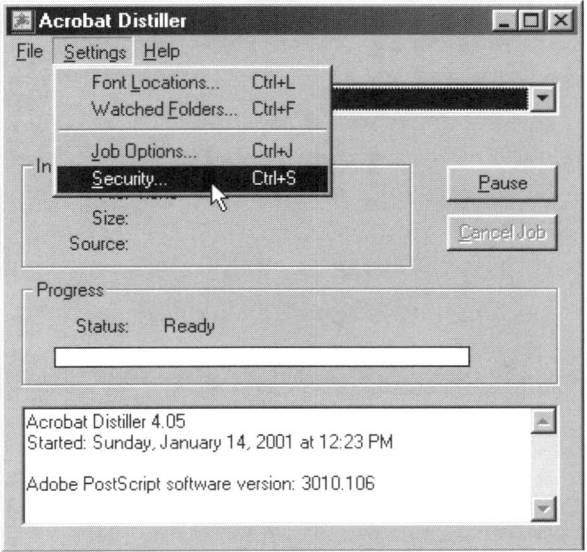

The Acrobat Distiller — Security dialog box appears.

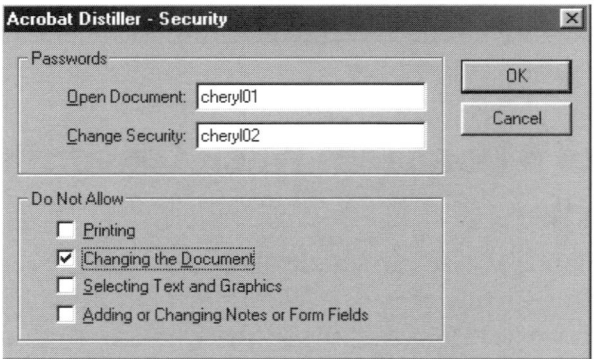

3. Enter a password in the Open Document field. This password provides you with the ability to open the document.

4. Enter another password in the Change Security field. This password lets you change the security settings of this document.

5. To disable certain functions, select options found in the Do Not Allow area.

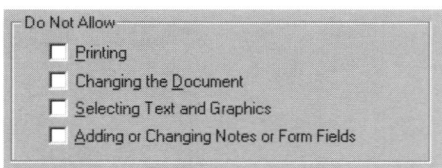

6. After all choices are made in the Acrobat Distiller — Security dialog box, click **OK** to save the settings.

7. Select **File | Open** in the Acrobat Distiller dialog box. The Acrobat Distiller — Open PostScript File dialog box appears.

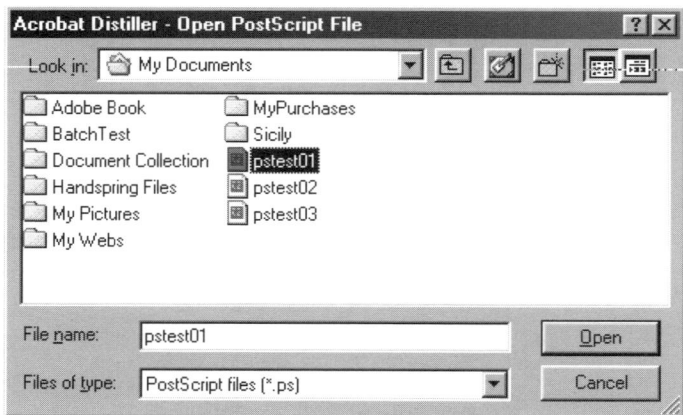

8. Select the PostScript file you want to convert to PDF format.

9. Click **Open**. The Acrobat Distiller — Specify PDF File Name dialog box appears.

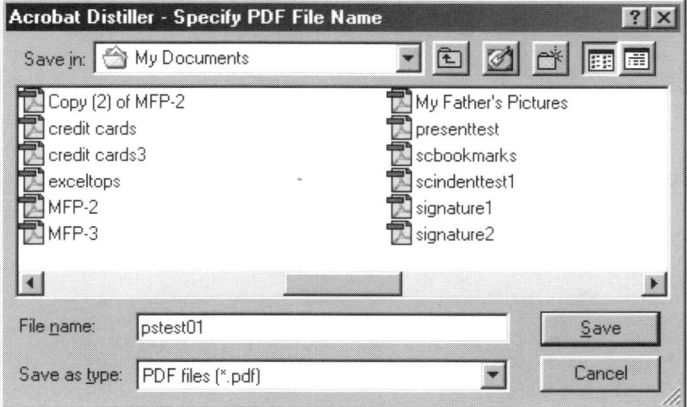

10. Select a filename for the PDF file that will be created by the Distiller conversion process.

11. Click **Save**. The Distiller process immediately begins to convert the PostScript file to PDF format. As the conversion progresses, the time line, found in the Progress section, shows the current status.

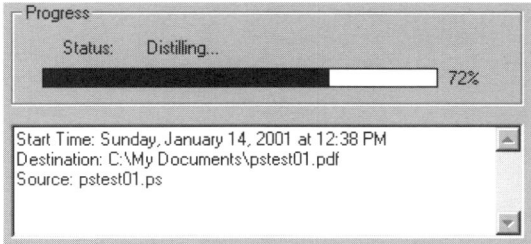

12. After the PostScript file is converted to PDF format, the Status field displays "Ready."

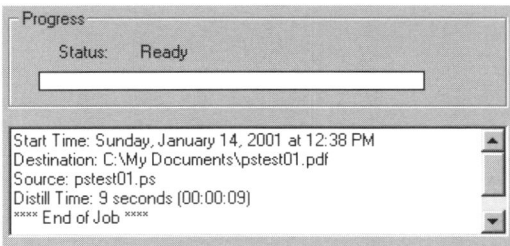

To view this new PDF file:

1. Launch Adobe Acrobat.

2. Open the new PDF file. The Password dialog box appears.

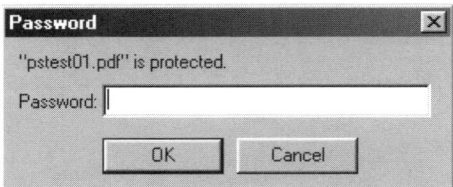

3. Enter the password and click **OK**. The new PDF document opens automatically.

*Note:* *You must enter the password you defined in Distiller's Open Document field.*

# Setting Security for More than One Document Using the Batch Process

When dealing with a number of PDF documents, a significant amount of time can be saved by setting security on the documents via a batch process. When this process is used, more than one document can be set up with identical security options.

To set the security features on more than one PDF document by using the batch process:

1. Add all documents to be batch processed to one folder.

*Note:* *Documents to be batch processed must be located in the same folder.*

At this point, these documents should not have pre-existing passwords.

2. On the menu bar, select **File | Batch Process**. The Select Folder To Process dialog box appears.

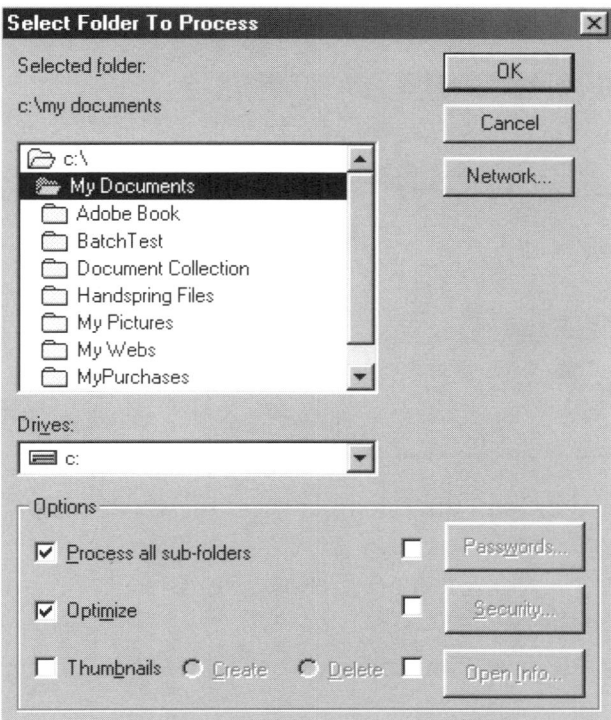

3. In the Selected folder and Drives fields, select the folder that contains the PDF documents to batch process.

4. In the Options area, enable the Security button .

   Other options available during batch processing include:

   - **Process all sub-folders** to batch process all subfolders of the selected folder.

   - **Optimize** to optimize the processing.

   - **Thumbnails** to automatically generate thumbnails for each of the PDF documents that have been batch processed.

   - **Security** to define the level of security to add to the PDF document.

   - **Open Info** to define the appearance of the PDF document when initially opened.

5. Click the **Security** button to display the Security dialog box.

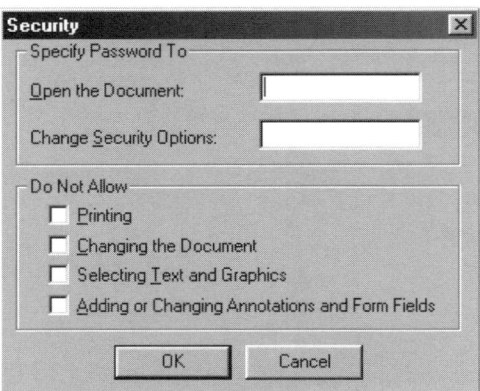

6. Enter the Open the Document and the Change Security Options passwords.

7. In the Do Not Allow area, choose those functions to which you want to add security.

8. Click **OK**. The Confirm Password To Open the Document dialog box appears.

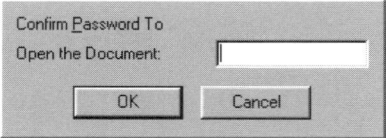

9. Enter the Open the Document password and click **OK**. The Confirm Password To Change Security Options dialog box appears.

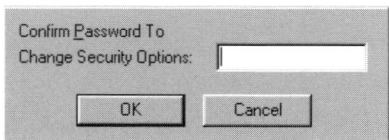

10. Enter the Change Security Options password and click **OK**.

11. Click **OK** to run the batch process. The Batch Processor Progress dialog box appears.

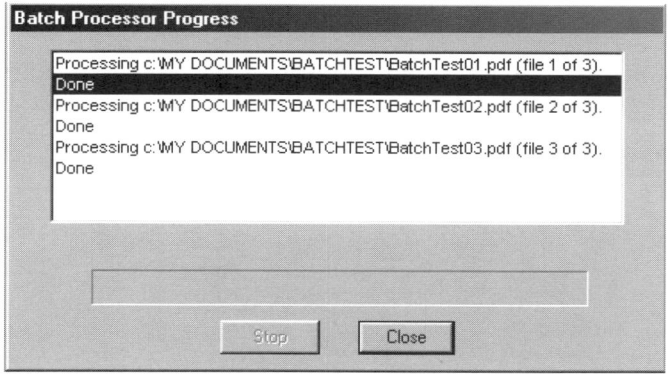

12. When the batch process has completed, click **Close** to close the dialog box.

# Changing Security on a PDF Document

When changes in the business have occurred, it is frequently desirable to change the existing security on a PDF document.

To change the security on a PDF document:

1. Open the PDF document.

2. On the menu bar, click **File | Save As**. The Save As dialog box appears.

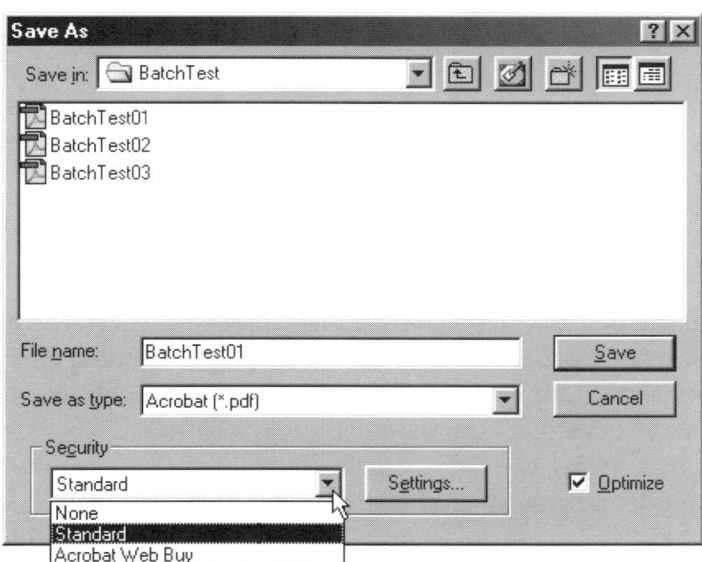

3. Select the correct file and directory in which to save the document.

4. Click the **Settings** button, found in the Security area. The Security dialog box appears.

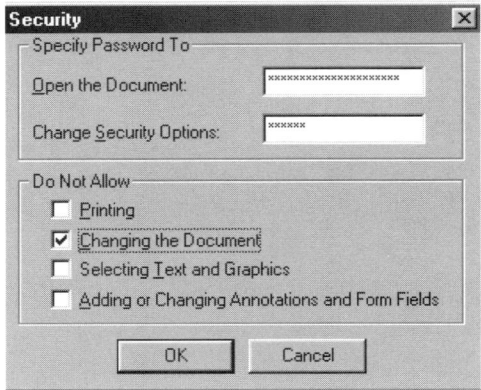

5. Select here all changes in security options.

6. Enter the Change Security Options password that was defined for this file.

7. Click **OK**. The Confirm Password To Change Security Options dialog box appears. Enter the Change Security Options password to confirm.

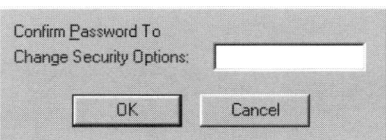

8. Click **OK**. The Save As dialog box appears.

9. Click **Save** to change the changes in security.

# Changing Passwords Using Batch Processing

Before distributing a collection of PDF files, check the current password for these documents. Is it suitable for the intended audience? If the answer to that question is "no," change that password to one better suited for the intended audience.

Changing the passwords to a group of PDF documents is most efficiently accomplished via batch processing, which enables you to change the passwords for a group of PDF documents at one time through one process. Important to note is the fact that the PDF files to be batch processed must be located in the same folder. Additionally, the passwords for each document in this collection must be identical. Unfortunately, if these passwords differ, you must process each document individually.

To change the passwords for a collection of documents via batch processing:

1. Select **File | Batch Process**. The Select Folder To Process dialog box appears.

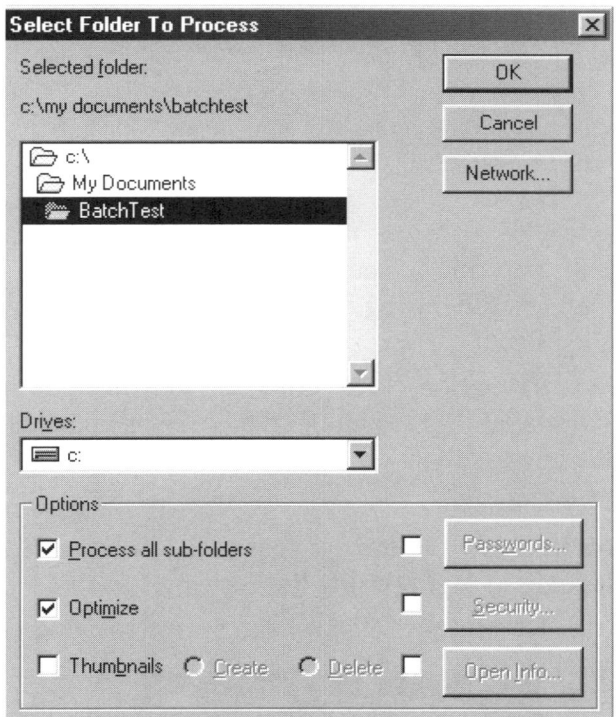

2. In the Selected folder and the Drives fields, choose the folder containing the collection of the PDF files that will have their passwords updated.

3. Under Options, select:

   ■ **Process all sub-folders** to process all folders and files within the chosen folder.

   ■ **Optimize** to significantly reduce the resulting file size.

*Note:* *The issue of optimization can become quite important when dealing with documents on the Internet. Consider this: How long do you really want to wait while a document downloads?*

- **Thumbnails** to either create or delete thumbnails.
- **Passwords** to input the current password of the files:

Press **Passwords** to display the Original Passwords dialog box.

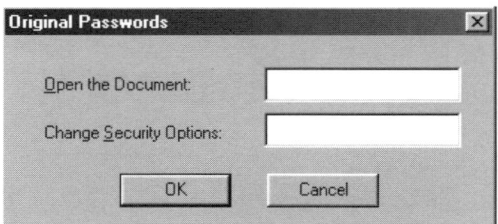

Enter the current PDF files' password in the Open the Document field. Entering the current password merely enables the system to open the file during batch processing.

Enter the password used to revise security options in the Change Security Options field. Entering this information provides you with the ability to change the password of the PDF files in the document collection.

Click **OK**.

- **Security** to add the new passwords to use when accessing the documents and revising the security options.

Press **Security** to display the Security dialog box.

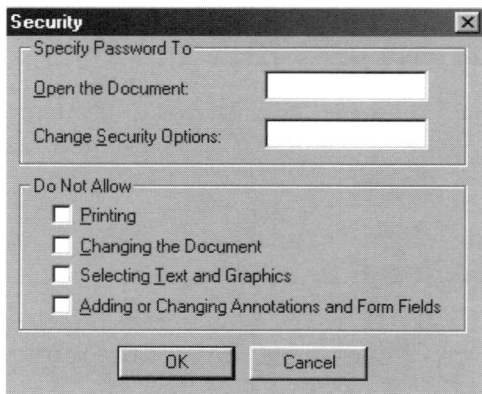

Add the new password to open the document in the Open the Document field.

Add the new password to change security options in the Change Security Options field.

Select the security options in the Do Not Allow section to apply to all documents within this collection.

Click **OK**.

■ **Open Info** to set the initial appearance and functionality of the PDF file when it is first opened. Here, you can set the initial view of the file, the window options, and the user interface options. Click **OK** after setting these options.

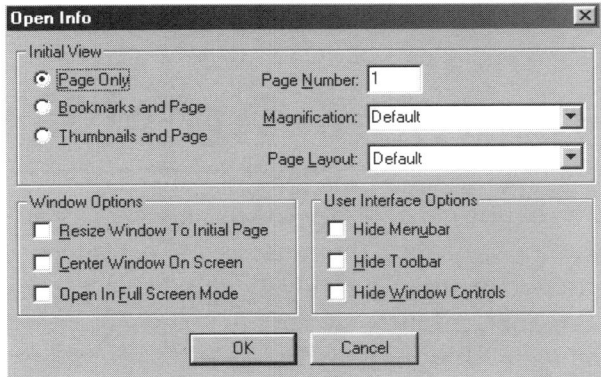

4. In the Select Folder To Process dialog box, choose **OK** to initiate batch processing.

5. During the process, a Batch Processor Progress box will display the results of the batch process. If any error occurred, the explanation will appear in this box.

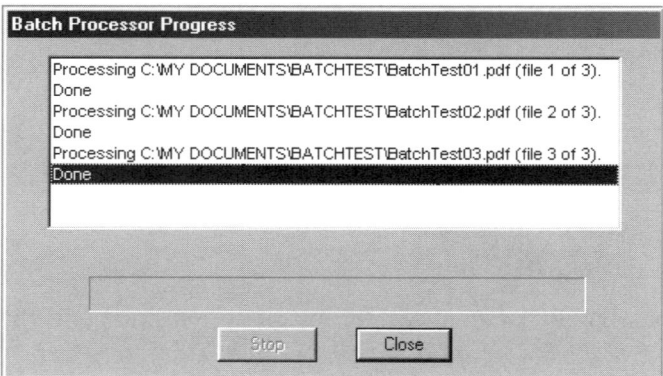

6. When "Done" appears in the Batch Processing Progress box, the process has completed.

# Ensuring Security with Digital Signatures

Digital signatures enable you to securely sign forms electronically. The following sections explain the processes of creating a signature profile, signing a document electronically, validating a signature, and personalizing a signature. Additionally, the process of creating electronic signatures by using Palm Pilot software is covered.

## What are Digital Signatures?

Digital signatures are user-defined profiles, or signatures, that are accessible only by the authorized person. They enable a user to add a uniquely identifiable mark to a document that identifies only the authorized person as the signer. The identification information that is embedded in the signature can add more validity (and, therefore, security) to a digital signature than is available in a handwritten signature.

The digital signatures in Adobe Acrobat include version stamping. In other words, when a PDF document is electronically signed, the signature is linked to one particular version of the document. If another user alters the document after it was electronically signed, a dialog box containing a warning appears. Version stamping ensures that no unauthorized changes will be added to the document during the approval process.

# Logging in to an Existing Signature Profile

If you will be doing a significant amount of work using one specific signature, you can save time by logging in to a particular signature. By doing so, the system will automatically default to that signature when you digitally sign a document.

To log in to an existing signature profile:

1. On the menu bar, select **Tools | Self-Sign Signatures | Log In**. The Acrobat Self-Sign Signatures — Log In dialog box appears.

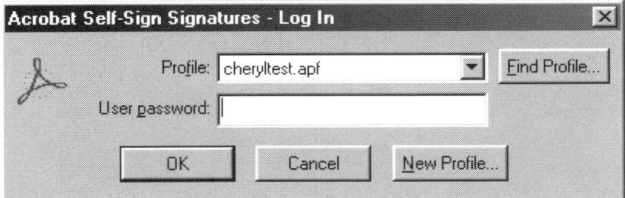

2. In the Profile field, click the drop-down arrow to choose a signature profile to log into.

3. Enter the password in the User password field.

4. Click **OK**.

# Adding Your Signature to a Signature Field

Frequently, signature fields are found on PDF forms. To add your signature to a signature field:

1. Navigate over the signature field. The cursor automatically displays as the digital signature tool cursor:

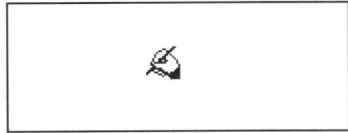

2. Click on the Signature field.

If you have not saved Acrobat Self-Sign Signatures as the default, the Acrobat Digital Signature Plug-in dialog box appears.

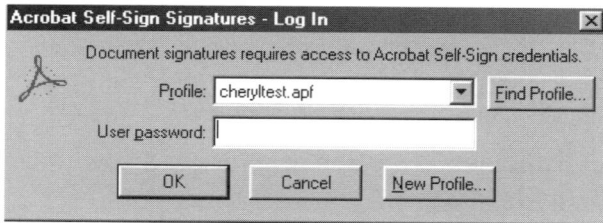

*Note:* Select **Save as default** *to eliminate the repeated appearance of this dialog box.*

Click **OK**.

3. If you have not yet logged into the system, the Acrobat Self-Sign Signatures — Log In dialog box appears.

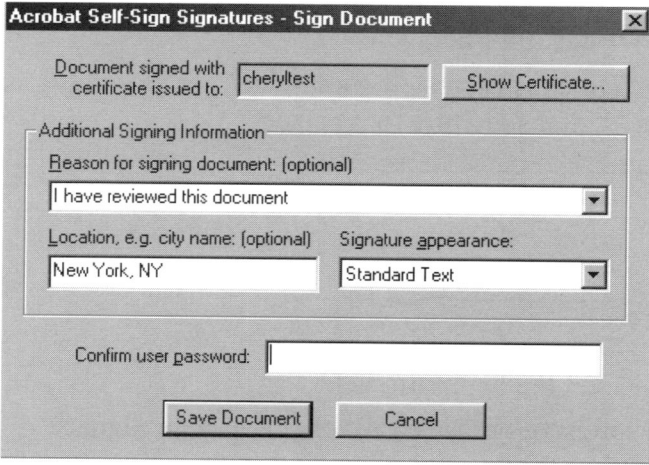

4. Enter your password in the User password field.

5. Click **OK**. Another dialog box, Acrobat Self-Sign Signatures — Sign Document, appears on the screen.

6. Type your password into the Confirm user password field. The other fields are optional.

7. Click **Save Document**.

8. The Save As dialog box appears on the screen. Choose the directory in which you want to save the signed document.

9. Click **Save**.

# Adding Your Signature to a Document without a Signature Field

When a PDF document does not contain a dedicated signature field, Adobe Acrobat provides you with the tools to add a signature to it. To add a signature to a document without a signature field:

1. On the toolbar, select the **Digital Signature** tool.

   The cursor changes to a cross hair.  -¦-

2. Position the cross hair cursor on the document and drag the cursor to create a signature box.

3. Release the mouse button. If you aren't logged into the system, the Acrobat Self-Sign Signatures — Log In dialog box appears.

**Note:** *If you haven't selected Acrobat Self-Sign Signatures as a default, the Acrobat Digital Signature Plug-in dialog box first appears.*

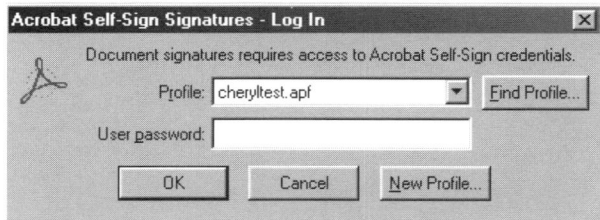

4. In the Profile field, click on the drop-down list to select a signature profile.

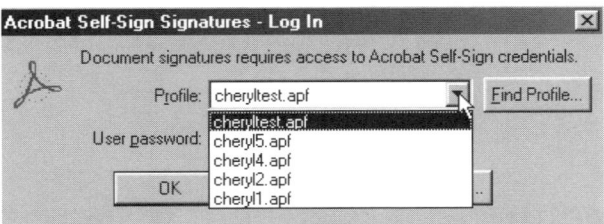

5. Enter the signature profile's password into the User password field.

6. Click **OK**. The Acrobat Self-Sign Signatures — Sign Document dialog box appears.

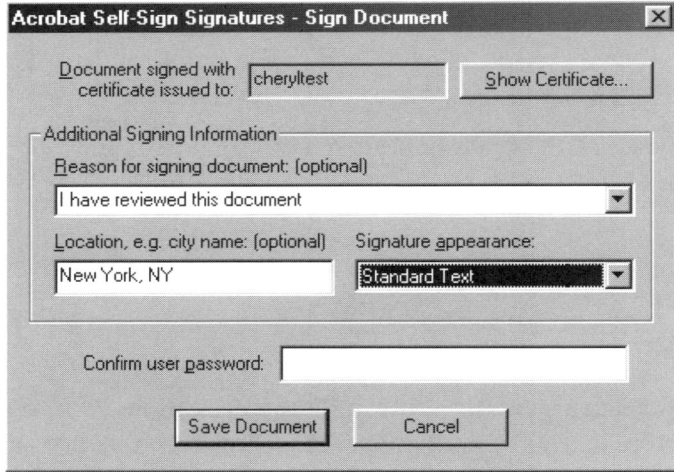

7. Click **Show Certificate** to display the signature certificate information in the Certificate Attributes for *Current User* dialog box.

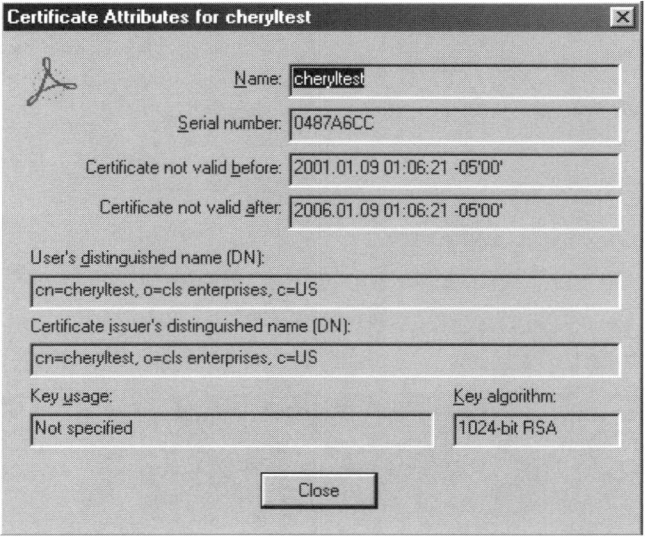

Click **Close** to close this dialog box.

8. Enter information into the Additional Signing Information section. The optional information entered into the Reason for signing document and/or Location fields will appear on the signature.

9. Add the password and click **Save Document** to save this new signature on the document.

> Digitally signed by Cheryl Stinerock
> cn=Cheryl Stinerock, ou=MIS, o=CLS Enterprises, c=US
> Date: 2001.01.14 15:46:29 -05'00'
> Reason: I have reviewed this document
> New York, NY

## Re-Signing/Revalidating a Document

If the document was changed during the approval process, the signature reverts to its pre-validated appearance.

> Digitally signed by Cheryl Stinerock
> cn=Cheryl Stinerock, ou=MIS, o=CLS Enterprises, c=US
> Date: 2001.01.14 15:46:29 -05'00'
> Reason: I have reviewed this document
> New York, NY

After you've reviewed the altered document, you'll need to re-sign/ revalidate the document.

***Note:*** *Re-signing a document automatically revalidates it if the certificate is present.*

To resign the document:

1. Click on the signature.

2. Right-click to display the context menu.

3. Select **Sign Signature Field**. The Acrobat Digital Signature dialog box appears.

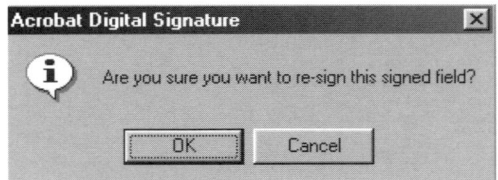

4. Choose **OK**. The Acrobat Self-Sign Signatures — Sign Document dialog box appears.

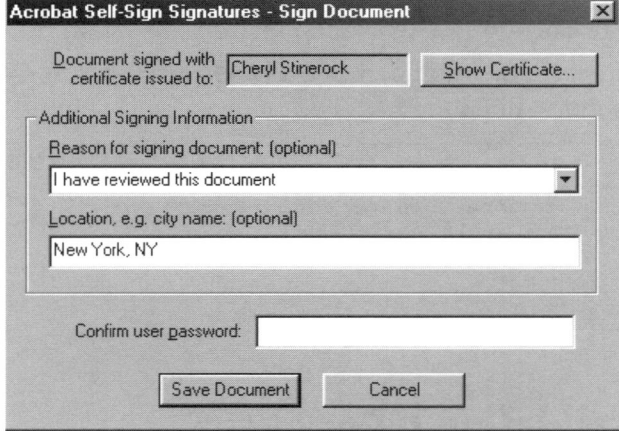

5. Fill in the Additional Signing Information (reason for signing document, location).

6. Enter the password for your signature in the Confirm user password field.

7. Click **Save Document**. The signature now appears as properly signed/validated.

# Creating a Signature Profile

Before a digital signature can be used, a signature profile must be defined. The signature profile defines the appearance of the digital signature. The initial signature definition automatically sets up a portion of the profile. However, to add a specific look to the signature, refinements must be added to the profile at a later date.

To create a signature profile:

1. On the menu bar, click on **Tools | Self-Sign Signatures | Log In** or **Tools | Self-Sign Signatures | Log In as Different User**. The Acrobat Self-Sign Signatures — Log In dialog box appears.

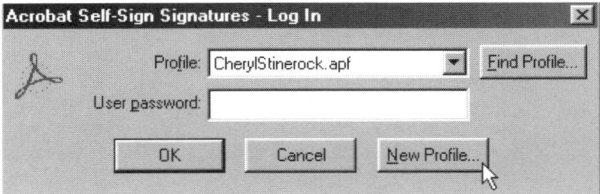

2. Click **New Profile**. The Acrobat Self-Sign Signatures — Create New User dialog box appears.

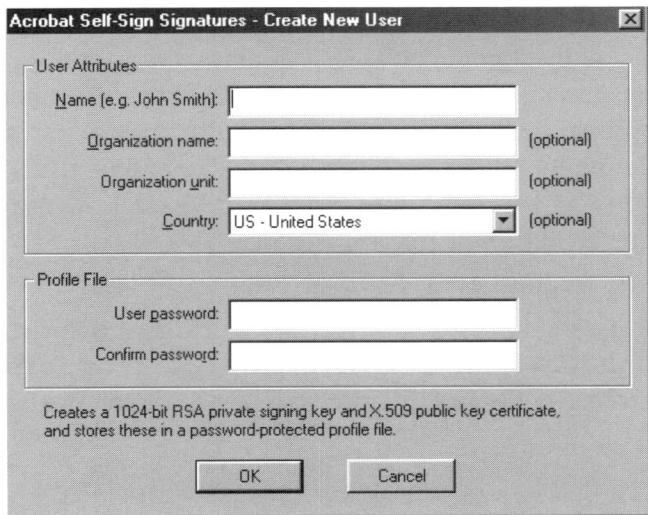

3. In the User Attributes section, add the Name, Organization name, Organization unit, and Country.

4. In the Profile File section, enter a password to be used each time this profile is accessed in the User password field. Verify that password by entering it into the Confirm password field.

*Note: This password must be at least six characters.*

5. Click **OK**. The New Acrobat Self-Sign Profile File dialog box appears.

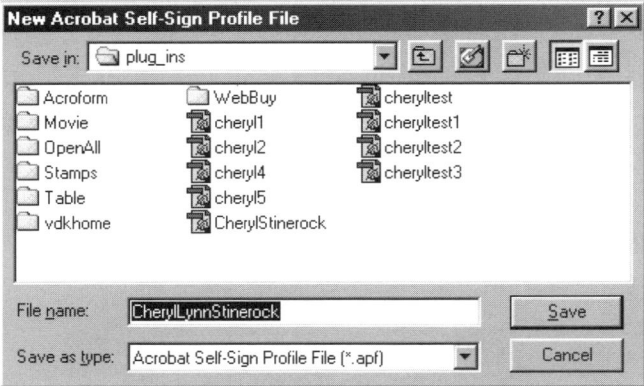

6. Choose the filename and the directory in which to save the profile file.

7. Click **Save**.

# Creating Additional Signature Profiles

In this rapidly changing business climate, many employees assume different roles in varying corporate situations. When documents move through the approval process, approvers frequently may be the same employee functioning in a different business role. To enable users to operate with a number of signature profiles, Adobe Acrobat allows users to create more than one signature profile.

To create an additional signature profile:

1. On the menu bar, select **Tools | Self-Sign Signatures | Log In** or **Tools | Self-Sign Signatures | Log In as Different User**. The Acrobat Self-Sign Signatures — Log In dialog box appears.

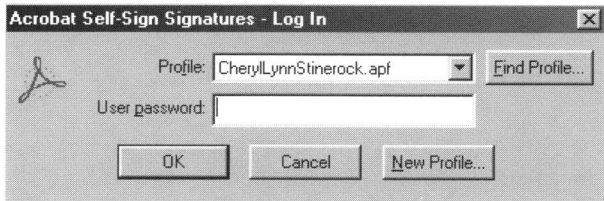

2. Click **New Profile**. The Acrobat Self-Sign Signatures — Create New User dialog box appears.

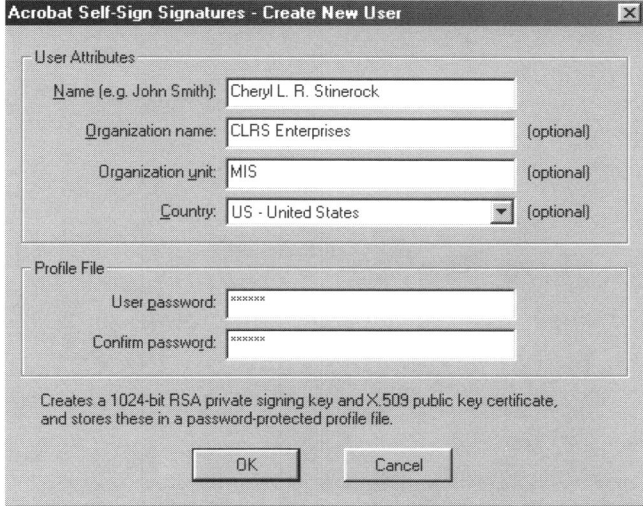

3. In the User Attributes area, add the information that will appear as part of the signature.

4. In the Profile File area, identify a password to ensure that the signature can only be used by the owner of the profile, and verify the password.

*Note: This password must be at least six characters.*

5. Click **OK** to save the profile. The New Acrobat Self-Sign Profile File dialog box appears.

6. Select the filename and the directory in which to save this signature profile.

7. Click **Save** to save the profile.

# Changing a Signature Profile

To add changes to a current signature profile:

1. Click **Tools | Self-Sign Signatures | User Settings** on the menu bar. The Acrobat Self-Sign Signatures — User Settings for *Current User* dialog box appears.

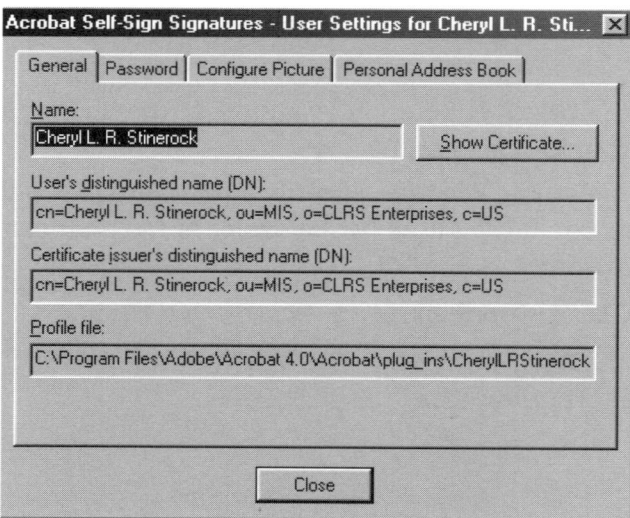

2. Click the **General** tab to view the current details regarding the signature profile.

3. Click the **Password** tab to define when the password is required to use the digital signature or to change the current password.

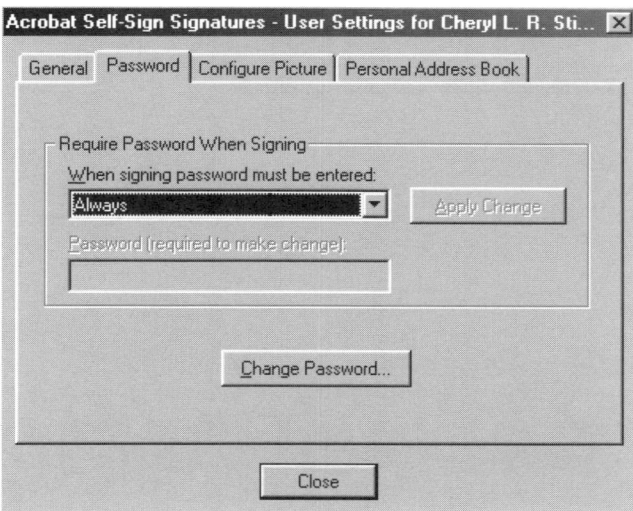

4. Click the **Configure Picture** tab to add a picture to the signature definition.

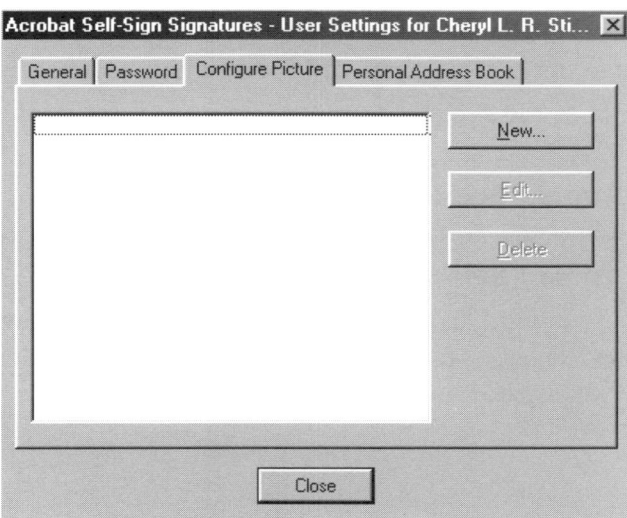

5. Click the **Personal Address Book** tab to export/import signature certificate information. This feature enables you to check the validity of the signature on a newly received PDF document.

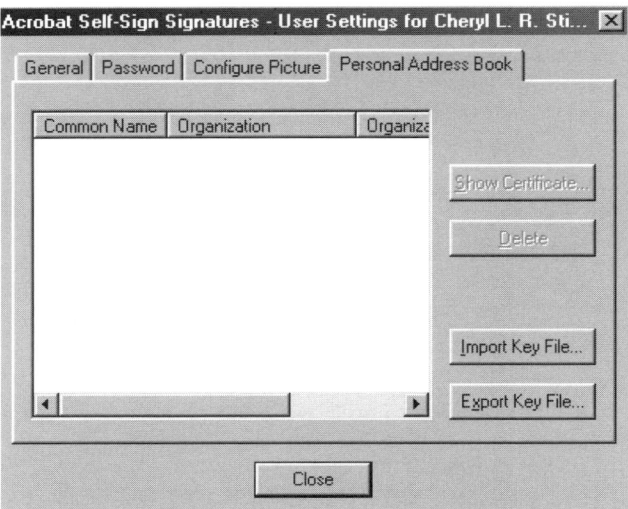

6. After all changes are added to the Acrobat Self-Sign Signatures — User Settings for *Current User* dialog box, click **Close**.

# Changing a Signature's Password

To change the current password for a signature profile:

1. Log in to the signature profile update.

   - If you are not currently logged into a signature profile, select **Tools | Self-Sign Signatures | Log In** on the menu bar.

   - If you are currently logged into another signature profile, select **Tools | Self-Sign Signatures | Log In as Different User**.

2. On the menu bar, select **Tools | Self-Sign Signatures | User Settings**. The Acrobat Self-Sign Signatures — User Settings for *Current User* dialog box appears.

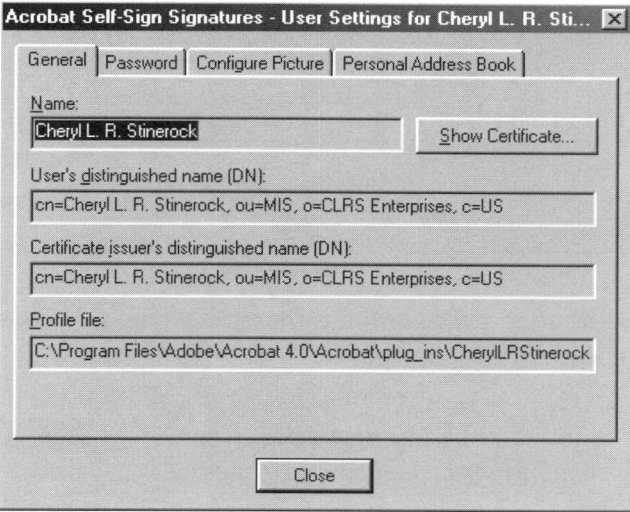

3. Navigate to the Password tab.

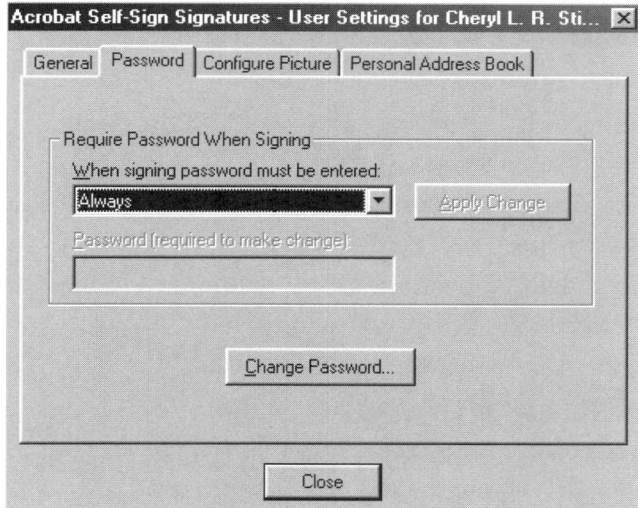

4. Click **Change Password**. The Acrobat Self-Sign Signatures —
   Change Profile File Password dialog box appears.

**Acrobat Self-Sign Signatures - Change Profile File Password**

Old password:

New password:

Confirm password:

OK        Cancel

5. Input the old password and the new password, and confirm the new password.

6. Click **OK** to accept the new password. If the password was changed, the system will respond with the following message:

7. Click **OK**.

8. Click **Close**.

# Deleting a Signature Field

To delete a signature field:

1. Highlight the actual signature field on the document or the signature field on the Signature palette.

2. Right-click to display the context menu.

3. Select **Delete Signature Field**. The signature field is deleted from the document and the Signature palette.

# Signature Validation Statuses

During the process of adding and validating signatures, you will notice that the icons appearing over the signature found on the document and on the Signature palette change depending on the current status of the signature.

After a signature field is added to a document, the unsigned field appears:

On the Signature palette, a signature tool icon appears in front of the signature field reference:

If a signature field is signed but not validated, the signature on the document appears:

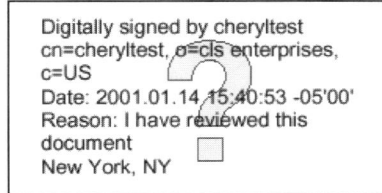

On the Signature palette, a question mark appears in front of the signature field reference:

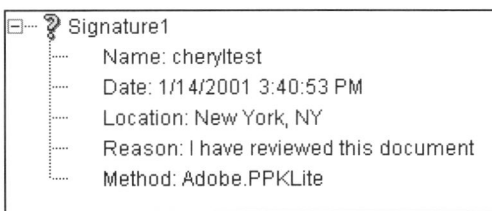

If a signature field is signed and partially validated, the signature on the document appears:

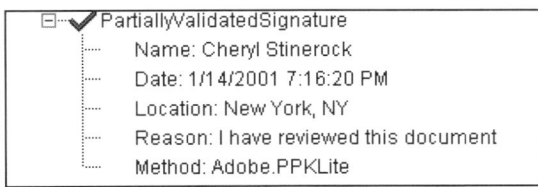

On the Signature palette, a check mark appears in front of the signature field reference.

If a signature field is signed and fully validated, the signature on the document appears:

> Digitally signed by Cheryl Stinerock
> cn=Cheryl Stinerock, ou=MIS, o=CLS Enterprises,
> c=US
> Date: 2001.01.14 19:26:03 -05'00'
> Reason: I have reviewed this document
> New York, NY

On the Signature palette, a check mark over a shield appears in front of the signature field reference:

> ⊟ 🛡 FullyValidatedSignature
>     Name: Cheryl Stinerock
>     Date: 1/14/2001 7:26:03 PM
>     Location: New York, NY
>     Reason: I have reviewed this document
>     Method: Adobe.PPKLite

**Note:** *A partially validated signature indicates that the document has not been changed since it was signed. A fully validated signature indicates that the document has not been changed since it was signed and a copy of the signer's certificate resides on the computer performing the validation.*

If a signature field is signed but invalid (e.g., if the document was altered after it was signed, then saved), the signature on the document appears:

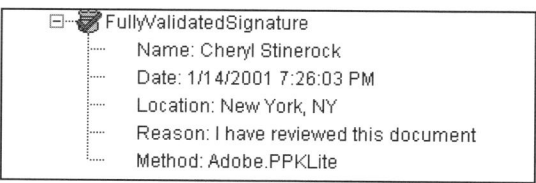

On the Signature palette, an "X" appears in front of the signature field reference:

> ⊟ ✗ Signature7
>     Name: Cheryl Stinerock
>     Date: 1/14/2001 7:25:30 PM
>     Location: New York, NY
>     Reason: I have reviewed this document
>     Method: Adobe.PPKLite
>     Changes: 1 field(s) filled-in

# Validating a Signature

To determine if a document was electronically signed by the correct person, you must validate the signature. During the validation process, there are two types of validation: partial validation and full validation. If the document was not altered after signing, then the system will partially validate the signature. If the signature also matches the signer's certificate, then the system will fully validate the signature.

To validate a signature:

1. Import the signer's certificate if it does not exist on your computer.

2. Navigate over the signature. The cursor becomes the signature cursor.

3. Right-click to display the context menu.

4. Click **Validate Signature**.

5. The validation is now complete. On the Signatures palette, this signature now displays a green check mark if the validation was partial ✔ or a green check mark and a shield if the validation was complete  . The actual signature now appears with the Adobe Acrobat icon over it.

```
Digitally signed by Cheryl Stinerock
cn=Cheryl Stinerock, ou=MIS, o=CLS Enterprises, c=US
Date: 2001.01.14 19:16:20 -05'00'
Reason: I have reviewed this document
New York, NY
```

# Exporting/Importing Signature Certificate Information

Adobe Acrobat provides you with the ability to verify the authenticity of a signature. To do this, you must have the signer's certificate available in your Personal Address Book (found in **Tools | Self-Sign Signatures | User Settings**). Obtaining the certificates of various users involves exporting and importing certificate files.

To export the signature certificate information to another computer:

1. On the menu bar, select **Tools | Self-Sign Signatures | User Settings**. The Acrobat Self-Sign Signatures — User Settings for *Current User* dialog box appears.

2. Select the **Personal Address Book** tab.

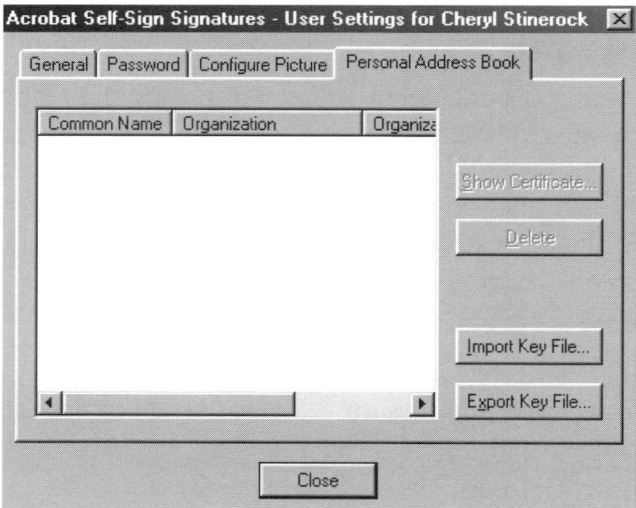

3. Click **Export Key File**. The Export Certificates As… dialog box appears.

4. Choose the directory and the filename.

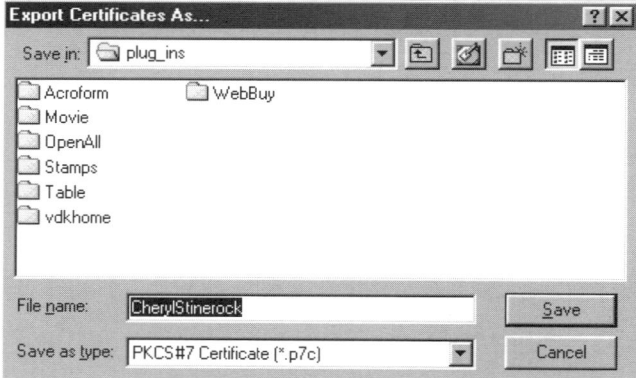

***Note:*** *Files of this type have an extension of .p7c.*

5. Click **Save**. The Export Validation String dialog box appears. Remember to keep a record of this string.

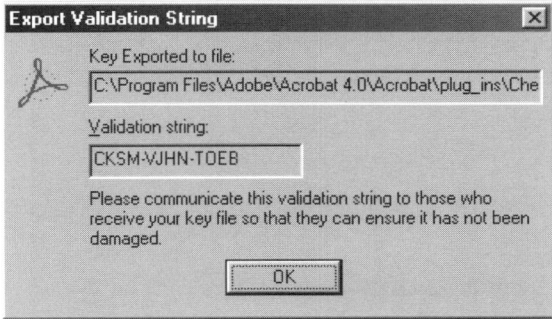

6. Click **OK** to close this dialog box.

7. Click **Close**.

To import the signature certificate information into another computer:

1. On the menu bar, select **Tools | Self-Sign Signatures | User Settings**. The Acrobat Self-Sign Signatures — User Settings for *Current User* dialog box appears.

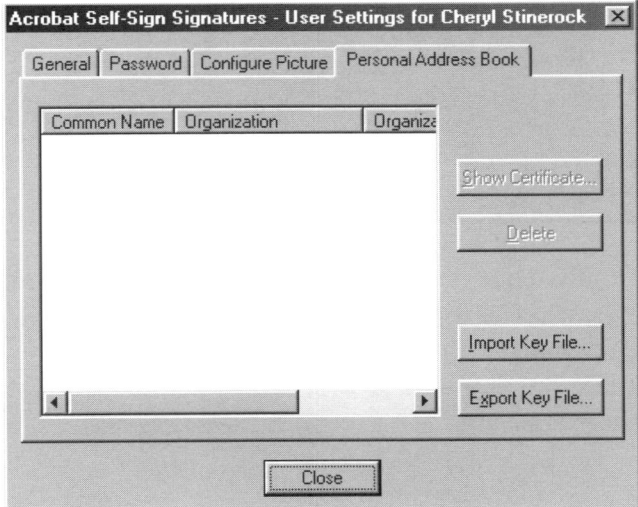

2. Select the **Personal Address Book** tab.

3. Click **Import Key File**. The Import Certificates dialog box appears.

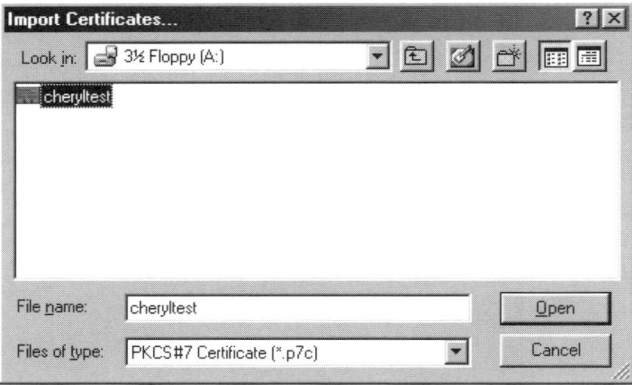

4. Select the file (with an extension of .p7c) to import.

5. Click **Open**. The Import Validation String dialog box appears.

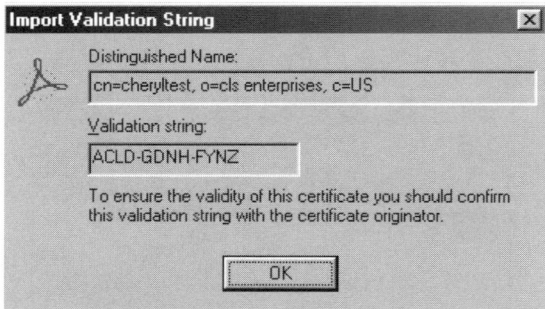

6. Click **OK**. The Personal Address Book tab now displays the imported certificate. The users on this computer can now validate the authenticity of that signature.

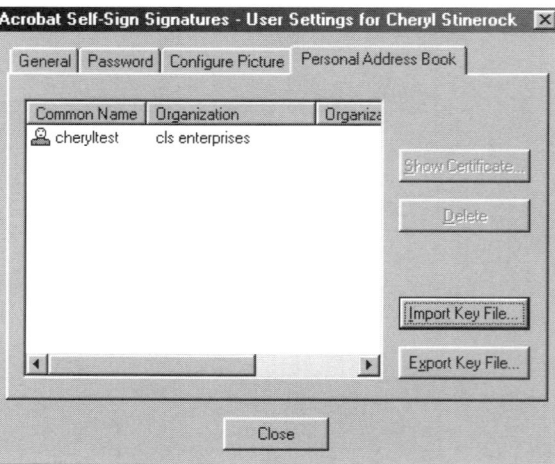

# Personalizing Your Signature Profile

You can either use the text signature, which is quickly and easily created, or add graphics to your signature profile. Typically, when a signature is initially created, a default signature version is added to your profile. Each time you add a new distinctive element to your signature (such as a picture of your signature), you create a new version of your signature. When a document is signed, you are given the choice to select the signature version.

## Adding Pictures to Your Signature Profile

To add a picture to your signature profile:

1. First, create a picture, then convert it to a PDF file.

2. Next, log in to your signature profile. (On the menu bar, select **Tools | Self-Sign Signatures | Log In**.)

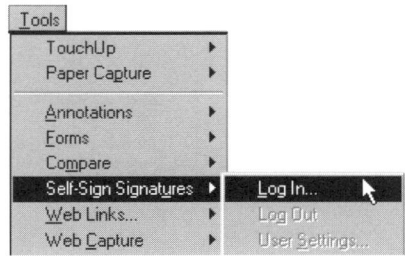

3. On the menu bar, select **Tools | Self-Sign Signatures | User Settings**. The Acrobat Self-Sign Signatures — User Settings for *Current User* appears.

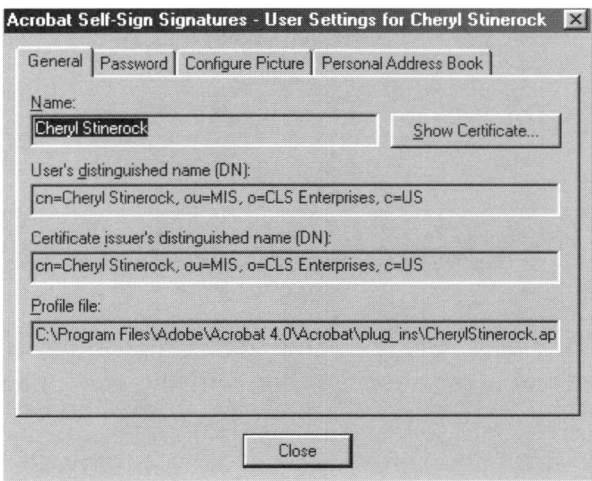

4. Select the **Configure Picture** tab.

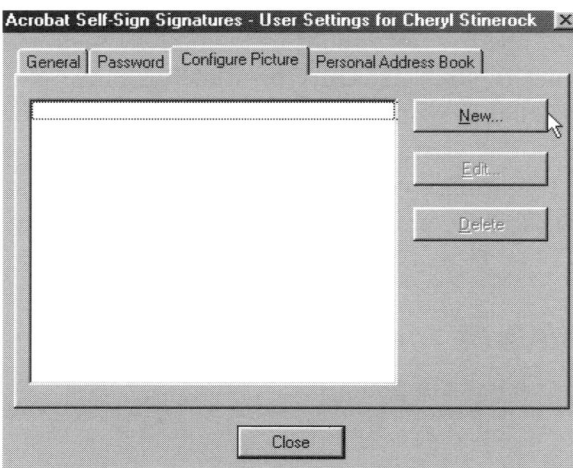

5. Select **New**. The Acrobat Self-Sign Signatures — Signature Picture Configuration dialog box appears.

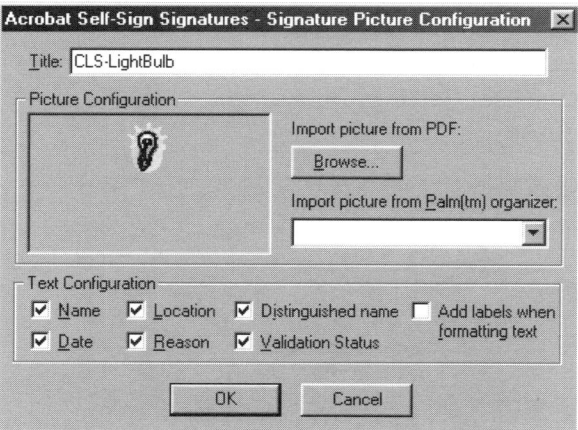

6. In the Title field, add the name of this version of the signature. It's a good idea to add a short but descriptive name for easy retrieval in the future.

7. In the Picture Configuration section, click **Browse** to import a picture from PDF. The Select Picture dialog box appears.

8. Click **Browse** to search for the PDF file containing the desired picture. The Choose a New Appearance File dialog box appears.

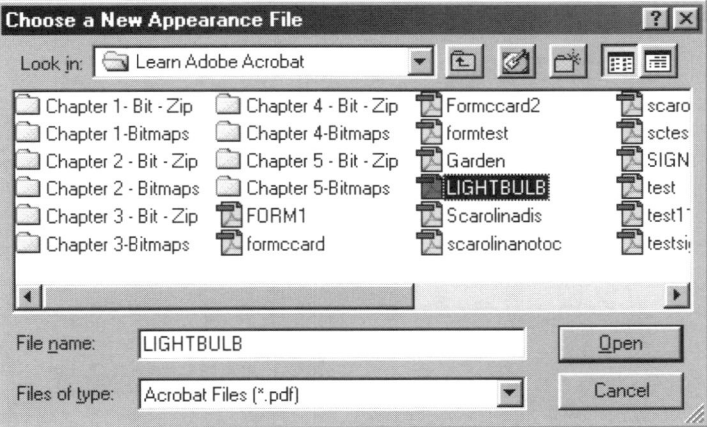

9. Select the PDF file and click **Open**.

10. In the Select Picture dialog box, click **OK**.

11. In the Text Configuration section of the Acrobat Self-Sign Signatures — Signature Picture Configuration dialog box, select options to include as part of the signature.

12. When all selections are made, choose **OK**.

13. Select **Close** to exit the Acrobat Self-Sign Signatures — User Settings for *Current User* dialog box.

To sign a document using the new signature version:

1.  Click on the **Signature** tool found on the toolbar.
2.  Using the Signature tool, create a signature field. The Acrobat Digital Signature Plug-in dialog box appears.

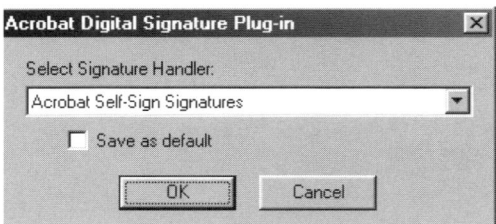

3.  Select **OK**. The Acrobat Self-Sign Signatures — Sign Document dialog box appears.

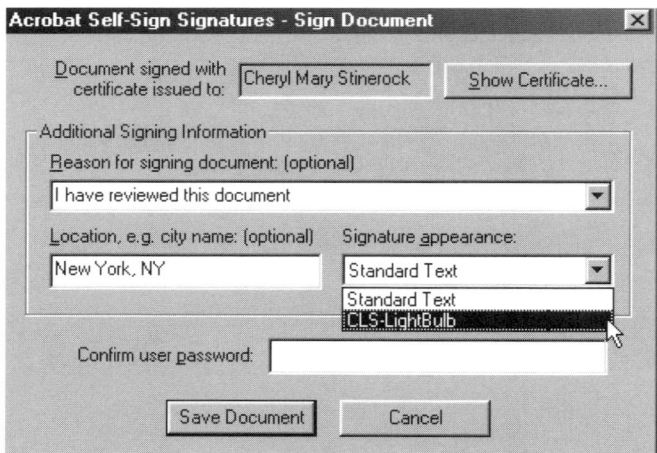

4.  In the Additional Signing Information section, choose the reason for signing document and the location. Click on the Signature appearance drop-down list to choose the version of the signature. Select the new signature version.
5.  Enter the password in the Confirm user password field.
6.  Click **Save Document**. The Save As dialog box appears.
7.  Click **Save**. The document is now saved and signed.

## Adding Your Signature to a Signature Profile Using MS Word and MS Paint

By adding a PDF file containing a picture of your written signature to your signature profile, you can create a unique signature.

### Creating Your Signature Using MS Paint

To add your written signature to your signature profile, create a picture of your signature using MS Paint:

1.  Launch MS Paint (or another application that provides you with similar functionality).
2.  In the toolbox, select the **Pencil** tool .
3.  Using the Pencil tool, write your signature.
4.  When completed, save this signature by selecting **File** | **Save As** on the menu bar.

### Add the Picture to an MS Word Document

1.  Launch MS Word.
2.  On the menu bar, select **File** | **New** to open a new document.
3.  On the menu bar, select **Insert** | **Picture** | **From File**. The Insert Picture dialog box appears.

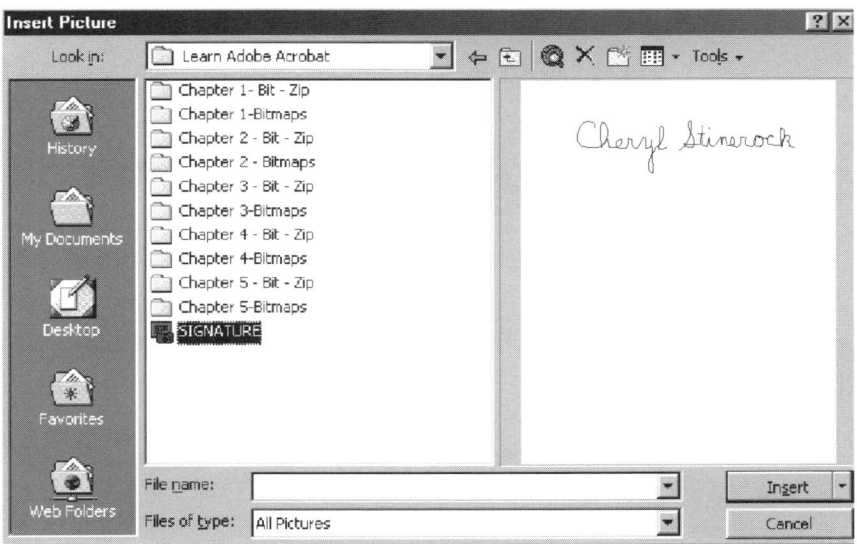

4. Select the file containing your signature and add it to the document.

5. Click **Insert**.

Next, convert the MS Word document to PDF format.

1. Click the **Create Adobe PDF** icon 🔁 to convert this document to PDF format.

   The Acrobat PDFMaker dialog box appears.

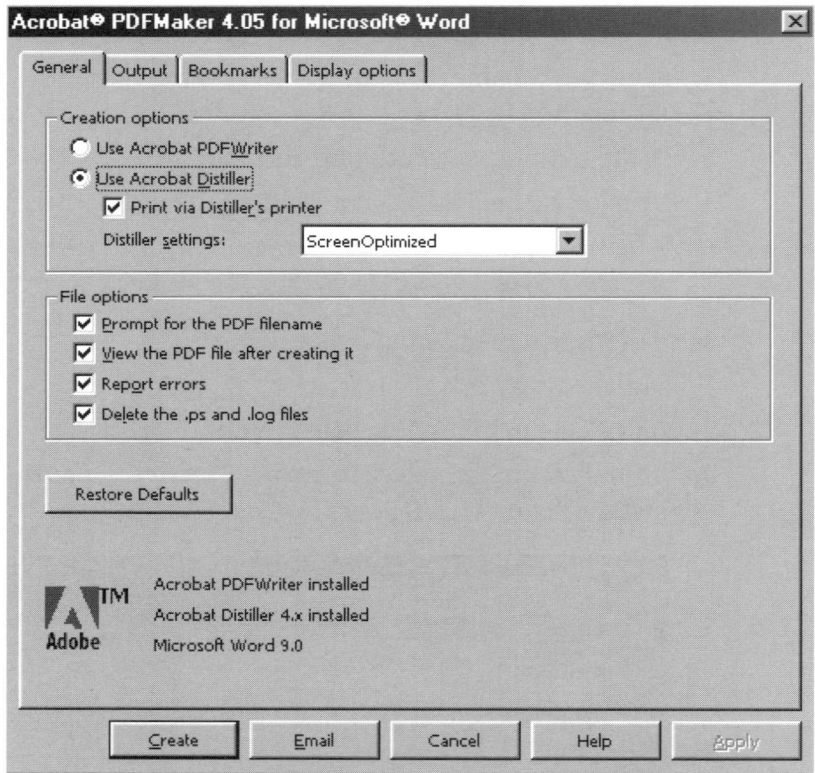

2. In the Creation options section, choose **Use Acrobat Distiller**.

3. Select all other necessary conversion settings, and click **Create**. The Acrobat PDFMaker for Microsoft Word dialog box appears, detailing the progress of the conversion process.

4. After the file is converted to a PDF file, the Save PDF file as dialog box appears.

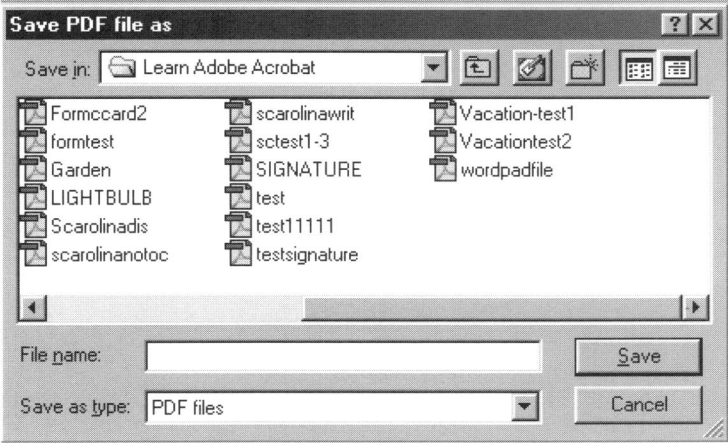

5. Add the filename, then select **Save**.

Finally, add the PDF file to your signature profile.

1. Return to Adobe Acrobat.

2. On the menu bar, select **Tools | Self-Sign Signatures | User Settings**. The Acrobat Self-Sign Signatures — User Settings for *Current User* dialog box appears.

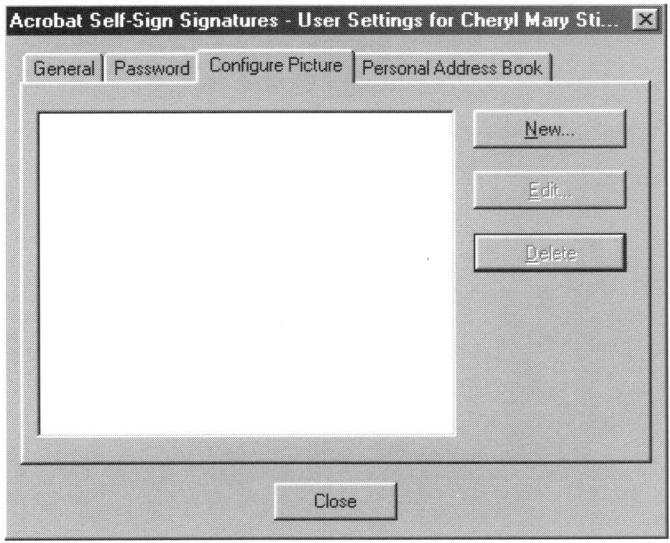

3. Select the **Configure Picture** tab.

4. Press **New**. The Acrobat Self-Sign Signatures — Signature Picture Configuration dialog box appears.

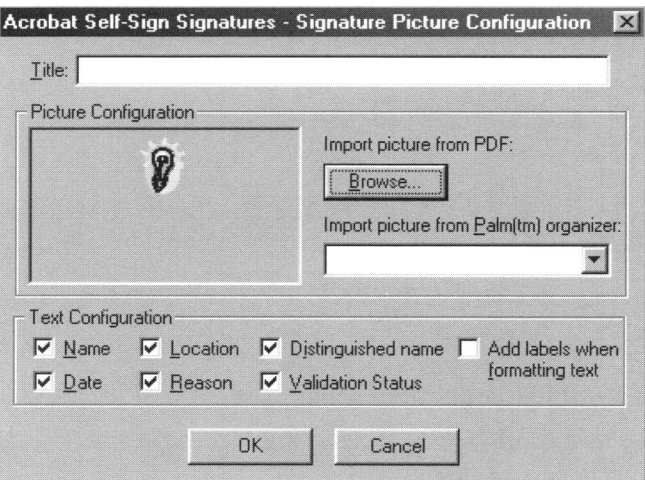

5. Add a title and select desired options in the Text Configuration area.

6. Click **Browse** to import a PDF file.

***Note:*** *Adobe Acrobat also provides you with the option of importing a picture from your Palm Organizer.*

The Select Picture dialog box appears.

7. Select **Browse** and then select the PDF file you created. Click **OK**. The new signature now appears listed in the Acrobat Self-Sign Signatures — User Settings for *Current User* dialog box.

8. Click **Close**.

Now you can sign a document with your written signature. To sign a document using the newest version of your signature:

1. Click the Signature field. The Acrobat Self-Sign Signatures — Sign Document dialog box appears.

2. Click the drop-down box found in the Signature appearance field.

3. Select the signature version to use.

4. Add your password to the Confirm user password field.

5. Click **Save Document**.

## Adding Your Signature to a Signature Profile Using Palm Pilot Software

A quick and easy way to add a signature or a graphic image created by freehand to a signature's design is to use your Palm Pilot (or any PDA that uses the Palm OS, version 2.0 or higher). However, before the image can be created, the Selfsign.prc file (distributed with the Adobe Acrobat software) must be installed on your hand-held organizer.

### Installing Selfsign.prc on Your Palm Pilot

1. Launch the Palm Pilot software installed on your computer.

2. Click **Install** to initiate the installation process. The Install Tool dialog box appears.

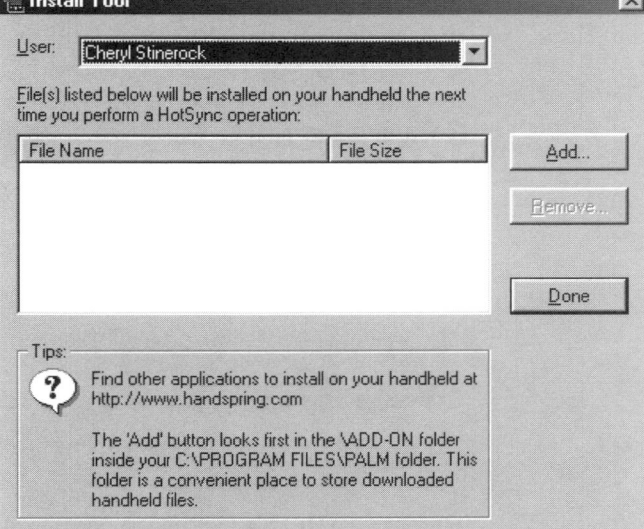

3. Click **Add**. An Open dialog box immediately appears.

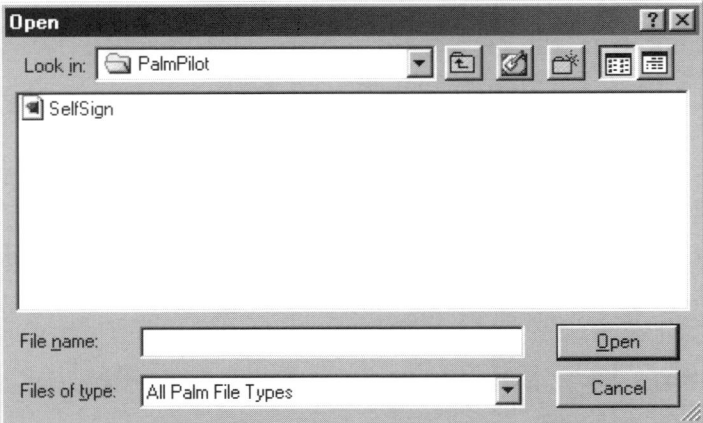

4. Navigate to Program Files\Adobe\Acrobat 4.0\Acrobat\Palm-Pilot\selfsign.prc.

5. Click **Open**. The Install Tool dialog box now displays the program to add to the Palm Pilot during the next HotSync operation.

6. Click **Done**. Immediately, the Install Tool dialog box appears, informing you that the next HotSync operation will install this file onto your PalmPilot.

7. Click **OK**.

8. Perform a HotSync operation.

9. When the PalmPilot displays "HotSync operation complete," the Selfsign.prc file has been added to your PalmPilot.

### Creating the Image Using Your Palm Pilot

1. Select the SelfSign application on your Palm Pilot. A screen divided by a horizontal line appears.

2. Using the stylus, write your first name in the top box and your last name in the bottom box.

3. Press **Done** when finished.

### Transferring an Image from Your Palm Pilot to Your Signature Definition

To transfer the new signature from the PalmPilot to your computer, perform a HotSync operation.

1. Click **OK** when the HotSync dialog box appears.

2. Launch Adobe Acrobat.

3. Log in to a signature.

4. On the menu bar, select **Tools | Self-Sign Signatures | User Settings**. The Acrobat Self-Sign Signatures — User Settings for *Current User* dialog box appears.

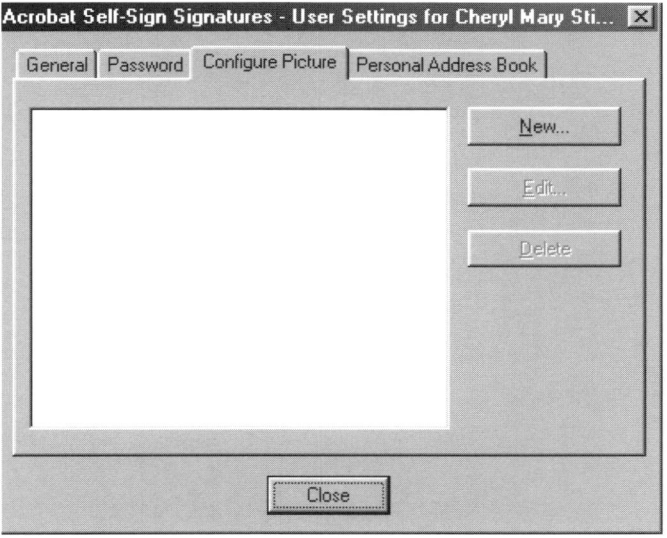

5. Select the **Configure Picture** tab.

6. Click **New**. The Acrobat Self-Sign Signatures — Signature Picture Configuration dialog box appears.

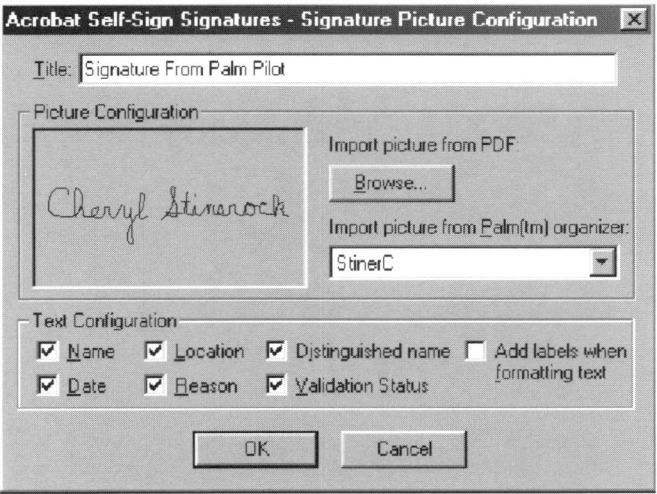

7. Add a name for this signature version into the Title field. Notice that the Import picture from Palm organizer field now points to the self-sign file you just imported.

8. Click **OK** to accept this definition.

9. Click **Close** on the Acrobat Self-Sign Signatures — User Settings for *Current User* dialog box.

## Chapter 6

# Acrobat and the Internet

In today's marketplace, a web site is almost a requirement for doing business. Large corporations and small upstarts alike have ventured onto the Internet. Among the multitude of URLs are those well-designed and truly functional sites that have incorporated PDF files into their pages.

More and more designers of web pages have discovered the benefits of using PDF files, including:

- **Ease of Creation**. By scanning existing documents into Adobe Acrobat, then enhancing them with Acrobat's tools, a once-tedious task now can be completed in a matter of minutes.

- **Accurate printing**. Frequently, printed web pages appear quite unattractive. PDF files print identically from the web site as they do from an application residing on your desktop.

- **HTML Compatibility**. By adding a few simple commands to your HTML file, it is quite simple to add PDF files to your site.

The following pages aim to familiarize you with preparing PDF documents for the web and using PDF files that reside on the web.

## Viewing PDF Files on the Web

When Adobe Acrobat is installed, the installation process automatically adds the nppdf32.dll file to Netscape's plug-ins. Immediately, you have the capability to view PDF files through your browser. However, if your browser (Netscape, or a compatible browser) was added after the Adobe

Acrobat installation, you must install this file yourself.

To install the nppdf32.dll file:

1. Navigate to C:\Program Files\Adobe\Acrobat 4.0\Acrobat\Browser.

2. Copy the file nppdf32.dll.

3. Navigate to C:\Program Files\Netscape\Plugins.

**Note:** *If you are using a browser other than Netscape, navigate to that browser's Plugins directory.*

4. Paste nppdf32.dll into that folder.

# Making PDF Forms "Web-Ready"

Before a PDF document can be added to a web site, you must determine what its purpose on the site will be, then prepare the document for that purpose. For example, do you intend for visitors to your site to view or print the document? Or, do you want to provide visitors with an interactive form that enables you to take merchandise orders, register students for classes, or record the results of a survey?

If the document on your site will only be read or printed, you only need to create or scan the document. However, if you want to provide visitors with the ability to fill out and submit a form, you need to add form fields and additional functionality by using the Form tool.

## Scanning the Form into Acrobat

Scanning the form directly into Adobe Acrobat eliminates the need to create a form from scratch. By adding functional fields to the scanned form, you can rapidly and easily create a ready-to-use form or revise an outdated form.

To scan a form in as a PDF file:

1. Place the form facedown on the scanner glass.

2. Launch Adobe Acrobat.

3. On the menu bar, select **File | Import | Scan**. The Adobe Acrobat Scan dialog box appears.

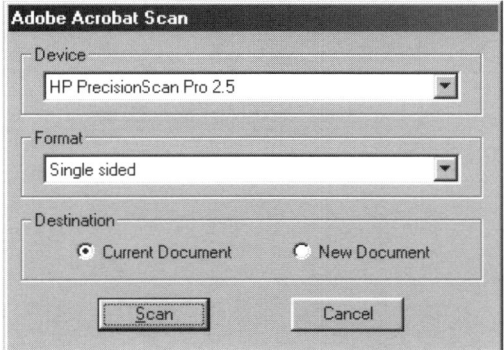

4. In the Device field, click on the drop-down list and choose your current scanner device.

5. In the Format field, select **Single sided** or **Double sided**.

6. In the destination field choose one of the following:

   ■ **Current Document** to add the scanned image to the currently opened document.

   ■ **New Document** to create a new document.

7. Click **Scan** to initiate the scanning process.

8. Depending on the manufacturer and model of your scanner, you will be provided with different scanning setup options.

   Using the HP ScanJet 5370C, the HP PrecisionScan Pro dialog box appears with a preliminary scan of the document.

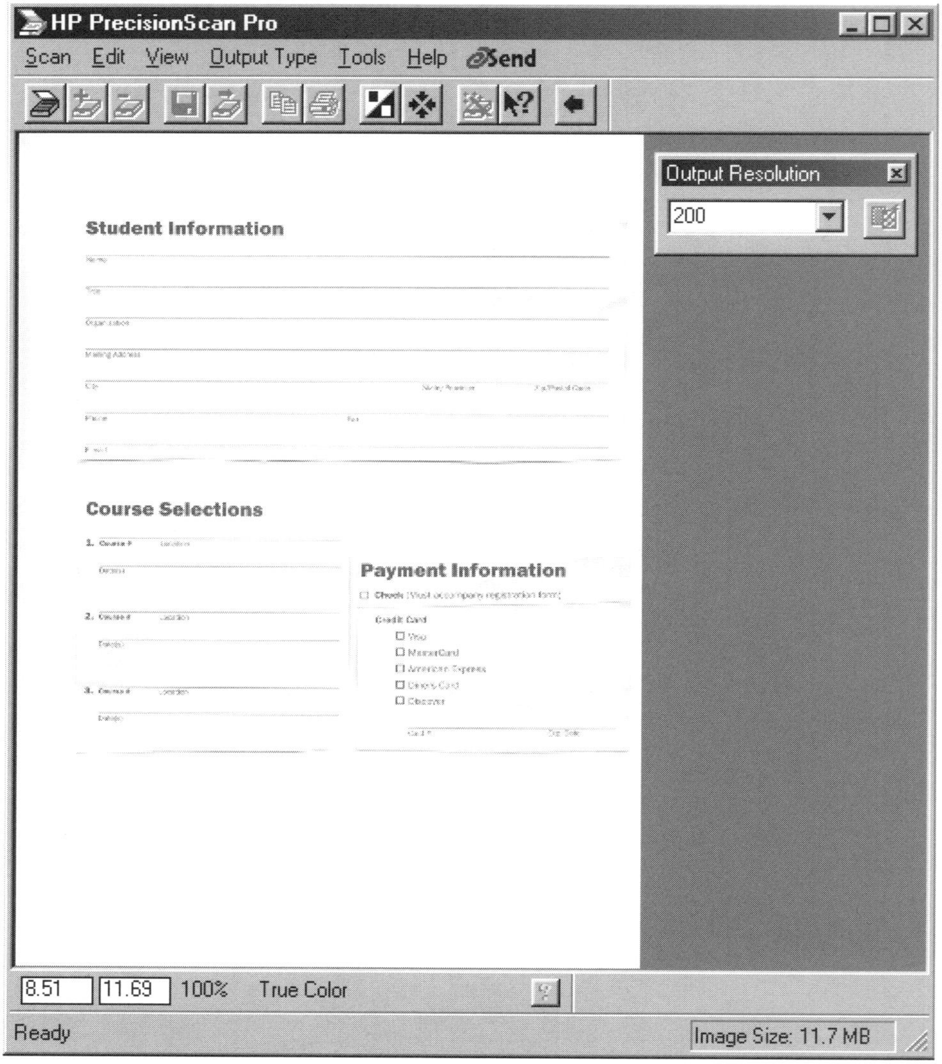

Using the cross hair cursor, select the area of the document you actually want to scan.

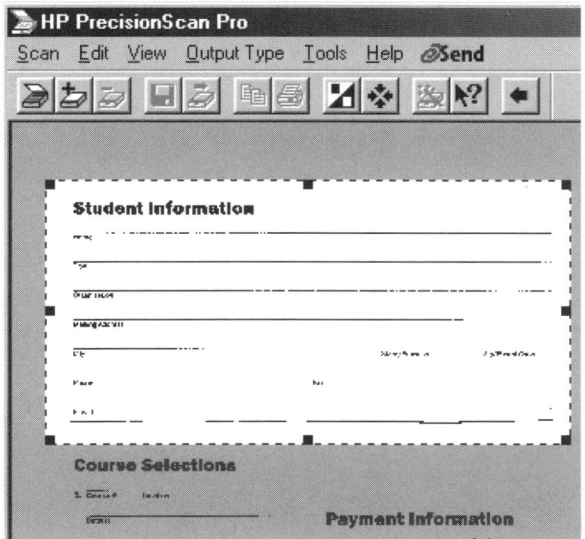

Select **Tools | Output resolution** to choose the actual resolution of the scanned document.

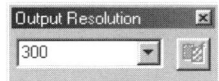

*Note:* *For black and white images and text, use a resolution of 200 to 600 dpi. For color images and text, use a resolution of 200 to 400 dpi. Usually, the resolution that produces the best, most space-efficient scanned documents is 300 dpi.*

To return to Adobe Acrobat to continue scanning, select **Scan | Return to Adobe Acrobat Scan**. The HP PrecisionScan Pro dialog box appears, displaying the progress of the scan.

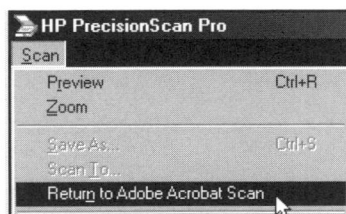

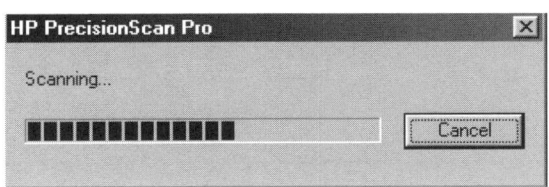

After the current document is completely scanned, the Adobe Acrobat Scan dialog box appears, indicating that the system is ready for a second page.

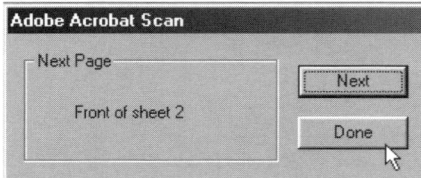

9. If no additional documents will be scanned, press **Done**. A dialog box appears, informing you that Acrobat Scan Plug-in is converting the scanned page to PDF format.

10. At this point, you can save your new PDF file and add the functionality of form fields.

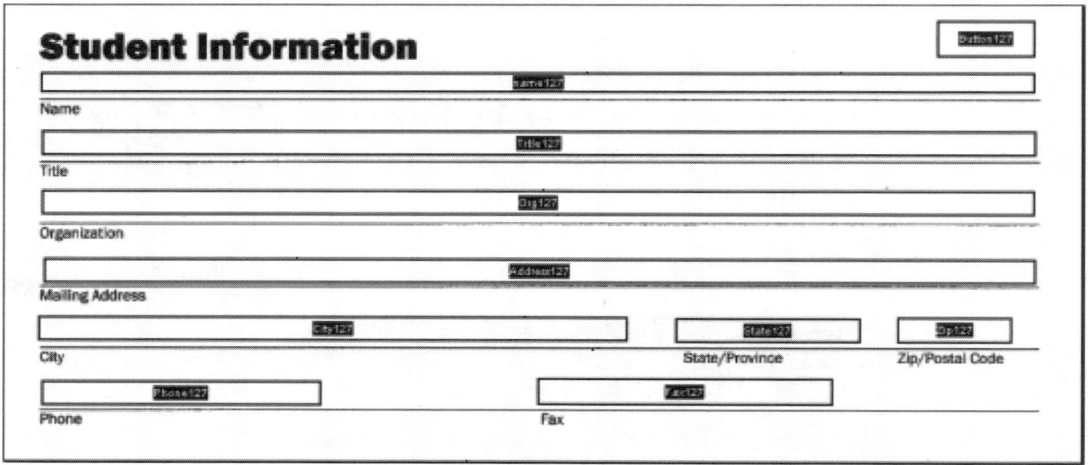

# Adding Interactive Functionality to the Form

After scanning the form into Adobe Acrobat, you can make the form truly interactive by adding input fields and action buttons. Submit, Refresh, and Send are only a few action buttons that can be added to a form by using the Form tool. These three are discussed in the following sections.

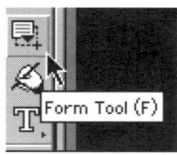

## Adding a Send Button to the Form

A Send button provides users with a quick way to forward the PDF document to one or more e-mail addresses. However, when a form is sent to an e-mail address, Adobe Acrobat uses the MAPI (Messaging Application Programming Interface) to interface with your e-mail application. Therefore, your e-mail application must be set up to use its MAPI server prior to successful usage of Acrobat's e-mail function.

To set up a Send button:

1. Using the Form tool , create a form field.

2. Select **Button** as the Type and define the appearance of the button on the Appearance and Options tabs. In the Button Face Attributes section, enter **Send** in the Text field.

3. On the Actions tab, select **Mouse Up** in the When this happens box.

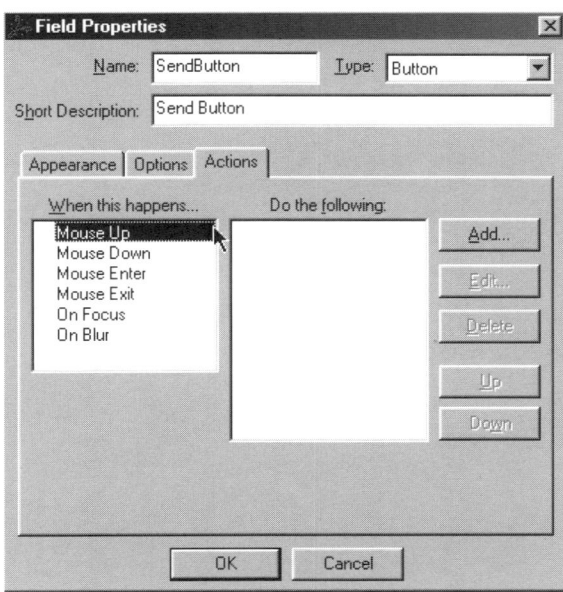

4. Press **Add**. Immediately, the Add an Action dialog box appears.

5. In the Type drop-down box, select **Submit Form**.

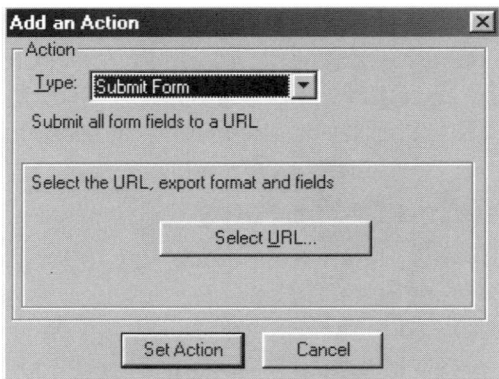

6. Press **Select URL**. The SubmitForm Selections dialog box appears.

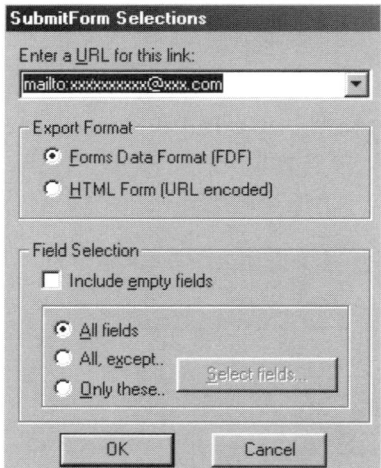

7. In the Enter a URL for this link field, enter **mailto:***YourEmailAddress*.

8. Click **OK**.

9. Click **Set Action**.

10. Click **OK**.

## Using the Send Button

To use the Send button:

1.  Click the **Send** button. The Untitled — Message (Plain Text) dialog box appears.

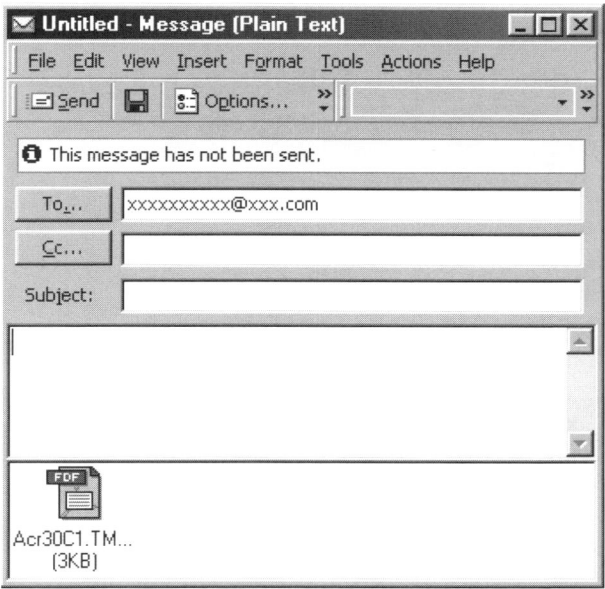

2.  At this point, you have the opportunity to add a message, add additional recipients of the e-mail, and change the e-mail address of the original recipient. After all changes/additions are made, click **Send** to send the message.

## Adding a Submit Button to the Form

A Submit button provides visitors to your web site with an efficient way to order merchandise or to submit an application online. In order for a Submit button to function correctly after your form is added to a web site, you must create a script to work alongside the form. Check with your ISP provider to determine the type of script to use.

***Note:*** *Possible types of scripts to use include JavaScript, VBScript, and Perl.*

To create a Submit button:

1. Using the Form tool, create a form field.

2. Select **Button** as the Type and define the appearance of the button on the Appearance and Options tabs. In the Button Face Attributes section, enter **Submit** in the Text field.

3. On the Actions tab, select **Mouse Up** in the When this happens box.

4. Press **Add**. The Add an Action dialog box appears.

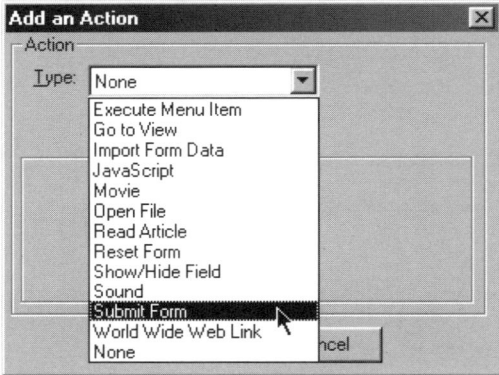

5. Select **Submit Form** in the Type drop-down box.

6. Press **Select URL**. The SubmitForm Selections dialog box appears.

7. In the Enter a URL for this link field, add the URL that will process the form. Be sure to enter the complete URL into this field (including the name of the script file).

8. Choose your export format and make your field selections.

9. Click **OK** to close the SubmitForm Selections dialog box.

10. Click **Set Action** to close the Add an Action dialog box.

11. Click **OK** to close the Field Properties dialog box.

## Adding a Reset Button to the Form

Visitors to your web page will inevitably add erroneous information to your form, no matter how well designed it is. A Reset button provides those visitors with a quick way to reset the form and begin anew.

To add a Reset button:

1. Using the Form tool, create a form field.

2. Select **Button** as the Type and define the appearance of the button on the Appearance and Options tabs. In the Button Face Attributes section, enter **Reset** in the Text field.

3. On the Actions tab, select **Mouse Up** in the When this happens box.

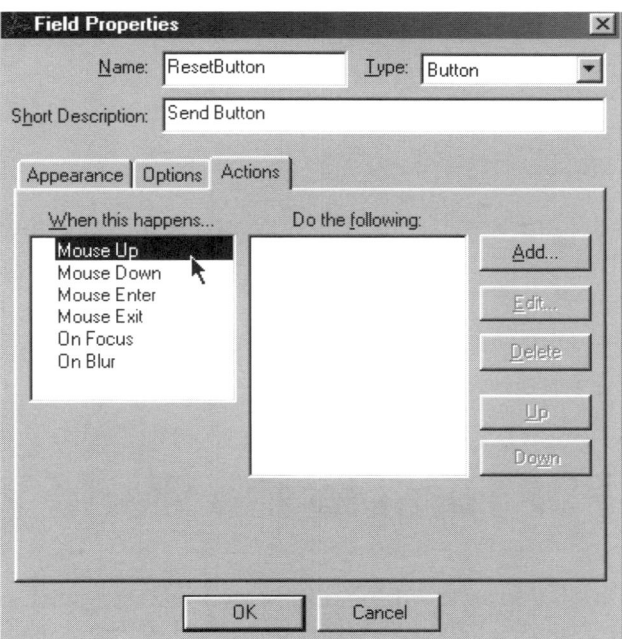

4. Press **Add**. Immediately, the Add an Action dialog box appears.

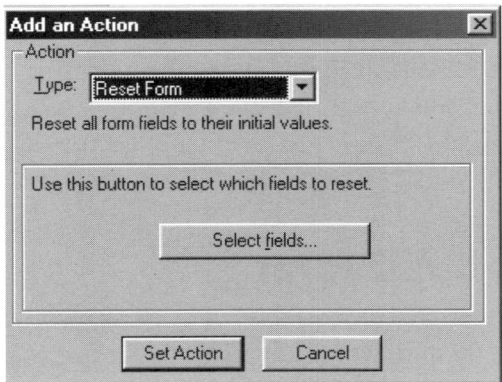

5. Select **Reset Form** for the action type and click **Select fields** to choose the fields to be refreshed when this button is pressed. The Field Selection dialog box appears.

6. The default is All fields. However, you can select only those fields you want refreshed when the button is pressed. Make your selection, then click **OK**.

7. In the Add an Action dialog box, click **Set Action**.

8. In the Field Properties dialog box, click **OK**.

# Adding the PDF Form to the World Wide Web

A form in PDF format can be added to a web site with or without interactive functionality. You can easily add a PDF form to a web site for the purpose of viewing and/or printing. Typically, user instructions or magazine articles are distributed in this manner. Or, with a bit more work, you can add input form fields to the form and interactive buttons which enable users to fill out and submit the form.

However your form is designed, your form must be accessible to your web site. Of course, the actual PDF file must be uploaded to your site's server. Additionally, a reference to the PDF file must exist in a script file or the HTML file.

## Using HTML to Link to a PDF Form

When designing web pages, you may want to provide visitors with documents that are easily and accurately printed. Notice that many web sites are difficult to print out. When PDF files are printed out from a web site, they appear identical to the original documents.

The simplest way to provide visitors to your web site with access to PDF documents is to add links to the documents in the HTML file.

To add links to PDF documents within an HTML file:

1. Create an HTML file.

**Note:** *Many tools available on your desktop can be used to create HTML files, including MS Word, MS WordPad, and MS Notepad.*

2. To create the link to the PDF file, add the following line within the body of the file: **<A HREF="YourForm.PDF">**

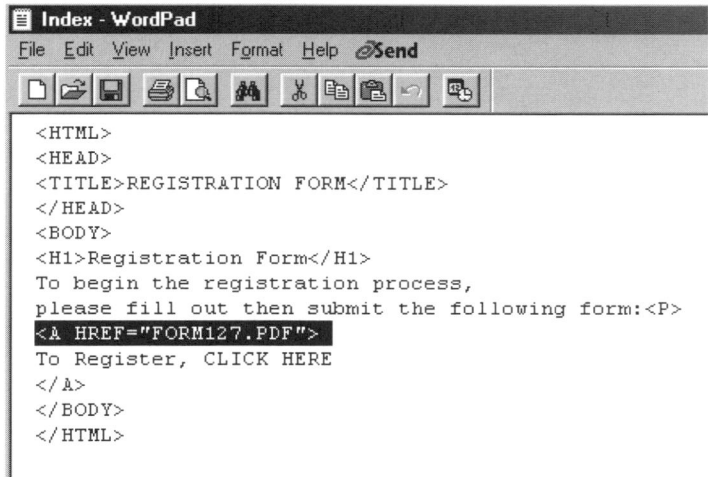

3. Directly below that line, add the text that will appear as the hyperlink to the PDF file.

**Note:** *When this text is double-clicked, Adobe Acrobat will launch and the PDF file will appear in the browser.*

You might want to add a comment with direction, such as: Click Here to Register.

4. On the next line, add **</A>** to complete the link.

5. Save the file.

# Testing Your HTML Code Using Internet Explorer

Prior to FTPing your new HTML file to your web server, you will want to test it to ensure that all links work properly.

To test your HTML code:

1. Launch a browser such as Internet Explorer or Navigator. (**Note:** *I used Internet Explorer in this example.*)

Internet Explorer

2. Click **File | Open**. The Open dialog box appears.

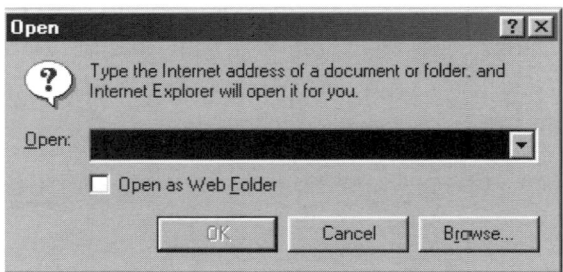

3. Press **Browse**. The Microsoft Internet Explorer dialog box appears.

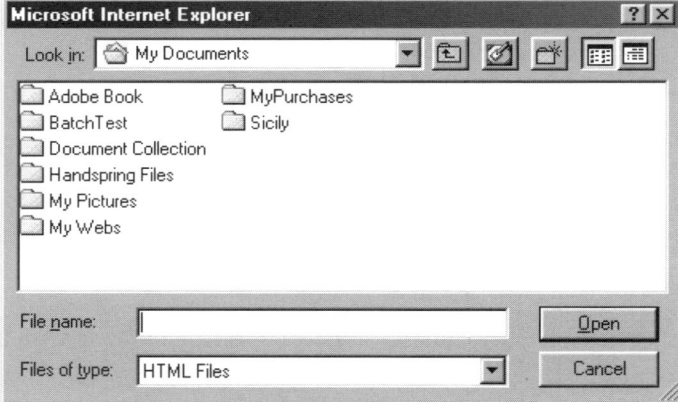

4. Select the HTML file you want to test, then select **Open**. The Open dialog box reappears with the path to the chosen HTML file in the Open field.

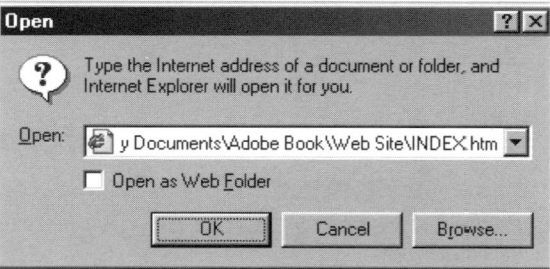

5. Click **OK**. Immediately, the HTML script runs, displaying the results in the browser.

# Registration Form

To begin the registration process, please fill out then submit the following form:

To Register, CLICK HERE

6. To ensure that the link executes properly, click the link on the browser.

Automatically, Adobe Acrobat launches and its splash screen appears.

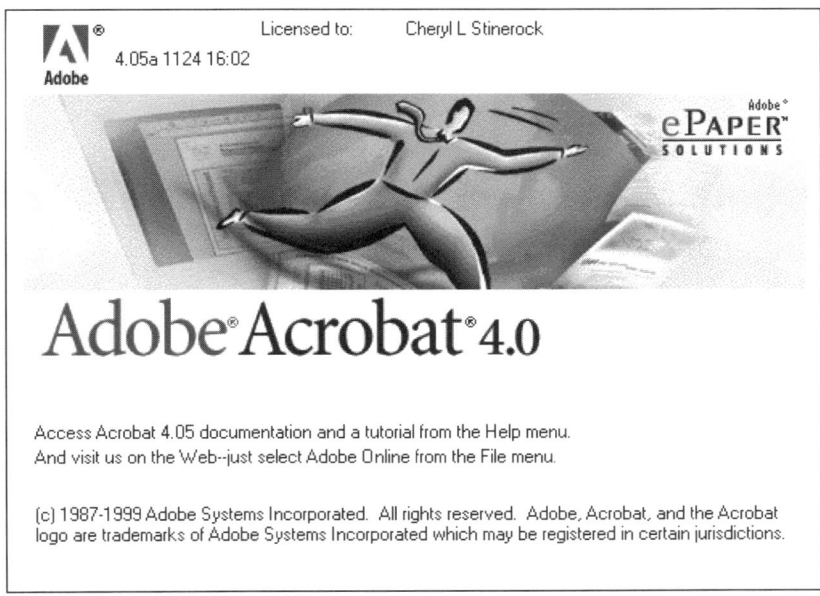

In a short time, the PDF file appears in the browser.

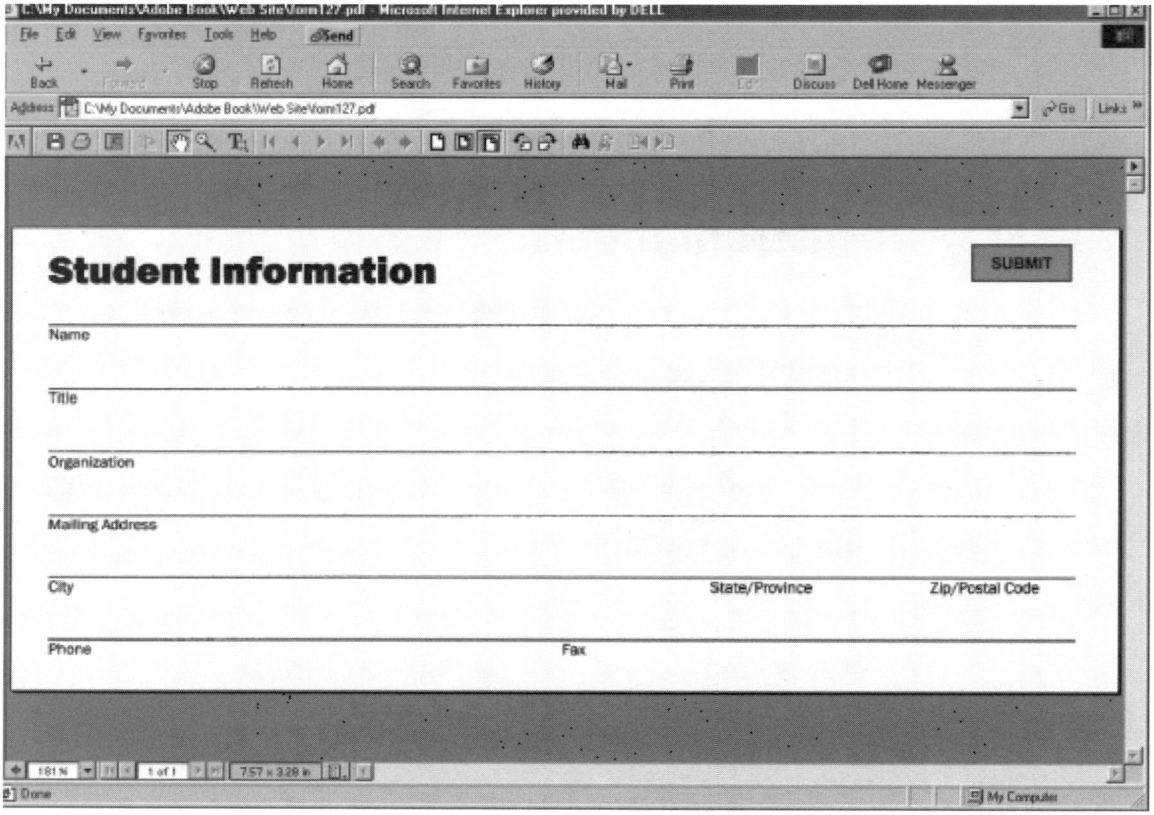

# Additional Requirements When Adding a Form to a Web Site

As you add a PDF document/form to a web site, there are a few details you should keep in mind:

■ Verify with your ISP your site's capability for handling interactive forms.

***Note:*** *Some smaller sites don't provide users with that ability.*

■ If a dynamic PDF form is added to a web site, an additional script is required to communicate with the server. Depending on the requirements determined by your ISP, you will need to write a script in Perl, JavaScript, VBScript, etc.

- Remember to optimize your PDF files. When you add your PDF forms to the web site, you need to keep the size of the PDF file as small as possible. Face it, visitors to your web site do not want to wait for long periods of time while a PDF file downloads. In Adobe Acrobat's Save As dialog box, always make sure the Optimize option is selected.

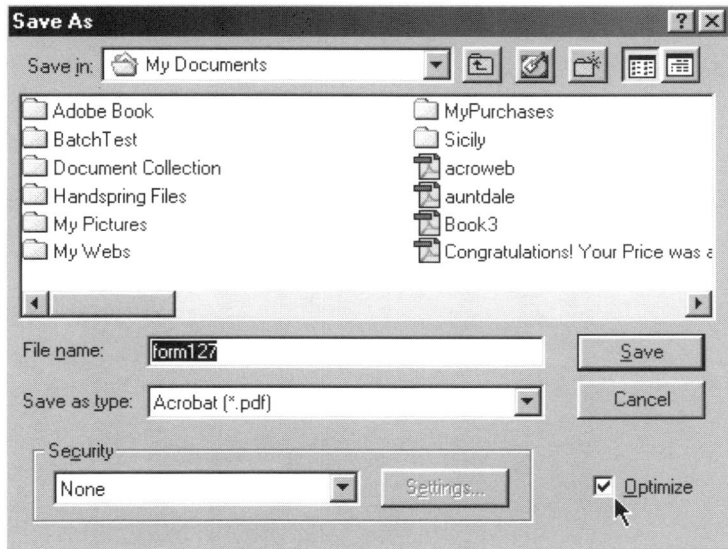

Throughout the past few chapters, you've been introduced to some of the functionality offered by Adobe Acrobat. With minimal complexity, Acrobat enables you to:

- Create a PDF file
- Convert a simple file to an interactive form by enhancing the PDF files with form fields
- Add security to documents
- Prepare forms for use on the Internet

By integrating Adobe Acrobat into your workflow, you'll discover the benefits of using this application to create, enhance, and manage PDF files.

# Index